THE ITALIAN ANTI-FASCIST PRESS (1919–1945)

THE ITALIAN ANTI-FASCIST PRESS (1919–1945)

FROM THE LEGAL OPPOSITION PRESS TO THE UNDERGROUND NEWSPAPERS OF WORLD WAR II

FRANK ROSENGARTEN

THE PRESS OF CASE WESTERN RESERVE UNIVERSITY CLEVELAND/1968

To the men and women of Italy who struggled
to liberate their country from fascism

ABBREVIATIONS USED IN TEXT AND FOOTNOTES

1. The following abbreviations are used in the text:

CLNAI Comitato di Liberazione dell'Alta Italia (Committee of National Liberation for Northern Italy)

CVL   Corpo Volontari della Libertà (Corps of Freedom Volunteers)

GAP   Gruppi di Azione Politica (Political Action Groups)

2. The following abbreviations are used in footnote references to indicate the location of underground newspapers and other documents mentioned in the text:

CDE   Centro di Documentazione Ebraica Contemporanea   via Guastalla, 19, Milan

CG   Centro Gobetti   via Fabro, 6, Turin

ICP   Italian Communist Party Documentation Center   via Botteghe Oscure, 4, Rome

IG   Istituto Gramsci   via del Conservatorio, 55, Rome

INS   Instituto Nazionale per la Storia del Movimento di Liberazione in Italia   Piazza Duomo, 14, Milan

ISRT   Istituto Storico della Resistenza in Toscana   Palazzo Medici Riccardi,   via Cavour, 1, Florence

LC   The collection of underground newspapers in the private possession of Laura Conti

MR   Museo del Risorgimento   via Borgonuovo, 23, Milan

NY   New York Public Library   New York City, New York

ACKNOWLEDGMENTS

I would like to express my thanks to the persons who, during the past four years, have offered me their guidance and encouragement.

I wish first of all to thank the directors of the American Philosophical Society for a research grant in 1964 that enabled me to spend the summer of that year working in the Resistance Institutes of Milan and Florence.

I owe a special debt of gratitude to the directors and staffs of four Resistance Institutes in Italy whose libraries are particularly important repositories of information on the history of Italian anti-fascism: the *Istituto Nazionale per la Storia del Movimento di Liberazione in Italia* in Milan; the *Centro Gobetti* in Turin; the *Istituto Storico della Resistenza in Toscana* in Florence; and the *Istituto Gramsci* in Rome.

While in Florence during the summer of 1963, at which time I began my study of the Italian anti-fascist press, I had the advantage of receiving the enthusiastic support of Professor Carlo Francovich, director of the *Istituto Storico della Resistenza in Toscana,* who greatly facilitated my research by providing me with valuable bibliographical information and especially by challenging some of the political assumptions that I had brought with me from the shores of America. Professor Francovich's colleague and assistant, Mr. Foscolo Lombardi, was also very helpful to me during the course of our conversations about the role played in the history of Italian anti-fascism by the Italian Socialist Party, of which Mr. Lombardi is a long-standing member. Mr. Gino Moncini, who serves as administrator of the Florentine Institute's library and documentation center, placed himself at my disposal with graciousness and generosity.

Among my most pleasant memories associated with the Florentine Resistance Institute is my meeting and subsequent friendship with Miss Maria Luigia Guaita, who is at present a publicist for art shows but who from 1943 to 1945 became known in Florence as an intrepid anti-fascist conspirator. Miss Guaita was in fact responsible for disseminating much of the clandestine propaganda of the Florentine Action Party. An excellent reporter and a charming woman, Miss Guaita provided me with valuable information regarding the organization and functions of the underground press in Florence.

I am especially grateful to Mrs. Carla Gobetti, director of the *Centro*

Gobetti in Turin. Mrs. Gobetti not only spent many hours on my behalf searching out books, articles, and various documents related to the Italian Resistance, but also gave me the benefit of her knowledge about Italian political history and personal experience as a representative of Italy's militant and intellectually independent left-wing movement. Through Carla, I met Ada and Paolo, the widow and son of the outstanding anti-fascist writer Piero Gobetti, in whose memory the Center in Turin has been named. Both Ada and Paolo were equally generous in furnishing me with firsthand knowledge of the origin and development of Italian anti-fascism, particularly with regard to the history of the Action Party and of the Italian Communist Party.

In Milan, Mr. Massimo Legnani and Miss Bianca Ceva, codirectors of the *Istituto Nazionale per la Storia del Movimento di Liberazione in Italia,* offered me numerous helpful comments and suggestions and were always willing to answer questions, locate documents, and point out possible areas of study that would have remained unknown to me without their guidance. Miss Maria Biga also willingly gave of her time and effort to help me orient myself amidst the myriad documents contained in the Milanese Resistance Institute.

It was also in Milan that I had the good fortune to meet Miss Laura Conti, who probably knows more than anyone else in Italy about the underground press of World War II. Miss Conti granted me permission to study her privately owned collection of clandestine newspapers, many of which are unavailable or difficult to obtain elsewhere. For this manifestation of confidence and solidarity, I am deeply grateful.

Among the many other persons in Italy whose guidance and interest were of crucial importance to me, the young Milanese journalist Giampaolo Pansa stands out in my mind because of his intellectual integrity and his infectious enthusiasm for every phase and aspect of recent Italian history.

Finally, I would like to express my gratitude to my wife, Lillian, whose moral support and intelligent criticism were indispensable to me in the writing of this book.

CONTENTS

PART III. THE UNDERGROUND PRESS OF THE ARMED
RESISTANCE (1943–1945)

INTRODUCTION

One of the characteristic features of World War II was the development of resistance movements in all countries occupied by the nazi and fascist armies. In some instances, such as in Yugoslavia and Greece, popular insurgency against the nazi-fascist forces was led chiefly by communists who, inspired by the example of the Bolshevik Revolution and by the achievements of the Soviet Army and partisans in World War II, based their struggle on the political principles of Marxism-Leninism and on the military strategy of organized guerrilla warfare. In other instances, such as France and particularly the countries of northern Europe, where liberal-democratic methods and ideals were firmly established, resistance leaders were identified with many diverse political movements and aimed essentially to liberate their lands from foreign oppression rather than to bring about a fundamental revolutionary transformation of their societies.

But the phenomenon of resistance was not limited to Yugoslavia, Greece, France, and northern Europe. It manifested itself also in countries whose governments either formed part of or were linked politically with the nazi-fascist alliance. There were conspiratorial anti-nazi movements in eastern Europe which, although led largely by communists, included men and women of all classes and political ideologies. In nazi Germany itself concentration camps were built as early as 1935 to silence the voices of a half million Germans, many of whom were non-Jews, who opposed Hitler's regime.

Of all the countries ruled by rightist totalitarian regimes, Italy was the one in which the forces of resistance waged the most successful and organized campaign in both a political and a military sense. From July 25, 1943, the day on which Benito Mussolini was ousted from power by a group of dissident members of the Fascist Grand Council in league with King Victor Emmanuel III and elements of the Italian Army, to April 25, 1945, a resistance movement grew and developed with impressive speed in Italy and, in fact, made an important contribution to the defeat of the German Army. This movement was buttressed by numerous partisan brigades and was supported by a political and propaganda apparatus that assumed the twofold task of educating and mobilizing the Italian people and of providing intelligence and other forms of assistance to the armies of the Western Allies engaged in combat in Italy. Yet despite these facts, and despite the appearance in recent years of some admirable studies of the Italian Resistance Movement, notably Charles Delzell's *Mussolini's Enemies: The Italian Anti-Fascist Resistance* (Princeton, 1961), many persons both in America and in Europe still react with surprise when told that there were some Italians who actively opposed Mussolini's regime during the fascist period itself, and that thousands of Italians took up arms against nazi-fascism after September 8, 1943, when the Italian government headed by Marshal Pietro Badoglio announced that it had accepted the armistice conditions laid down by the Allies. Persons who are unaware of the realities of recent Italian history often assert that there was no resistance at all in Italy, that the Allies alone liberated Italy while the Italian people simply waited passively for the war to end in order to see which side would win before taking sides.

Certainly there were millions of Italians who were pro-fascist or who remained uncommitted either to fascism or to anti-fascism. It is also true that the Resistance Movement in Italy was initiated by a small and courageous minority of individuals and that the Allied campaign was a necessary precondition for the decisive defeat of the fascist regime. The fact is, however, that without the contribution of Italian partisans and of various Italian anti-fascist movements engaged in propaganda warfare, it is likely that the Italian campaign would have been far more costly for the Allies and that Italy would have emerged from the war in a totally demoralized and debilitated state. The ability of the Italian people not only to recover rapidly from the devastation caused by the war, but also to recreate a political democracy within the framework of fundamental institutional reforms, was primarily due to the efforts of the Italian Resistance Movement. With or without the help of Italian partisans, the Allies would have eventually conquered Italy and defeated the Germans, but it was not within their power to shape the democratic consciousness of the Italian people. This task could be accomplished only by persons who were intimately acquainted with the nature and purposes of the fascist regime and with the diverse sources of anti-fascist thought and action which, at the time of the Allied invasion, were latent or already active in various strata of the Italian population itself.

This book aims primarily to provide an analysis of one significant component of the Italian Resistance—the ideas and programs of the underground newspapers that were produced by various anti-fascist movements in Italy during the years 1943 to 1945. These ideas and programs, however, did not come to sudden fruition in 1943. On the contrary, the fascist assault on freedom of the press, which began even before Mussolini took power in October 1922 and which from 1922 to 1926 was implemented through a whole series of authoritarian decrees and laws, galvanized into opposition many outstanding Italian journalists, who first laid the ideological groundwork for the campaign waged two decades later by the underground press of World War II. Of even greater relevance to our purposes in this study is the history of the anti-fascist press from 1926 to the first years of World War II, since during this period the spirit of active resistance, the idea of intransigent opposition to Mussolini's regime, was kept alive by groups of anti-fascist Italians both within Italy itself and in various foreign countries. Indeed, without the examples of *Non Mollare!, Quarto Stato, Avanti!, Giustizia e Libertà, L'Unità, Lo Stato Operaio, Battaglie Sindacali,* and many other newspapers illegally circulated in Italy or published abroad during the fascist era, the Italian Resistance Movement would have lacked an essential point of reference for the struggle it waged against fascism and nazism from 1943 to 1945.

The history of the anti-fascist press in Italy tends therefore to fall naturally into three periods: 1919 to 1926, which witnessed the progressively militant fascist assault on freedom of the press that culminated in the totalitarian "Special Laws for the Defense of the State" of November 1926; 1926 to the first years of World War II, when anti-fascist journalists either carried on clandestine propaganda in Italy or continued to challenge the legitimacy of the fascist regime as political exiles in France, Switzerland, the United States, and other friendly countries; and 1943 to 1945, the period of armed resistance that gave birth to well over five hundred underground newspapers and many thousands of pamphlets and manifestoes.

The first chapter of this study has as its chief purpose the description of the legal and extralegal methods with which the fascist regime crushed the opposition press. It also attempts to indicate the attitudes and ideas underlying the fascist assault on freedom of the press and includes as well a brief discussion of the role assigned to the press by the fascist state.

Chapters II and III deal with the political ideas and moral principles that guided the anti-fascist press from 1919 to the early years of World War II. Chapter II is a discussion of the thought of six representative leaders of the anti-fascist press during the first legal phase of opposition from 1919 to 1926. It was in those years that the fundamental ideological bases of anti-fascism were established as guidelines for the future action of Mussolini's enemies in the 1930's and 1940's. Chapter III traces the development of various currents of anti-fascist thought and action during the years 1925 to 1939, as embodied in the clandestine newspapers circulated in Italy and especially in the numerous newspapers and magazines produced by groups of anti-fascist émigrés in Paris. I have not included in chapter III a discussion of newspapers published by groups of anti-fascist exiles in London, Brussels, New York, and other foreign cities, since during the 1920's and 1930's Paris was the main center of Italian émigré journalism, and it was there that the various components of anti-fascist thought were most consistently and effectively articulated.

Chapters IV through IX provide a systematic analysis of the ideas, ideals, and political programs of the underground press during the period of armed resistance from 1943 to 1945.

Chapter IV begins with a brief description of some of the national and international events during the latter years of the fascist epoch that contributed to the development of an organized Resistance Movement in Italy in 1943. Its principal concern, however, is with the methodology of underground journalism, and it therefore discusses the types and functions of underground newspapers, explains how they were produced and distributed, and relates the experiences of some of the men and women who participated in the Resistance as anti-fascist propagandists.

Since the Italian Resistance Movement achieved a substantial unity of purpose, chapter V deals first with the ideas and ideals shared in common by the five principal anti-fascist parties, as reflected in the work of the Committees of National Liberation formed in the latter part of 1943 in Turin, Milan, Padua, Genoa, Florence, and other Italian cities. This chapter also discusses some of the divisive issues that occasionally threatened the unity of the committees during the period of the Resistance and that foreshadowed the tensions and conflicts of the postwar era.

In their effort to demonstrate that the anti-fascist struggle formed part of a native tradition of democratic values, Italian Resistance leaders were compelled to reexamine the whole course of their nation's history and in particular the age of the Risorgimento, the period from the latter part of the eighteenth century to 1870 during which the Italian people struggled to achieve national unity and political independence. Chapter VI is concerned chiefly with the historical links and parallels that Italian anti-fascists sought to establish between the Risorgimento and the Resistance.

Chapter VII is an examination of the anatomy of fascism, and discusses the diverse opinions expressed by the underground newspapers as to the reasons underlying the fascist conquest of totalitarian power in Italy.

Chapter VIII first provides a summary of some of the military, political, and social achievements of the Italian Resistance Movement and then proceeds to an explanation of the postwar goals of the main groups and parties that participated in the Resistance.

Italian underground newspapers reveal a strongly international commitment on the part of Resistance leaders, who saw events in Italy as part of a single, massive struggle waged in the name of ideals that transcended national or narrowly political ambitions. Chapter IX seeks to explain the specific forms of thought and action through which this international commitment was expressed.

Until very recently, historians interested in the underground press were severely hampered by the inadequate way in which all primary documents related to the Resistance were collected and made accessible to scholars in Italy. Toward the mid-1950's, the various Resistance Institutes that were established in most of the principal Italian cities began to function on a reasonably efficient basis; yet even today these Institutes operate in a somewhat improvised manner and only by virtue of the zeal of small groups of individuals. As a consequence, it was not until 1959 that a serious effort was made, under the auspices of the Feltrinelli Institute in Milan, to locate and identify all of the clandestine literature belonging to the period of the Resistance. The result of this effort was the publication in 1961 of a four-hundred-page bibliographical guide compiled by Laura Conti and Giampaolo Pansa.[1] This bibliography contains the titles, locations, and political classifications of more than five thousand clandestine publications—newspapers, magazines, pamphlets, manifestoes—and is therefore of great value to students of the Italian Resistance.

The work produced thus far by American and non-Italian European historians interested in recent Italian history, although illuminating with regard to the political and military aspects of the Resistance Movement, provides relatively little information on the fundamental ideas and ideals of the major anti-fascist groups and parties. The underground press remains, with the exception of Charles Delzell's *Mussolini's Enemies,* to which I am indebted for a variety of facts, judgments, and interpretations regarding the history of Italian anti-fascism, an entirely unexplored area. But even Professor Delzell's work makes only passing reference to the "luxuriant clandestine press" in Italy, and in a few pages mentions some of the principal newspapers and the men who created them.[2]

Research on the underground press undertaken in Italy during the past twenty years also points to the need for a comprehensive study of the type that this book intends to make. Italian historians who have dealt with the underground press have uniformly limited their field of interest to newspapers belonging to a single geographical area or political party. For example, in *Un anno di lotta contro il nazismo e il fascismo* (Rome, 1944), Orazio Barbieri illustrates only the communists' position during the

---

[1] *La Resistenza in Italia 25 luglio 1943–25 aprile 1945,* edited by Laura Conti.
[2] See *Mussolini's Enemies: The Italian Anti-Fascist Resistance,* pp. 351–53.

Resistance by summarizing and quoting extensively from articles that appeared in the communist clandestine press in Florence; Giuseppe Gaddi restricts the scope of his study to the region of Veneto in *Saggio sulla stampa clandestina della Resistenza veneta* (Bologna, 1955); Carlo Ventura deals exclusively with the newspapers published by the anti-fascist parties in Trieste in *La stampa a Trieste 1943–1945* (Udine, 1958); Filippo Jacini exemplifies the positions taken by the Liberal Party press in *Carattere* (Milan, 1947); and Luigi Longo's anthology *Sulla via dell'insurrezione nazionale* (Rome, 1954) contains selections of writings that appeared in the Italian Communist Party's two most important clandestine publications, *L'Unità* and *La Nostra Lotta*. In the many books and articles not primarily concerned with the underground press but in which there are pages or chapters devoted to the subject, one finds the same tendency to limit discussion to the contributions made by particular individuals, groups, regions, and political parties.

The Italian historians mentioned above have performed a valuable service for students of the Italian Resistance in that they speak from firsthand experience of the problems with which persons engaged in clandestine press activities had to cope and often shed light on the inception and development of the main currents of thought characteristic of the different groups that participated in the anti-fascist struggle. Yet the anti-fascist press, and especially the underground press in Italy during the years 1943 to 1945, is of sufficient importance to warrant a broader and more thorough treatment than it has received thus far. In most cases, the individuals active in the clandestine press were fully conscious of the moral and political issues at stake in the struggle against nazism and fascism. The newspapers and other publications that are discussed in this study raise all the questions and deal with all the ideological problems that concerned Resistance leaders not only in Italy but also in other countries of western and eastern Europe.

PART 1

THE PRESS AND THE FASCIST STATE

CHAPTER ONE

THE FASCIST ASSAULT ON FREEDOM OF THE PRESS (1919–1939)

I
All Power to the Fascist State

Within a period of five years, from 1922 to 1927, the fascist regime succeeded in destroying all legal opposition to its power and in creating a political dictatorship, one of whose principal features was its incorporation of the Italian press into a totalitarian state apparatus.

The fascist assault on freedom of the press was motivated by a repudiation of what Benito Mussolini referred to contemptuously as the "immortal principles" of liberal parliamentary democracy as practiced by the United States and England and by many of the countries of western Europe. Despite his intense hatred for the doctrines of socialism and communism, whose elimination from Italian political life represented one of the chief aims of his career after his defection from the Socialist Party in 1914, Mussolini often expressed a certain grudging admiration for the methods and structure of the Soviet state.[1] The Italian dictator saw clearly that Soviet

[1] Many of Mussolini's speeches and writings collected in his *Opera Omnia,* edited by Eduardo and Duilio Susmel, reveal his admiration for the durability and toughness of the Soviet state. This admiration was most often expressed by Mussolini during the early years of his regime, when he was frequently compelled by both his supporters and his enemies to defend the rigorous repressive methods used by the fascists against members of the opposition parties.

In an article entitled "Force and Consent," published in the magazine *Gerarchia* in March 1923, Mussolini asserted that though liberalism had been constructive and necessary in the nineteenth century, it was not suited to the development of "modern" states in the twentieth century. He cited fascist Italy and Soviet Russia as examples of modern states that had successfully vanquished the liberal order: "Events are worth more than books; experience more than doctrine. *Now the greatest experiences of the postwar period,* those which are in movement in front of our eyes, mark the defeat of liberalism. In Russia and in Italy it has been demonstrated that men can govern outside, above and against the whole liberal ideology. Communism and fascism are outside the boundaries of liberalism." (Italics mine; *Opera Omnia,* vol. 19, pp. 195, 196.)

In a speech to the Italian Senate on June 8, 1923, Mussolini spoke of the accomplishments of his regime during its first months in power. He warned his op-

Russia, like fascist Italy, had embarked on an experiment in political organization whose purpose was to integrate and coordinate the activities of each individual under its control within the framework of a centralized, totalitarian state. The humanistic and democratic aspects of the Soviet experiment were despised and ridiculed by Mussolini. What he respected was the ruthless manner in which the leaders of the Soviet Union had crushed

---

ponents not to exaggerate the danger to fascism of occcasional minor crises, for the fascist government, he said, like the Soviet government, was well able to defend itself against its foes: "Fascism is still and will remain for a long time a simply formidable party. Don't make the mistake of the Western bourgeois who, every minute, . . . used to think that those little [anti-Bolshevik] bands of unarmed and barefoot men could demolish the Soviet government. The other day Lloyd George said that it is a very solid government. In the same way, if you see that there is a dispute in one of the many villages of Italy, don't argue from that that fascism is in crisis. It is necessary, gentlemen, to introduce into the examination of the phenomena of history the element of duration, the element of time. And when a party has the government in its hands, it holds it, if it wishes to hold it, because it has formidable powers to use in order to establish its dominion more and more firmly." (*Opera Omnia,* vol. 19, p. 260.)

On July 15, 1923, in a speech to the Chamber of Deputies, Mussolini responded to Socialist Arturo Labriola, who had stated that there was nothing in common between the dictatorship of the proletariat in the Soviet Union and the fascist dictatorship in Italy: "The guilt attributed to us by the Honorable Labriola, who accuses us of finding an unfounded analogy between the methods and development of the Russian Revolution and the methods and development of the Italian Revolution, is itself unfounded, inasmuch as I am making here a simple assertion of an historical order. It is a fact that both revolutions tend to surpass all ideologies and in particular the liberal and democratic institutions that emerged from the French Revolution." (*Opera Omnia,* vol. 19, p. 310.) Five months later, on December 5, 1923, Mussolini again referred to the analogous durability of the fascist and Soviet governments in resisting the attacks of their liberal opposition: "There is no greater strength for a government than the certainty of enduring. Nothing so cuts into the nerves of the opposition as this sense of the ineluctable stability of a government. Let me tell you something that will seem strange to you: the same capacity for resistance in Russia consists, above all, in the determined conviction of its rulers that they will endure and resist." (In an interview with a reporter of *Il Giornale d'Italia, Opera Omnia,* vol. 20, pp. 126, 127.)

One other example of Mussolini's admiration for the power of the Soviet government will suffice to show to what extent his domestic policy of violent anti-communism did not prevent him from feeling a certain sense of identification with the rulers of the Soviet Union. In an article published in the newspaper *Il Popolo d'Italia* on March 15, 1924, Mussolini referred to the recent efforts made by Italian socialist and communist leaders to expose fascist violence during the electoral campaign of 1924: "With what criminal brazenness do these filthy snakes of Italian subversivism not yet crushed by the fascist heel dare to utter cries of protest if some betrayer of fascism is punished more or less noisily? We are still very far from the system in Russia. Anyhow, when a party has assumed the tremendous responsibility of directing the destiny of the nation, especially in the present historical period, it has the perfect right and the duty to be inflexible against its deserters who pass over to the enemy. In any case fascism is following the example of your 'comrades' in Russia, oh zealous and putrid men of the socialist movement!" (*Opera Omnia,* vol. 20, p. 205.)

their liberal opposition; for it was the philosophy of liberalism, embracing in particular freedom of the press and the right to political dissent from established governmental policy, that Mussolini was most intent on destroying.

Anti-socialism and anti-communism, of course, became equally important ingredients of Mussolini's political philosophy as soon as he was firmly in power and no longer had to make constant appeals for support to the Italian working classes. Indeed, much of his early financial backing was provided by Italian industrialists, landowners, and other segments of the middle and upper classes who saw fascism as a solid bulwark against the threat of socialism. In December 1922, the Italian dictator declared that he saw no possibility of any agreement between fascists and socialists, since socialist ideas were an obstacle to the achievement of "national unity and national discipline." [2] Fascism, he said, was the surest defense of "Western civilization" against the "spiritual epidemic" spread by the Bolshevik Revolution.[3] In January 1923, he warned a group of Genoese workers to be on guard against the myth of "Asiatic utopias coming from Russia," [4] and in June of that year he praised the Florentine fascist leaders for their victory over "the bestiality of Red demagogy." [5] In March 1924, in an interview with an American journalist, Mussolini explained that "the fascist movement was born five years ago, for the purpose of fighting against the aberrations of bolshevized socialism, and began to develop rapidly when the workers proceeded to the occupation of the factories. Subsequently, faced with the indecisive attitude of the government, fascism resolved to act to reestablish national order." [6]

As previously suggested, however, Mussolini almost always attacked liberalism with far more élan and conviction than he did socialism and communism, for he aspired above all to create a compact, unified, totalitarian state.

Mussolini's contempt for liberalism lay at the very core of his personal political philosophy, which he sought to articulate in a short treatise entitled *La dottrina del fascismo,* published in 1933. In this treatise Mussolini stresses the fact that fascism did not come into being on March 23, 1919, as a political party with a coherent program of ideas and aims but was born instead as a movement, as a dynamic faith, as a creative assertion of the essentially spiritual nature of man. Fascism arose in reaction to the

---

[2] Mussolini, *Opera Omnia,* vol. 19, p. 61.
[3] *Ibid.,* vol. 19, p. 68.
[4] *Ibid.,* vol. 19, p. 92.
[5] *Ibid.,* vol. 19, p. 278.
[6] *Ibid.,* vol. 20, p. 188.

materialistic positivism of the nineteenth century, which produced "skeptical pessimistic, agnostic" men who were deprived of the two values that render life worth living: religious belief in a power that transcends the individual and a will to action motivated not by selfish aims but rather by a desire to serve the higher aspirations of the national collectivity. The ideology of liberalism and the practice of parliamentary democracy, Mussolini said, were the political manifestations of a widespread rejection of monarchical absolutism and for a certain period fulfilled a creative function in European political life. But very soon it became evident that the rampant individualism unleashed by the French and American Revolutions was destined to destroy the vital purpose in which political man ought to find his reason for being, namely, the welfare and power of the state to whose needs and aspirations each citizen must ideally subordinate himself. Liberalism gave rise to futile parliamentary bickering and incessant factious disputes between individuals, parties, and social classes. It made freedom into a cult, a fetish; it degraded the state to the level of a tax-collecting agency that served the interests of this or that segment of society; it exalted the principle of majority rule, whereby individuals of high intellectual ability were frequently voted out of office by the ignorant, semiliterate masses.

Fascism, Mussolini asserted, had once and for all put an end to the absurd contradictions inherent in liberalism, "which denied the state in the interests of the particular individual; fascism reaffirms the state as the true reality of the individual. . . . Fascism is for the only freedom that can be a serious thing, the freedom of the state and of the individual within the state. For the fascist, everything is within the state, and nothing human or spiritual exists, or still less has value, outside the state. In this sense fascism is totalitarian, and the fascist state, the synthesis and unity of every value, interprets, develops, and strengthens the whole life of the people." [7]

Mussolini indicated that it was in 1921 and 1922, the years during which gangs of blackshirts began making armed raids on socialist and communist labor organizations, that fascist doctrine was first "refined and elaborated" in systematic fashion. It was during those years of "punitive expeditions" that fascism began considering "the problems of the individual and the state, the problem of authority and freedom, and the political, social, and specifically national problems; the struggle against liberal, democratic, socialistic, and masonic doctrines was waged contemporaneously with the punitive expeditions." [8] Out of this struggle, declared Mussolini, were born the laws and institutions of the fascist state that took shape in the years 1926 to 1928.

La dottrina del fascismo ends with an attempt to define fascism in both

[7] Benito Mussolini, *La dottrina del fascismo,* p. 4.
[8] *Ibid.,* p. 9.

negative and positive terms: its chief enemy is the ideology and practice of liberalism which, according to the Italian dictator, long ago outlived its usefulness. Fascism does not believe in the possibility or usefulness of perpetual peace. It therefore repudiates pacifism, "which hides a renunciation of struggle and cowardice." It believes instead in the virtue of war, "which alone brings all human energies to a maximum of tension and stamps an imprint of nobility on peoples who have the courage to confront it." Fascism is against all forms of internationalism and exalts the principle of nationalism. It is intransigently opposed to Marxian socialism and believes that "saintly and heroic action," not class struggle, is the main agency of social change. Fascism is unalterably opposed to all traditional democratic ideologies and affirms instead "the irremediable, fruitful, beneficial inequality of men." Fascism is a new type of democracy, "an organized, centralized, authoritarian democracy." Finally, fascism is ardently imperialistic, deriving its belief in imperialism from the Roman tradition. "For fascism," Mussolini asserted, "the tendency toward empire, that is, the expansion of nations, is a manifestation of vitality; its opposite, or the policy of remaining comfortably at home, is a sign of decadence." [9]

In the process of justifying and elaborating the fascist conception of the totalitarian state, Mussolini was able to rely on the supportive labors of a host of philosophers, historians, jurists, and political thinkers, some of whom belonged to the upper echelons of the Italian intellectual community. The profoundly anti-liberal and anti-democratic attitudes that characterize Mussolini's *La dottrina del fascismo* abound, for example, in the works of the historian Gioacchino Volpe and the idealist philosopher Giovanni Gentile, who in November 1922 was appointed Minister of Education in Mussolini's first cabinet. The responsibility of these men for the destruction of freedom in Italy in 1922 cannot be overestimated, for their support gave fascism a prestige and an aura of legitimacy that greatly facilitated the regime's effort to suppress its anti-fascist opposition.

Both Volpe and Gentile, like other Italian intellectuals whose names are legion, embraced fascist totalitarian doctrine with disconcerting enthusiasm. Both men had utter contempt for the liberal constitutional monarchy that preceded fascism. Both saw "ineffectual liberalism" and "parliamentary anarchy" as the main obstacles to the creation of "a great, unified, powerful Italy." [10] Both were convinced that what Italy needed above all was a virile, totalitarian conception of the state and of life. Both agreed

---

[9] *Ibid.*, pp. 11–22.
[10] Volpe justifies fascist totalitarianism in the name of a "great, unified, powerful Italy" in "Genesi del fascismo," reprinted in *Il fascismo,* edited by Costanzo Casucci, pp. 68–92.

that the ideals of the Risorgimento, Italy's struggle for national unity and independence in the nineteenth century, were at long last being realized by the fascist state. They were capable of believing this despite the fact that most of the men who led the Risorgimento were inspired by the very principles of liberal democracy that were crushed by Mussolini's regime.

In 1927, readers of Gentile's *Origini e dottrina del fascismo* learned that Italy had not entered World War I for idealistic or even political reasons but rather for the sake of war itself, to test her strength in a military conflict. Fascism, Gentile said, reflected the desire of worthy Italians to create a state that, once and for all, would be respected and feared. Instead of placing emphasis on the distinctions between social, economic, political, and cultural phenomena, fascism championed an ideal synthesis of them; in place of decadent liberalism and parliamentarianism, fascism substituted totalitarianism and integralism; as opposed to socialist internationalism, fascism promoted belief in the sacred value of national pride and national traditions; instead of equality, fascism correctly stressed the natural differences between men and the necessity for order, hierarchy, and obedience to authority. In Gentile's view, fascism represented a creative leap forward in the history of mankind made possible by the genius of the Italian race.[11]

Historians tend to disagree as to the particular event or legislative action that was of preeminent importance to the triumph of the fascist dictatorship in Italy. Some believe that the electoral "reform" of December 13, 1923, which stipulated that the party receiving the largest number of votes in the national elections scheduled for April 5, 1924, would obtain two-thirds of the seats in the Chamber of Deputies, gave the regime an indispensable "legal" status that formed the basis of its subsequent continuity and power.[12] Others regard the "Special Legislative Provisions for the Defense of the State," known as the *leggi eccezionali* of November 25, 1926, as marking the beginning of absolute totalitarian rule. These laws for the defense of the fascist state deprived all Italian exiles known to be engaged in anti-fascist activity of their citizenship and, in the case of their capture, imposed on them from five to fifteen years imprisonment; required the immediate dismissal of the managing editors of all non- or anti-fascist

[11] Giovanni Gentile, "Origini e dottrina del fascismo," the central part of which is reprinted in *ibid.*, pp. 15–50.

[12] The key articles of, and legal justifications for, the electoral reform of December 13, 1923, and the plebisicitary reform of September 2, 1928, are published in *La legislazione fascista 1922–1928*, edited by Annibale Alberti, vol. I, pp. 141–42, 153–55. By reason of fascist violence and intimidation, but also because of a genuine hope among many Italians that the Fascist Party would restore order to Italian political and social life, the fascist-endorsed list of candidates in the elections of April 5, 1924, received 64.9 per cent of the vote.

newspapers; declared illegal and demanded the abolition of all anti-fascist political parties, associations, and organizations; established the death penalty for attempts on the life of Mussolini and members of the Royal family; and instituted a Special Tribunal for the Defense of the State to try political crimes.[13]

Historians may continue to differ for many years to come about when and how the fascist regime gained absolute power. There is no doubt, however, that by the early part of 1927 the Italian people were living under a highly centralized political dictatorship that, moreover, enjoyed the full support of the Army, the Monarchy, and many of Italy's most prominent business and industrial leaders.

II
Fascist Decrees and Legislation on the Press

The various decrees and laws on the press that were promulgated by the fascist government from 1923 to 1929 formed an integral part of Mussolini's "organized, centralized, authoritarian democracy." Mussolini was always acutely sensitive to the power of the press to mould public opinion. Even if many of his countrymen revered him as a man of infallible judgment who "was always right" and who "always told the truth," Mussolini himself clearly recognized that truth in the arena of political debate was protean and elusive, that victory in the struggle to win the loyalty of men required control over the most important means of communication with which political ideas are brought to the attention of the public. His own remarkably successful career as an editorial writer for the socialist newspaper *Avanti!* and then as founder and chief editor of *Il Popolo d'Italia,* the official fascist organ in Rome, had taught him how quickly people could be swayed to this or that policy position, how readily men responded to programs and appeals that gratified their emotional needs and promised them a better future. For Mussolini, the press was never basically a means with which to inform people on the significant domestic and international issues of the day, but rather an instrument with which to acquire and maintain state power.

We shall examine in this chapter several of Mussolini's more important pronouncements on the role of the press in the fascist state. It will suffice at this point to make mention only of one incident in Mussolini's career that reveals much about the personal psychology of the man and about his attitude toward the function of newspapers.

---

[13] The main provisions of the *leggi eccezionali* of November 25, 1926, are published in *La legislazione fascista 1922–1928,* vol. I, pp. 59–60.

On October 17, 1922, exactly two weeks before his assumption of power, Mussolini called a meeting in Milan of the directors of the leading fascist daily and weekly newspapers. Present at the meeting were Roberto Farinacci, Dino Grandi, Giuseppe Bottai, and many other future stars in the fascist firmament. Toward the end of his speech, Mussolini told the assembled journalists that it was vitally necessary that all fascist newspapers be up-to-date and thoroughly efficient, since "it is quite possible that at a certain point we may no longer feel like tolerating the survival of some prominent newspapers." He then turned to Sandro Giuliani, the managing editor of *Il Popolo d'Italia* and, "smiling ironically," said: "We understand each other, don't we, Giuliani; you won't write anything about all this in your report for *Il Popolo d'Italia*!" The fate of Italy's anti-fascist newspapers was already sealed.[14]

One major obstacle stood in the way of the fascist regime's effort to suppress opposition newspapers, namely, the edict on the press issued on March 26, 1848, by King Charles Albert of Sardinia-Piedmont. It will be useful, therefore, to indicate some of the basic features of this document.

The opening paragraph of the Albertine edict affirmed that freedom of the press constitutes "a necessary guarantee for the institutions of every well-ordered representative government" and that this freedom "must be upheld and protected in such a way as to assure its beneficial effects." [15] This edict formed the basis of the constitutional provisions guaranteeing freedom of the press in the Italian state following unification in 1861 and was later extended to the region of Veneto, which became part of united Italy in 1866, and to Rome in 1870. Thus from 1870 to the advent of the fascist era, Italy was among the nations of the Western world in which freedom of the press was considered an indispensable prerequisite for a liberal, democratic society. Newspapers reflecting the full spectrum of political opinion usually had complete freedom in pre-fascist Italy to express their views.

It must also be said, however, that a series of restrictive and qualifying clauses in the Albertine edict, although only rarely applied in pre-fascist Italy, provided Mussolini and his followers with a convenient pretext for the application of punitive measures against the anti-fascist press. In the first place, the edict left a wide margin of control to the government to punish offenses against generally accepted standards of good taste and

---

[14] Mussolini's remarks at this meeting are reported by Piero Pedrazza, a fascist journalist, in *Giornalismo di Mussolini*, p. 59.

[15] *Codice della stampa e degli autori,* edited by Giulio Benedetti, p. 61. The full text of this edict is published on pp. 61–72 of the *Codice*.

morality. Needless to say, the fascist authoritarian mind easily extended the concept of "good taste and morality" to include spoken or written offenses against the person of the dictator of Italy: the first case tried by the Special Tribunal created in November 1926 involved a worker named Giuseppe Piva, who had insulted Mussolini in true Roman fashion by saying "li mortacci sui, sto puzzolento!" Piva was sentenced to nine months in prison.[16] Secondly, the edict contained an extraordinary number of articles in which various "abuses of freedom of the press" were defined. Article nineteen stated, for example, that "anyone who by means of printed matter of any kind is guilty of offenses against the Holy Person of the King, or the Royal Family, will be punished with up to two years of imprisonment" (*Codice,* p. 64). Articles twenty-one and twenty-two imposed up to two years imprisonment on "anyone who insults the Senate or the Chamber of Deputies," and on those "who have publicly declared their adherence to any other form of government" or who have "vowed or threatened to destroy the constitutional monarchical order" (*Codice,* p. 65.) Article twenty-four was particularly illiberal in character. It stated that "any offense against the inviolability of the right of property, the sanctity of the oath of loyalty [to the Savoy Monarchy], and the respect due to the laws, every justification of acts considered by the penal code to be crimes, *every provocation of hatred between the various social classes and against the order of the family,* will be punished with up to one year in prison." (Italics mine; *Codice,* p. 65).

It is clear, then, that although the Albertine edict sought to guarantee freedom of the press, its various restrictive clauses could easily be interpreted or slightly modified to suit the needs of an authoritarian regime. With the exception of the law of June 28, 1906, which declared the preventive confiscation of newspapers to be illegal, all of the other legislation on the press enacted by the Italian state from 1871 to 1922 simply restated or clarified the meaning of the "abuses" of freedom of the press as defined by King Charles Albert in 1848.

It should also be noted that, in addition to the legal loopholes provided by the Albertine edict, one other important precedent for press censorship existed in recent Italian history: during World War I, the socialist newspaper *Avanti!* and other publications that echoed the socialists' refusal to support Italy's intervention in the war were periodically subjected to rigorous censorship. In fact, in all the provinces of the country that were regarded as military territory and placed under the jurisdiction of

[16] Piva's offense and trial are mentioned by Cesare Rossi in his *Il Tribunale Speciale,* p. 23. Roughly translated, "li mortacci sui, sto puzzolento!" means "May this stinker's ancestors be damned!"

military authority, the distribution of *Avanti!* was forbidden entirely. Thus Mussolini's regime could also cite the wartime censorship of *Avanti!* as a precedent for punitive measures taken by the Italian government against publications that provoked dissension and thereby threatened to undermine a transcendent national cause.

On July 15, 1923, King Victor Emmanuel III placed his signature of approval on the first of two fateful decrees on the press that were the fruit of the collective labors of Mussolini and of Luigi Federzoni and Alfredo Rocco, the Ministers of the Interior and Justice in the first fascist cabinet. In their message to the King on July 8, 1923,[17] requesting his approval of the new decree, Mussolini, Federzoni, and Rocco noted that the lack of specific regulations for the execution of the edict of March 26, 1848, and in particular the failure of that edict to define the functions and obligations of the *gerente responsabile*—that is, the person who is legally responsible for what is printed in a newspaper—had recently resulted in numerous abuses of the freedom granted to the press in Italy. The Italian state and nation had been exposed to grave danger by the excesses of anti-fascist newspapers, which were undermining public confidence in the government and demeaning the prestige of Italian political and religious institutions.

Article thirty-seven of the edict of 1848 had simply stated that "every newspaper must have a *gerente responsabile*." According to the three authors of the new decree, the owners and editors of subversive newspapers had resorted to the practice of hiring individuals as *gerenti responsabili* who were paid handsomely to run the risk of fines or imprisonment in the event that the government sought to press charges against an offending publication, thus protecting the real culprits from any punitive action. Article one of the decree of July 15, 1923, rectified this situation by asserting that the *gerente responsabile* "must be the director or one of the principal editors of the newspaper or publication and must obtain the official approval of the Prefect of the province where the newspaper or publication are printed." [18] The real force of the new decree lay, in fact, in the punitive power it gave to the Prefects, who were of course appointed in 1923 primarily on the basis of their proved loyalty to fascism. Article two authorized the Prefects to issue an injunction to the *gerente* of a newspaper or other periodical in the following cases:

(*a*) if the newspaper or other publication with false or tendentious news hampers the diplomatic action of the government in its relations with

---

[17] The message to the King sent by Mussolini, Federzoni, and Rocco on July 8, 1923, is published on pp. 109–10 of the *Codice della stampa e degli autori*.

[18] *Codice della stampa e degli autori*, p. 110. The full text of the decree of July 15, 1923, is published on pp. 110–11 of the *Codice*.

other powers or damages national prestige within Italy or abroad or arouses unjustified alarm among the population or causes a disturbance of public order;

(*b*) if the newspaper or other publication with articles, comments, notes, headlines, illustrations, or cartoons instigates the commission of crimes or provokes class hatred or disobedience of the laws or the orders of the authorities or interferes with the discipline of public employees or favors the interests of foreign states, organizations, or individuals to the detriment of Italian interests or insults the Fatherland, the King, the Royal Family, the Pontiff, the Religion of the State, the institutions and the power of the State or of friendly Powers . . . . [*Codice,* p. 110.]

In the event that the *gerente* of an accused publication refused to heed the Prefect's injunction, Article four stated that "the newspapers or other writings published in illegal defiance of the regulations in Article two are to be confiscated. The confiscation is to be carried out by the persons responsible for public security without requiring any special authorization. Those guilty of the abusive publications are to be punished according to existing laws" (*Codice,* p. 111).

A year later, on July 10, 1924, King Victor Emmanuel III issued a second decree on the press which, although adding nothing substantially new to the previous decree, further strengthened the investigative and punitive powers of local and regional Prefects and defined more precisely the methods with which preventive and repressive action could be taken against offending publications.[19] As we shall see in chapter II this second decree was a countermeasure to the intensified anti-fascist campaign of the opposition press that followed the assassination of the socialist deputy Giacomo Matteotti on June 10, 1924.

The decrees of July 15, 1923, and July 10, 1924, were both converted into law, in the face of strong opposition from various members of the Liberal, Popular, and Socialist Parties,[20] on December 31, 1925, when another law on the press, entitled "Regulations Pertaining to the Periodical Press," [21] also received the official approval of the King. The key articles of the new law, numbers one, two, three, and seven, although not immediately applied, thereby allowing opposition newspapers to appear

[19] The full text of the decree of July 10, 1924, is published in the *Codice,* pp. 112–13.

[20] Parliamentary opposition to the new Regulations pertaining to the periodical press was led by the liberal Senators Luigi Albertini, the managing editor of *Il Corriere della Sera,* Marcello Soleri, Leone Wollemborg, and Nino Tamassia. The final votes in the Senate on the conversion of the two decrees into law were 151 for and 45 against, and 143 for and 53 against. The final Senate vote on the Regulations pertaining to the periodical press was 150 for and 46 against.

[21] The full text of the Regulations pertaining to the periodical press is published in the *Codice,* pp. 113–15.

for another year, were in full force by the end of 1926 and as a consequence effectively reduced Italian journalists to the status of servants of the fascist regime.

Article one stated first of all that "the director or managing editor [of every periodical publication] must be listed in the professional directory of journalists" (*Codice,* p. 113). Needless to say, this directory was open only to journalists whose loyalty to the regime was beyond question. Second, Article one required that the managing editors of every periodical publication "obtain the official approval of the attorney-general of the Court of Appeals under whose jurisdiction the newspaper or periodical is printed" (*Codice,* p. 113). Third, Article one stipulated that the attorney-general could "deny or revoke his approval to those who have been condemned two times for crimes committed by means of the press" (*Codice,* p. 114). Article two stated that no periodical could be legally published unless the attorneys-general (of the relevant city or region) officially recognized its *gerente responsabile,* and sanctioned the immediate confiscation of any periodical whose *gerente* had not been accorded such recognition (*Codice,* p. 114). Article three stated that, along with the application for the recognition of the *gerente responsabile,* "the printer and publisher of a newspaper or periodical must present to the attorney-general a declaration containing the vital statistics of all the owners of the newspaper or periodical [and indicate the addresses] of their place of business and their private residence" (*Codice,* p. 114). Article seven announced "the institution of an Order of Journalists that will have its offices in cities where there exists a Court of Appeals. The Order will establish its professional directories that will be deposited at the chancelleries of the Courts of Appeal. *The practice of the profession of journalism is allowed only to those whose names are listed in the directories"* (italics mine; *Codice,* pp. 114, 115).

The establishment in 1925 of an Order of Journalists and of a Professional Directory of Journalists foreshadowed the Royal decree of April 7, 1927, which incorporated all Italian newspapermen within a National Fascist Syndicate of Journalists. This syndicate was integrated into a National Confederation of Professional Men and Artists, which was one of thirteen National Confederations that formed part of the corporate state created by the fascist government.[22] Another Royal decree of

---

[22] The thirteen National Confederations, as listed in *La legislazione fascista 1922–1928,* vol. I, p. 156, are National Confederation of Agricultural Land Owners; National Confederation of Agricultural Workers; National Confederation of Industrialists; National Confederation of Industrial Workers; National Confederation of Businessmen; National Confederation of Business Workers; National Confederation of Owners of Marine and Air Transport Companies; National Confedera-

February 10, 1927, brought the owners and publishers of newspapers within the corporate system by making the National Fascist Association of Newspaper Publishers a part of the National Fascist Confederation of Industrialists. The purposes of this Association were "to safeguard the general welfare of the industry for which it is constituted and to favor the industry's technical and economic development in harmony with the general interests of the nation and of its productive activity." [23]

A Royal decree of February 26, 1928, established norms for the institution of the professional directory of journalists. The decree stated that every journalist had to have his name listed in the directory in order to practice his profession; that control of the directory and the discipline of its members would be exercised by the Journalists Syndicate through a committee; and that the members of the committee were to be appointed by the Minister of Justice, the Minister of the Interior, and the Minister of Corporations.[24]

In conformity with its proclaimed intention to help Italian journalists understand their mission in the new order, the fascist government instituted a series of special university chairs in journalism in 1928 and 1929. A Royal decree of March 15, 1928, announced the founding of a new Fascist Faculty of Political Science at the University of Perugia, the purposes of which were "to promote knowledge and awareness of fascism and to prepare fascists for careers in public administration, syndical-corporative organization, consular-diplomatic work, colonial administration, and journalism." [25] The course in journalism was divided into two sections, the history of journalism, taught by Professor Paolo Orano, and domestic and comparative legislation on the press, taught by Senator Silvio Longhi. Other chairs in journalism were created in 1929 at the University of Ferrara, the Catholic University of Milan, and the Royal University of Economic and Commercial Studies of Trieste.

In the latter part of 1927, a professional school for journalists was founded in Rome, under the auspices of the Ministry of Corporations, by the National Fascist Syndicate of Journalists. This school had less

---

tion of Workers in Marine and Air Transport Industry; National Conferation of Owners of Land and Internal Navigation Transport Companies; National Confederation of Workers in Land and Internal Navigation Transport; National Confederation of Bankers; National Confederation of Bank Employees; National Confederation of Professional Men and Artists.

[23] *Codice della stampa e degli autori,* p. 259. The full text of the decree of February 10, 1927, is published in the *Codice,* pp. 258–66.

[24] The full text of the decree of February 26, 1928, is published in the *Codice,* pp. 126–31.

[25] The full text of the decree of March 15, 1928, is published in the *Codice,* pp. 231–35.

exalted but infinitely more practical aims than the university programs and sought primarily "to furnish those who have an aptitude for journalism with the technical preparation necessary for the practice of this profession that the fascist regime has tried to purify of all the intellectual and moral dross of the past." [26]

Finally, on May 1, 1929, Alfredo Rocco, the Minister of Justice, announced to the Senate the founding of a special High Commission for the Press that completed the work of the fascist government in "the juridical organization of the journalistic profession." This Commission, headed by Mussolini's brother Arnaldo, one of the major theorists of fascist journalism, was described by Rocco as "the supreme organ of control over the disciplinary functions attributed by the law to the regional Committees of Journalists, a true High Court of justice for everything that pertains to the discipline of the journalistic profession. An organ of state but composed exclusively of eminent journalists, it makes possible at one and the same time the autonomy of journalism and its link with the state." [27]

Thus, just as Mussolini could, without any apparent sense of philosophical inconsistency, define fascism as an "organized, centralized, authoritarian democracy," so in the same way Alfredo Rocco could speak of the "autonomy" of Italian journalism while at the same time advocating the integration of Italian newspapermen within a totalitarian political and juridical state apparatus.

III
The Destruction of the Opposition Press

To what extent did the fascist regime actually apply the decrees of 1923 and 1924 and the law of December 31, 1925, regulating the periodical press? As already suggested, the answer to this question is that the Prefects chosen by the regime for their zealous devotion to the cause of fascism applied the law stringently and efficiently. But before discussing the consequences of the legally sanctioned measures taken by the regime against anti-fascist newspapers, it is necessary to describe the extralegal methods with which Mussolini and his more ardent followers carried out their campaign against the opposition press. The word extralegal is often used as a euphemism for violence, and indeed it was precisely physical violence, mere brute force and terror, that formed the real basis of the fascist assault on freedom of the press in Italy.

[26] *Ibid.*, p. 235.
[27] *Ibid.*, p. 139.

Many incidents of fascist raids on socialist and communist newspapers took place in the years immediately following the end of World War I. On April 1, 1919, for example, a group of blackshirts invaded and destroyed the offices of the socialist newspaper *Avanti!* in Milan; on February 27, 1921, fascists raided *L'Azione Comunista* in Florence, and murdered the newspaper's editor, Spartaco Lavagnini; in Turin, in 1921 and 1922, the offices and presses of the communist organ *L'Ordine Nuovo* were repeatedly sacked by gangs of armed blackshirts. Similar violent tactics were employed by fascist authorities in almost all of the principal Italian cities from 1923 to 1926 and were not halted until the regime felt sufficiently confident of its power to rely on nonviolent methods of control and repression.

Mussolini himself had a somewhat ambivalent attitude toward the use of violence as a means of achieving political ends. He usually frowned upon anarchic, undisciplined gestures but on the other hand had great respect for organized violence that was carefully calculated to achieve its purpose: On October 4, 1922, Mussolini addressed the "Antonio Sciesa" action squad in Milan and referred to a successful raid on the socialist newspaper *Avanti!* carried out two months earlier, on August 3, by a group of fascist hoodlums. "Here we have the real violence of Milanese fascism," Mussolini said. "Not small, sporadic, often useless individual violence, but the great, the beautiful, the inexorable violence of the decisive hours." [28] There can be no doubt that the Italian dictator was in large measure responsible for the wave of violence that accompanied and followed the fascist conquest of power.

Immediately after Mussolini took power on October 30, 1922, an atmosphere of terror pervaded all of Italy and especially Rome. In early November 1922, the offices of many of Rome's principal anti-fascist newspapers were invaded and devastated, including *Il Paese,* which ceased publication, *L'Epoca, Avanti!,* and *Il Comunista.* When Salvatore Barzilai, the President of the Italian National Press Federation, sent a telegram to Mussolini protesting these raids and the forced twenty-four hour suspension of the Milanese daily *Il Corriere della Sera,* the new Prime Minister replied that freedom was not only a right, but also a duty; the government therefore had the obligation to intervene when threatened by certain types of hostile propaganda.[29]

During the period just prior to the elections of April 5, 1924, anti-

[28] Mussolini's remarks addressed to the "Antonio Sciesa" action squad are reported by the fascist historian Gioacchino Volpe, "Storia del movimento fascista," appended to Mussolini's *La dottrina del fascismo,* p. 88.

[29] These events are described by Luigi Salvatorelli and Giovanni Mira in their *Storia d'Italia nel periodo fascista,* pp. 227–29.

fascist politicians and journalists were subjected to constant intimidation and violence. Several months before the elections, more than one hundred fascist demonstrators invaded the home of the former liberal prime minister, Francesco Saverio Nitti, and reduced it to rubble and ashes. The reason for this "punitive expedition" was revenge against Nitti for having recently published an article unfavorable to fascism in a South American political review.[30] Another grave incident, which took place on December 26, 1923, was the beating sustained at the hands of four blackshirts by Giovanni Amendola, the combative editor of the liberal newspaper *Il Mondo* of Rome. Amendola refused to be intimidated by this assault and subsequently paid for his courage with his life; on July 20, 1925, he was again savagely beaten while vacationing at the resort town of Montecatini. He died of his wounds in France less than a year later, on April 7, 1926.[31]

In 1926, two attempts were made on Mussolini's life, the first on April 7 by a mentally deranged Englishwoman named Violet Gibson, the second on October 31 in Bologna by someone (whose identity has never been established) standing in the crowd listening to a speech by Mussolini. Within a few seconds after the crime, the finger of guilt was pointed at a fifteen-year-old student named Anteo Zamboni, who was immediately and brutally killed by some enraged fascists who had come to Bologna to hear the Duce commemorate the fourth anniversary of fascist power. Both assassination attempts provoked a tremendous intensification of fascist violence against the opposition press. On April 8, the offices and presses of *Il Mondo* and *La Voce Repubblicana* were devastated by squads of Roman fascists. On November 1, reprisals were unleashed against anti-fascist newspapers and journalists throughout Italy. In Genoa, the office of the socialist newspaper *Il Lavoro* was burned in an attack so violent in nature that the police fired at random at the demonstrators, killing three persons and wounding twenty before order could be restored.[32]

But fascist action squads and propagandists did not need the pretext of assassination attempts to carry out their assaults, for violence was an integral component of the regime's method of acquiring and wielding power. The primary victims of course were the outspoken writers, editors, and publishers of the anti-fascist press, including Giuseppe Donati, the editor of the Christian Democratic *Il Popolo* in Rome, who was forced into exile in June 1925 after being subjected to incessant death threats

30 *Ibid.*, p. 281.
31 *Ibid.*, p. 282.
32 *Ibid.*, p. 357.

against himself and his family; Piero Gobetti, the founder and editor of *Rivoluzione Liberale* in Turin, who was harassed and beaten at the express orders of Mussolini [33] and who subsequently died an exile in Paris on February 13, 1926; Roberto Bencivenga, the President of the National Press Federation, whose home was devastated on October 31, 1926, and who was later deported to the island of Ustica along with hundreds of other political prisoners; Ferdinando Schiavetti, the managing editor of *La Voce Repubblicana,* who was severely beaten in early November 1926 and then forced into exile; Alberto Giannini, the publisher of the satirical review *Il Becco Giallo*; Gaetano Consolo and Gaetano Pilati, who were murdered in Florence on October 5, 1925, because of their association with the anti-fascist *Italia Libera* circle and, in particular, because of the support they had given the clandestine newspaper *Non Mollare!* The fact is that the fear of "punitive expeditions," of direct physical assault, hung over the heads of every notable anti-fascist journalist and politician from the very day the fascists took power.

Yet it is also true that rank-and-file supporters of the opposition press were exposed to risks almost equal to those undergone by prominent anti-fascist journalists. Beginning in 1924, Mussolini obtained from all anti-fascist newspaper publishers a list of the names and addresses of their subscribers, which he then forwarded to the heads of local and regional *Fasci* throughout the country. The *Fasci* bosses were told to threaten certain selected readers of the subversive newspapers and, if necessary, to use the favorite fascist weapons against recalcitrant foes of the regime: the blackjack followed by a cod-liver oil purge.[34]

It is well known that the fascists directed their violence most consistently and ferociously against the socialist and communist press. Yet the case of Italy's leading liberal newspaper, *Il Corriere della Sera* of Milan, illustrates that bourgeois respectability and conservative political views were no guarantee of safety against the wrath of militant fascists.[35]

In July 1921, fifteen months before the March on Rome, the editors of *Il Corriere della Sera* cautiously and quite objectively suggested that recent fascist "punitive expeditions" in the region of Tuscany were un-

---

[33] On June 1, 1925, Mussolini sent the following telegram to the Prefect Palmieri in Turin: "It has been reported to me that the well-known Gobetti has recently been in Paris and is today in Sicily. I beg you to keep me informed and to remain vigilant in order to make life doubly difficult for this stupid opponent of the government and of fascism." The telegram is published in *Le riviste di Gobetti,* edited by Lelio Basso and Luigi Anderlini, p. LXVIII, n. 2.

[34] Salvatorelli and Mira, *Storia d'Italia nel periodo fascista,* p. 282.

[35] The information on the events leading to the suppression of *Il Corriere della Sera* has been obtained from Alberto Albertini, *Vita di Luigi Albertini,* passim.

worthy of men who aspired to participation in the Italian government. Milanese fascists promptly responded to this criticism by burning thousands of copies of the newspaper on Milan's Piazza Duomo. On December 18, 1922, eleven anti-fascists were murdered in Turin in reprisal for the accidental killing of a Turinese fascist functionary in a dispute that later proved to be entirely private in character. *Il Corriere della Sera* protested the mass killing, and as a consequence the newspaper's managing editor, Luigi Albertini, became the recipient of hundreds of insulting and threatening letters that arrived at his office almost every week for the following three years. In the latter part of March 1923, Giacinto Menotti Serrati and Pietro Nenni, the coeditors of the socialist newspaper *Avanti!*, were arrested on the charge of having "defamed" the Italian government. *Il Corriere della Sera* protested the illegality of this arrest. *Il Popolo d'Italia, L'Idea Nazionale, L'Assalto*, and other fascist newspapers immediately demanded the suppression of the Milanese daily. Mario Carli, the editor of the fascist *L'Impero*, warned Albertini: "Either keep quiet or disappear!" was Carli's edifying response to Albertini's protest. Whole truckloads of the guilty issue of *Il Corriere della Sera* were publicly burned in Milan, Bologna, and Florence. On September 10, 1923, two bombs were thrown at the central office of *Il Corriere della Sera* in Milan. Bomb-throwing vandals again attacked the newspaper's office after the elections of April 5, 1924, because *Il Corriere della Sera* had not supported the fascist-sponsored list of candidates.

The violent incidents referred to above frightened the Crespi brothers, two Milanese industrialists who held majority ownership of *Corriere* stock as per a corporate agreement signed in 1919 by themselves and Luigi and Carlo Albertini. In November 1925, the Crespi brothers demanded that the corporation be liquidated, availing themselves of the banal oversight of a notary who had failed to have the signed agreement officially registered in accordance with proper legal procedure. The Albertini brothers had no choice except to yield to this pressure, since they knew that, even if some legal recourse were still available, further collaboration with their frightened partners would be unfeasible and that the ever-vigilant fascist authorities in Milan would not desist in their effort to suppress the newspaper. On November 29, 1925, Luigi Albertini published his last article as editor of *Il Corriere della Sera* in which he eloquently defended his career as an independent journalist and expressed hope that Italy would one day return to the practice of constitutional government in which freedom of the press was regarded as an inalienable right. In a gesture of solidarity with the Albertini brothers, practically all of the newspaper's anti-fascist reporters and correspondents resigned from their jobs.[36] Within a matter of months, nothing remained of *Il Corriere della Sera* except its name, for the newspaper came under the control of persons thoroughly loyal to the fascist regime. On November 30, 1925, the *London Times* published a long and appreciative article lamenting the fate of the Milanese daily. The article stated: "The end of the independent *Corriere* is a serious loss for European civilization." [37]

Italy's other nationally important liberal newspaper, *La Stampa* of Turin,[38] suffered essentially the same fate as befell *Il Corriere della Sera*. In September 1925, *La Stampa* was suspended for a month by fascist authorities in Turin for having published "offensive articles against the army." The newspaper's chief editorial writer, and one of Italy's most gifted historians, Luigi Salvatorelli, was compelled to resign from his position. *La Stampa's* director and publisher, Senator Alfredo Frassati, was told that he could remain at his post as long as he no longer concerned himself with political questions of vital interest to the fascist government. A year later, after being warned that his offices and presses would be destroyed unless he abstained entirely from political polemics, Frassati ceded a portion of his partnership to two liberal but more politically pliant individuals, Luigi Barzetti and Alfredo Pestelli. But soon after, fascist authorities in Turin demanded that *La Stampa* be controlled by someone absolutely loyal to the regime. Following Frassati's resignation, a new managing editor, the fascist deputy Andrea Torre, was therefore chosen by the newspaper's board of directors. Torre was one of many ex-liberals who in 1923 had swung over to fascism.

The end of *Il Corriere della Sera* and *La Stampa* as politically independent newspapers coincided with a whole series of actions taken against the anti-fascist press—progressing from periodic suspensions, censorship, and confiscation to final complete suppression—which were legally sanctioned by the new decrees and laws of the years 1923 to 1926.

The socialist newspaper *Avanti!*, which in 1924 had a daily circulation

---

[36] Among the men who resigned from *Il Corriere* with Albertini were Alberto Tarchiani, Luigi Einaudi, Count Carlo Sforza, Francesco Ruffini, Augusto Monti, Guglielmo Emanuel, Armando Rossini, Luciano Magrini, and Ferruccio Parri.

[37] Alberto Albertini, *Vita di Luigi Albertini*, p. 261.

[38] The information on *La Stampa* up to 1926 has been obtained from Salvatorelli and Mira, *Storia d'Italia nel periodo fascista*, pp. 228, 243, 260, 335. The events leading to the "fascistization" of *La Stampa* are described in a volume published by a group of Italian anti-fascist journalists who participated in an International Press Exposition in Cologne, Germany, on June 10, 1927, *Exposition de la Presse Antifasciste Italienne*, p. 32. For a thorough account of the economic and political pressures brought to bear by fascist authorities on two other liberal daily newspapers, the *Gazzettino di Venezia* and *Il Mattino* of Naples, see Giuseppe Cuomo, *La libertà di stampa ed impresa giornalistica nell'ordinamento costituzionale italiano*, pp. 80–85.

of about two hundred thousand, was confiscated thirty-seven times in 1924, sixty-one times in 1925, and thirty-four times from January to October 31, 1926, when it was definitively suppressed.[39] *La Voce Repubblicana,* which had the honor of being the first newspaper to receive an official injunction in July 1924, was twice suspended, in January and November 1925, and finally suppressed entirely in October 1926.[40] The weekly political review of Turin, *Rivoluzione Liberale,* was suppressed on November 25, 1925, for having refused to desist from its "defamatory writings directed against the authority of the state." [41] *L'Unità,* the daily organ of the Italian Communist Party, was officially supressed in November 1926. The suppression of *L'Unità,* which was preceded four months earlier by a successful operation carried out by fascist political police against a group of communists engaged in clandestine press activities, led in 1927 and 1928 to the imprisonment or trial *in absentia* of nearly all of the Italian Communist Party's leading propagandists and organizers.[42] Injunctions and confiscations, for offenses ranging from incitement of class hatred to contemptuous remarks directed against the established political order, were imposed on the Christian democratic *Il Popolo,* the satirical magazine *Il Becco Giallo,* the reformist socialist review *Critica Sociale,* and the liberal *Il Mondo,* which were officially suppressed in November 1925, December 1925, September 1926, and November 1926 respectively. Other, lesser-known political newspapers, mostly socialist or communist in point of view, also fell under the fascist assault. Sixteen such newspapers were suppressed in the regions of Piedmont and Liguria, thirty-six in Lombardy, sixteen in Emilia-Romagna, twenty in Tuscany, twelve in Rome, and twenty in southern Italy and Sicily. In addition, in 1926 thirty-six newspapers published by various labor unions and syndicalist groups affiliated with the anti-fascist Italian General Confederation of Labor were also suppressed.[43]

Beginning in 1927, the fascist secret police launched a methodical and highly successful effort to ferret out anti-fascist propagandists that resulted in the capture and trial of many Italian journalists and printers who had remained in Italy to wage a clandestine campaign against the regime. A vast network of spies and informers was created throughout

[39] *Exposition de la Presse Antifasciste Italienne,* p. 26.

[40] *Ibid.,* p. 27.

[41] The text of the injunction against *Rivoluzione Liberale* is prominently displayed in the apartment that today houses the *Centro Gobetti* at via Fabro, 6, Turin, where Piero Gobetti lived in 1924.

[42] For an account of the capture of the underground Communist journalists in 1926, and the subsequent trials of 1927 and 1928, see Cesare Rossi, *Il Tribunale Speciale,* pp. 136–42.

[43] *Exposition de la Presse Antifasciste Italienne,* p. 33.

Italy, and indeed the betrayal of paid informers proved to be the most effective means of apprehending the regime's underground opponents, as the testimony of Guido Leto and other functionaries in the fascist secret police during the 1920's and 1930's indicates.[44]

But the fascist regime was not content merely to silence its adversaries. The elimination of the anti-fascist press was only the first step toward the creation in Italy of a new type of journalism that would no longer be held back by what the fascists regarded as the decadent prejudices and practices of the past. With the advent of fascism, journalism ceased being a trade or at its best a profession and became instead a calling, a mission.

IV
The Mission of the Press in the Fascist State

As in many other areas of Italian political and cultural life during the fascist epoch, the dominant ideas regarding journalism were formulated by Mussolini himself. He made what is perhaps his first important official pronouncement on the role of the press in the fascist state on November 27, 1922, in reply to a group of Senators who had expressed disapproval of some of the illiberal, authoritarian actions already taken by the regime during its first month of power. Addressing himself particularly to Senator Luigi Albertini, the managing editor of *Il Corriere della Sera*, Mussolini asked rhetorically: "But, let's understand each other, what is this liberalism, this practice of liberalism? Because, if there is someone who claims that in order to be a perfect liberal one must give freedom to a few hundred stupid, fanatical scoundrels, the freedom to ruin forty million Italians, I energetically refuse to give this freedom." Adopting a stern mien, Mussolini then told the Senate: "Gentlemen, I have no fetishes, and, when the interests of the nation are at stake, I don't even have the fetish of freedom. This is why, after some people have talked to me about freedom of the press, I, who am a journalist, I have said that freedom is not only a right, it is also a duty." [45]

The conviction that dutiful subordination of the individual to the national interest takes precedence over the right to express dissenting views dominated all of Mussolini's speeches and writings on the press during

[44] For a remarkably objective description of the methods with which the fascist political police operated in the 1920's and 1930's see Guido Leto, *Ovra, Fascismo-Antifascismo*. Many significant aspects of the subject are also discussed by Cesare Rossi in *Il Tribunale Speciale*.

[45] Benito Mussolini, *Scritti e Discorsi*, vol. I, pp. 31–32.

the 1920's. On February 16, 1923, he announced to the Chamber of Deputies that the difference between the liberal state and the fascist state lay in the fact that "the fascist state not only defends itself, but attacks. And those who intend to defame the fascist state abroad or to undermine it within Italy must realize that their trade involves very grave and unpredictable consequences." [46] A month later Mussolini published an article in the magazine *Gerarchia,* entitled "Force and Consent," in which he spoke derisively of "this poor Italian liberalism" that was being so easily overcome by the faith of the new generation in different values, in "order, hierarchy, discipline." These values had rendered sterile and useless such old-fashioned notions as unqualified belief in freedom of the press.[47] Journalism was a noble career, said Mussolini on October 24, 1923, in his address to a group of Piedmontese newspapermen; it was noble "when it did not serve clandestine or picayune interests, when it was a weapon in defense of an ideal." [48] What ideal was Mussolini referring to? The next day in Milan he explained himself further by declaring that journalism was a "mission," an apostolate "whose end was collaboration with the nation" in building the fascist state.[49]

On January 24, 1924, speaking in Rome at a convention of the National Press Syndicate, Mussolini referred again, in commenting on the enormous power of the press in modern, technologically developed societies, to the mission of fascist journalism. "It is well to repeat," he said, "that the so-called freedom of the press is not only a right, it is a duty! It is well to repeat that today a simple news item, whether it be true or tendentious, can bring incalculable harm to the nation. If we wish, as we do wish, that journalism be a mission, well then, every mission is irrevocably accompanied by an extremely lofty sense of responsibility. Outside this frame of reference, there is no mission, but a trade." [50]

Mussolini added nothing substantially new to his doctrine of the press during the following years; but one other of his speeches on the matter,[51] delivered on October 10, 1928, to the directors of fascist newspapers assembled at Palazzo Chigi in Rome, deserves special comment for what it reveals about the mentality of the men who ruled and "educated" the Italian people from 1922 to 1943.

[46] *Ibid.,* p. 60.
[47] *Ibid.,* p. 79.
[48] Piero Pedrazza, *Giornalismo di Mussolini,* p. 71.
[49] Benito Mussolini, *Scritti e Discorsi,* vol. I, p. 222.
[50] *Ibid.,* vol. II, p. 28.
[51] This speech of October 10, 1928, is published in its entirety in the *Codice della stampa e degli autori,* pp. 5–9.

Mussolini began this speech, which elicited "the thunderous applause" of the assembled journalists, by affirming that during the preceding two years, the problem of the fascist press had been faced and resolved. "In a totalitarian regime," he said, "as a regime that has arisen from a triumphant revolution must necessarily be, the press is an element of this regime, a force in the service of this regime; in a unitary regime, the press cannot remain outside this unity. This is why all the Italian press is fascist and should feel proud to struggle compactly under the banner of the *Littorio*." [52] Mussolini then proceeded to laud the accomplishments of fascist journalism, for in Italy, he said, more than in any other country, journalism was a mission of singular importance. Second only to the schools, he continued, newspapers are a society's most powerful ideological weapon because they constantly "circulate among the masses and perform their functions of providing information and moulding character." What is all this talk, Mussolini asked, about the death of the free press in Italy? "The freest press in the entire world is the Italian press." In other countries, he noted, newspapers are controlled by plutocrats, by political parties, by self-seeking individuals; elsewhere newspapers are filled with sensational news because they form part of an industry. "Italian journalism," on the other hand, "is free because it serves only a cause and a regime."

The speech had hardly begun. Mussolini warmed to his subject and used a convincing analogy to make his point. Fascist newspapers, he said, can be compared to a symphony orchestra. Like the various instruments in a great orchestra, they all have the note "A" in common. This note "A" is not sounded by the government through its press offices, but is an "A" that fascist newspapermen voluntarily impose upon themselves, their common point of reference being "service to the Regime." Within this common framework, diversity of opinion was possible and desirable. Mussolini then waxed lyrical. Conformity with the "A" of service to the regime avoided cacophony and instead produced "complete and divine harmony."

Mussolini had still not ended his speech. His tone changed from that of a lyrical poet to that of a stern but loving father. He welcomed honest criticism, he deplored servility; he wanted his listeners to realize that under fascism, "aside from strictly political questions, or those which are fundamental in the revolution, for all other questions criticism can be

[52] The "Littorio" (English lictor) was, in ancient Rome, an officer who bore the fasces as the insignia of his office. The fasces were a bundle of rods having among them an ax with the blade projecting, borne before Roman magistrates as a badge of authority. Thus Mussolini's *Fascisti* were supposed to typify obedience to the law as did the lictors in ancient Rome. (*Webster's New International Dictionary*.)

expressed within limits." He assured his audience that poets, writers, musicians, and philosophers would be judged on their own merits and not according to the political acceptability of their works.

The directors of fascist newspapers, Mussolini concluded, had a twofold duty, domestic and international. In Italy, he said, within a few months the Italian people would be summoned to "plebiscitary assemblies" to show their support for the regime. "It is necessary to prepare for this great event, and you, with your newspapers, have the means to do it in a worthy manner." On an international level it was evident that the stronger fascist Italy became, the more intense would the reaction of the anti-fascist world be. To meet this challenge, "it is necessary that the press be vigilant, efficient, and equipped in a modern fashion; it is necessary that the press have men who are able to polemicize with adversaries beyond our borders, men, above all, who are inspired not by material objectives, but by ideal purposes."

This speech was an extraordinary performance, worthy of the man about whom Winston Churchill remarked, on January 20, 1927, that "his only thought is the enduring welfare of the Italian people." [53]

The elaboration of a fascist doctrine of journalism was not, however, the work of Mussolini alone. He was assisted in this endeavor by, among many others, his Ministers of the Interior and Justice, Luigi Federzoni and Alfredo Rocco, by his brother Arnaldo, the managing editor of *Il Popolo d'Italia,* by Paolo Orano, who was appointed to the Chair in the History of Journalism at the University of Perugia in 1928, by Ermanno Amicucci, the general secretary of the National Fascist Syndicate of Journalists, and by rank-and-file fascist journalists, such as Piero Pedrazza of the newspaper *Camicia Nera* of Treviso, Stanis Ruinas of *L'Impero* in Rome, Giulio Benedetti, the editor of the fascist government's official *Codice della stampa,* and Arturo Assante, author of *Contributo ad una critica di Il Giornale ed il Giornalismo di Stato* (Naples, 1937).

Federzoni and Rocco usually limited themselves in their statements on the press to certain practical bureaucratic defenses of the disciplined state created by fascism, a state that had eliminated, according to Federzoni, "the excesses of the factious press." [54] Rocco, however, occasionally soared to loftier doctrinal heights as when, on May 1, 1929, he

[53] Churchill's remark is quoted by Salvatorelli and Mira, *Storia d'Italia nel periodo fascista,* p. 390.

[54] Federzoni made this comment in a speech to the Chamber of Deputies on November 22, 1924, which is published in the *Codice della stampa e degli autori,* p. 32.

announced to the Senate the founding of a High Commission for the Italian Press. The "anarchic irresponsibility" of pre-fascist journalism, Rocco said, had been replaced by "a sense of responsibility and duty." Nor could it be justly said that the regime had killed freedom of the press. "Freedom of the press is not hindered by the establishment of moral and intellectual requirements for the practice of journalism," since similar requirements must also be fulfilled by all other professions. The obedience and discipline of journalists were indispensable in a regime that "considers loyalty to the Fatherland not as a political or party question, but as a problem of civic morality." [55]

In a series of articles in *Il Popolo d'Italia* in 1928, Arnaldo Mussolini declared that most newspapers in pre-fascist Italy had been frivolous, concerned mainly with petty intrigues, and entirely irresponsible in their emphasis of sensational news. Fascist newspapers, on the other hand, were fulfilling the real purposes of modern journalism, namely the discussion of serious problems and the instruction and education of the general public. In Italy, he maintained, fascist journalists had to reach a people that "did not read very much and that has had schools and a church which have been traditionally far removed from daily life." Therefore fascist newspapers had the obligation of filling in this gap and of becoming "the source of moral and political principles, the most rapid vehicle for reaching the mentality of the whole people, the most suitable organism for stimulating, shaping, and educating the spirit of the citizens." [56]

Ermanno Amicucci described the newspapers of pre-fascist Italy, indeed the newspapers of all liberal, democratic states from the time of the French Revolution on, as forming part of "the famous and infamous Fourth Estate" that had become a state within a state, a separate, autonomous force whose aim was to undermine the legitimate authority of civil, religious, and military institutions. Fascism, he said, had eliminated this infamous Fourth Estate from Italian life because it had "entirely repudiated the liberal and social-democratic conception of an irresponsible power that rose above and often against the state in the name of the myth of freedom of the press, which was nothing but the domination of private and particular interests over the general interests of the country and the superimposition of a so-called individual freedom and authority

---

[55] *Codice*, p. 140.

[56] Arnaldo Mussolini's articles on fascist journalism in 1928 are published in their entirety in the *Codice*, pp. 12–20. The article quoted above, entitled "La stampa e lo stile," is reprinted on pp. 13–14, and appeared originally in *Il Popolo d'Italia* on August 25, 1928. His other articles on the subject appeared in *Il Popolo d'Italia* on January 11, 1928, August 26, 1928, and October 12, 1928.

over the only legitimate freedom and authority of the state." [57] Amicucci later developed these concepts in a book entitled *La stampa della rivoluzione e del regime* (Milan, 1938), in which he attributed the degeneration of pre-fascist journalism to the general degeneration of national political life in Italy after the Risorgimento, with its parliamentarianism, its *trasformismo,* its compromises, its class warfare, its masses seduced by anti-state and anti-capitalist propaganda.

In his inaugural address [58] on April 28, 1928, opening the course on the History of Journalism at the University of Perugia, Professor Paolo Orano asserted that his speech would be "a declaration of principles, even more, an act of faith." His central theme, he said, hinged on "the formidable polemic that fascism has stimulated in the world between the democratic thesis and the authoritarian thesis." The democrat maintains that journalism contains in its history that of all freedoms; the fascist is convinced that in the history of journalism are to be traced "many of the causes of the gravest and most persistent errors of the modern political and social consciousness, that this history must serve to emancipate modern man from those errors by helping the regime of discipline to transform journalism from an abusive instrument of propaganda and irresponsibility into a responsible and avowed collaborator in national construction."

Professor Orano maintained that subsequent to the democratic triumph of the French Revolution, journalism became a powerful weapon of political aggression and counteraggression, until finally it emerged as a power unto itself, manipulated public opinion at will, and led to the ultimate "degeneration of the democratic, representative, electoralistic type of regime." Journalism first created the Third Estate as the heir of the *ancien régime* and gave it power. Journalism then became the notorious Fourth Estate, that "state of opinion that can always determine the totality of the political life of the State itself." Suddenly, those entrusted with power "became aware that they had abdicated in favor of the political press." Real power was lost the day in which the state no longer had any freedom to grant nor any to limit or take away. "The triumph of public opinion, of freedom of the press . . . is equivalent to the negation of power," a situation which in Italy, as elsewhere in western Europe, produced a chaotic, floundering political order.

The basic alternatives, Professor Orano concluded, were therefore,

---

[57] Amicucci expressed these ideas on journalism in a reply to Mussolini's speech of October 10, 1928, to the National Fascist Syndicate of Journalists. His reply is published in the *Codice,* pp. 10–11.

[58] Professor Orano's address, entitled "Per una dottrina storica del giornalismo," is published in its entirety in the *Codice,* pp. 42–57.

"Either journalism takes over political power, or the political power also governs journalism." Fascism, he said, has resolved the problem by choosing the second alternative. Fascism is not an opinion, it is a faith, a faith "that condemns and annuls the irresponsible superficiality of opinions and especially of those opinions converted into political enterprises that are called parties. . . . The newspaper of faith has won out in fascist Italy against the newspaper of opinion, the newspaper of sincerity and will has defeated the newspaper characterized by hypocrisy and fear of reponsibility."

As for the contribution to a fascist doctrine of the press of such journalists as Piero Pedrazza, Stanis Ruinas, and Arturo Assante, it must be said that they added nothing significant except their blind, unquestioning faith in the omniscience of Benito Mussolini. Ruinas was typical of these men in his belief that Mussolini's journalistic style and doctrine were unsurpassable. "The Duce has taught us the art of speaking clearly, without frills and stupid fears," Ruinas wrote in 1932. Prefects and the heads of local *fasci* were fallible men, he said, and should not be given the power of life and death over journalists. "There is only one infallible man in Italy: the Duce who always tells the truth. There is only one irreplaceable man in Italy: the Duce who is always right. All the others can make mistakes and can be replaced." [59]

Inspired by Mussolini and other theorists of journalism and carefully instructed by the Press Office of the Head of Government and by the Ministry of the Press and Propaganda,[60] the fascist press obediently fulfilled its responsibilities to the domestic and international goals of the regime. In 1935, continuing and developing a practice initiated soon after the March on Rome by Mussolini's Press Office, the Ministry of the Press and Propaganda began to send directives twice and three times a day to all editors of fascist newspapers. The purpose of these directives was to make sure that the editors understood completely and gave the proper tone and emphasis to, the leading events of the day. Even apparently insignificant news items were carefully screened. A Ministry directive on June 28, 1935, told newspaper editors "not to publish photographs of Primo Carnera lying on the canvas." [61] Another of November 8, 1938, stated: "Lady Rachele Mussolini requests that the newspapers not concern themselves with her imminent private journey to Milan." [62]

[59] Stanis Ruinas, *Appunti sul problema della stampa fascista,* p. 57.

[60] This Ministry was the nucleus of the *Ministero di Cultura Popolare,* founded in June 1937.

[61] This directive is cited by Salvatorelli and Mira, *Storia d'Italia nel periodo fascista,* p. 856.

[62] This directive is cited by Salvatorelli and Mira, p. 857.

But matters of state and international policy were most often covered in the directives. During the Ethiopian war, for example, the Ministry sent the following directives to all Italian newspapers on November 23, 1935: "Do not speak of our military reverses on the Ethiopian front; give broad coverage to the news from Egypt on the anti-British movement there without, however, above all in headlines, giving the impression that we are pleased about this event; do not publish reports of our aerial bombardments in East Africa." [63] The directives of 1938 and 1939 reflected in particular the new alliance between fascist Italy and nazi Germany and the Italian government's hostility to the Western democracies. A directive of May 31, 1938, stated laconically: "Ignore France." Another of July 3, 1939, said: "Complete solidarity with Germany on the question of Danzig." [64]

On January 15, 1938, the editors of all fascist newspapers received a directive concerned with an event in the history of Italian anti-fascism that brings us to the subject matter of the following chapters. The directive stated: "Ignore completely everything that regards the inquest concerning the murder of the Rosselli brothers." [65] Carlo and Nello Rosselli, Florentine Jews who played a leading role in organizing resistance to fascism first in Italy and later abroad, in France and in Spain, had been brutally murdered on June 9, 1937, by a band of French right-wing terrorists in the pay of the fascist government.[66] The murder provoked the outrage and sorrow of anti-fascists throughout Europe. The Rosselli brothers, and particularly Carlo, belonged to the small but determined legion of Italian journalists and intellectuals who, during the fascist era, laid the ideological groundwork for the Italian Resistance Movement of the years 1943 to 1945.

[63] This directive is cited by the anti-fascist émigré newspaper *Giustizia e Libertà* in an article entitled "Gli ordini segreti di Mussolini alla stampa," in the issue of January 3, 1936, p. 1. (NY)

[64] This directive is cited in *Stampa dell'era fascista*, edited by Francesco Flora, p. 55.

[65] *Ibid.*, p. 47.

[66] The circumstances surrounding the murder of the Rosselli brothers and the subsequent inquest initiated by French police authorities are described by Alessandro Levi, *Ricordi dei fratelli Rosselli*, pp. 193–219.

PART II

FROM LEGAL OPPOSITION TO ARMED RESISTANCE

CHAPTER TWO

REPRESENTATIVE LEADERS OF THE LEGAL OPPOSITION PRESS (1919–1926)

It is true that the fall of Mussolini on July 25, 1943, and the announcement on September 8 of Italy's surrender to the Allies greatly intensified and enlarged the power of Italian anti-fascism by bringing thousands of heretofore uncommitted persons into the Resistance Movement. But the essential moral, political, and historical bases of opposition to fascism, as articulated by the underground newspapers of the years 1943 to 1945, were in most instances first developed by the Italian journalists who fought against Mussolini's regime during the 1920's and 1930's. In this chapter we shall discuss the ideas of six representative leaders of the anti-fascist press during the initial legal phase of opposition from 1919 to 1926.

I
Luigi Albertini and Il Corriere della Sera

On November 29, 1925, an article entitled "Farewell" appeared on the first page of one of Italy's oldest and most widely respected daily newspapers, *Il Corriere della Sera* of Milan. The article, written by the newspaper's director and managing editor, Luigi Albertini, ended with these words: "I am losing something that was supremely dear to me, but I conserve intact a spiritual patrimony that is still more dear to me, and I save my dignity and my conscience." [1] Thus Albertini chose to sever his connection with a newspaper with which he had been associated since 1898 rather than acquiesce in a political doctrine and system that were repugnant to him.

The chain of events leading to Albertini's "Farewell" and to the end of *Il Corriere della Sera* as an independent newspaper have already been discussed. As we have seen, he yielded to virtually irresistible political and economic pressures. The decision to resign must have been particu-

[1] The article is cited textually by Alberto Albertini, *Vita di Luigi Albertini*, p. 259.

larly painful for Albertini, since he himself had often expressed a certain cautious approval of the very regime that had so brutally trampled on his right to express himself freely. Despite the manifestly anti-liberal and anti-democractic character of Mussolini's pronouncements prior to the March on Rome, Albertini had welcomed Mussolini's proclaimed intention to "restore order" and to "reestablish the authority of the Italian state" in the face of widespread "socialist and communist subversion." Like his more eminent contemporary, the philosopher Benedetto Croce,[2] he had looked with sympathy on the fascist regime's efforts to quell the social disorder and factional strife that had characterized Italian life in the years immediately following World War I. What then, in view of this initial tendency to regard the fascists with some favor, were the principles that formed the basis of Albertini's subsequent repudiation of fascism?

As indicated in the preceding chapter, Albertini was first of all offended by the vulgar political style and violent methods of the fascists. He belonged to a generation accustomed to resolving problems through orderly debate and discussion. He revered Italy's great liberal statesman, Count Camillo Cavour, whose career represented to him a model of political style and sagacity. Second, Albertini believed profoundly in freedom of the press. This belief, which he first derived from the teachings of Cavour and other founders of united Italy,[3] was further strengthened during

2 For a precise understanding of the reasons that led Croce to give his tentative approval to certain aspects of the fascist movement during the early 1920's, see the last section of the second volume of his *Pagine sparse*, which contains a series of interviews that Croce had with fascist journalists from 1922 to 1924 prior to his definitive break with fascism as revealed in his "Protest against the Manifesto of the Fascist Intellectuals" of May 1925.

3 The struggle for freedom of the press in Italy during the early decades of the nineteenth century was waged most consistently in Milan by the liberal Italian intellectuals who founded the newspaper *Il Conciliatore*, and in Florence by the liberal editors of *Antologia*. During the climactic phase of the Risorgimento, in the 1840's and 1850's the struggle was continued mainly in Turin by the Neapolitan Bertrando Spaventa, who had fled to the Piedmontese capital from Naples, by Luigi Carlo Farini, who founded the magazine *Il Cimento* in 1852, and by Count Camillo Benso di Cavour, founder of *Risorgimento* in 1847 and chief spokesman for the cause of Italian liberalism. Among Cavour's most important statements on freedom of the press was a speech he delivered to the Piedmontese parliament on February 5, 1852, in which he defended the right of newspapers to express dissenting views and denied the efficacy of either legally sanctioned or strong-arm measures against the press. Cavour did not then or later speak very passionately on behalf of freedom of the press. He even had serious doubts about the wisdom of granting unlimited freedom to newspapers to become embroiled in foreign policy matters. By temperament cautious and sober, he believed simply that ideas could not and should not be suppressed by force, and that a climate of freedom was much more conducive to the development of a healthy body politic than one of fear and intimidation. For

a period in his early twenties that he spent in London studying economics and journalism. "London and the *Times*," according to Albertini's brother and colleague Alberto, "confirmed in him the faith in ideas and in the possibility, in a free country, of promoting the elevation of minds through discussion and objective, unprejudiced criticism." [4] Third, Albertini was opposed in principle to the concentration of unlimited political power in the executive branch of government and consequently rejected the various fascist decrees and laws that enabled Mussolini to reduce Parliament to the status of a rubber-stamping agency. It was his commitment to constitutional, parliamentary government that compelled him, in October 1924, to write an editorial in which he spoke out forcefully against the dictatorial powers granted to Mussolini, denounced the undemocratic character of the "electoral reform" of December 1923, and criticized Italy's liberal ruling class for its failure "to remain worthy of the tradition left by the founders of national unity." [5]

II
Giovanni Amendola and Il Mondo

Luigi Albertini taught by example. He was willing to sacrifice his career for the sake of principle. In this way he won the loyalty of his fellow workers on *Il Corriere della Sera*. The same was true of Giovanni Amendola, who in December 1921 founded the liberal newspaper *Il Mondo* of Rome.

But Amendola's liberalism differed sharply from that of Albertini. A combative, intransigent Neapolitan, he never entertained any illusions about the capacity or desire of the fascists to restore order within the framework of constitutional procedure. For Amendola, there could be no compromise between freedom and dictatorship. No possible progress in social and economic democracy, no guarantee of public tranquility and order, could ever be justified if such progress and guarantees impinged on the freedom of individuals, groups, and political parties to advance their ideas freely.

Amendola was an enemy of all extremists whether left or right. During the months prior to the March on Rome, he was acutely aware of the crisis through which Italy's liberal institutions were passing and struggled

---

an enlightening discussion of the struggle for freedom of the press in Italy during the period of the Risorgimento, the reader is referred to Ugo D'Andrea's chapter "Libertà di stampa nella rivoluzione liberale," in *Saggi storici sul liberalismo italiano*, edited by Panfilo Gentile, pp. 201–82.

[4] Albertini, *Vita di Luigi Albertini*, p. 55.
[5] The editorial is cited by Albertini, *ibid.*, p. 236.

mightily to restore the Italian people's confidence in liberal democracy and representative government. On August 24, 1922, he called on all men loyal to Italian democracy to defend the liberal state against the threat of fascism and communism and spoke of the need for a "democratic federation" of men who, above and beyond all specific political programs, would unite in defense of liberty.[6] The following month, in an article entitled "Glorification of the Mass," he analyzed the contradictions inherent in Mussolini's tendency to idolize the proletarian masses while at the same time advocating a form of authoritarian elitism alien to the Western democratic tradition. The cult of the mass man and elitism, wrote Amendola, were contrary to the principles of liberal democracy, which repudiated both demagoguery and paternalism.[7]

One of Amendola's most important editorials [8] in *Il Mondo* appeared on February 8, 1924, when the fascist government had already begun to "prepare" the Italian people for the coming elections in April. Entitled "The Crisis of Authority," this editorial resolutely defined the nature of the challenge posed to Italian democracy by fascism:

> Fascism has enclosed itself in an insoluble contradiction. Since it is the antithesis of the fundamental conceptions and of the constitutional basis on which the Italian state was built and since it declares that it is not a party in government but instead the state itself, the entire state as spirit and will, it must face an inexorable dilemma: either declare that the Italian state is not amenable to the application of its theories, or agree that the fundamental bases of the state have been harmed and altered and that we are, in a few words, outside the framework of the Constitution.

Amendola continued his editorial with an affirmation of faith in liberal, multiparty democracy:

> The authority of the state does not lie in the annulment of parties but in their development; it does not result from their abdication of responsibility but from their conflicts. . . . The authority of the state grows and becomes strengthened to the extent that the state is capable of freedom, that is, to the extent that the state is capable of having parties in government without ever being forced to tolerate a government dominated by a single party.
>
> Now fascism has denied this essential principle of the life of a modern state. It has not aspired to be a party in government but rather the government itself.

The assassination of the socialist deputy Giacomo Matteotti on June 10, 1924, marked the beginning of a concerted but ultimately unsuccessful

---

[6] Giovanni Amendola, "I nemici interni della democrazia," reprinted in *La democrazia italiana contro il fascismo,* pp. 16–18.

[7] Amendola, "Glorificazione della massa," reprinted in *ibid.,* pp. 23–26.

[8] Amendola, "La crisi dell'autorità," reprinted in *ibid.,* pp. 250–53.

effort on the part of the opposition parties to bring about the fall of Mussolini's regime. In his editorials in the newspaper *La Giustizia*[9] and in a speech delivered to the Chamber of Deputies on May 30, 1924, Matteotti had denounced the violent methods used by the fascists to assure their victory in the elections of April 5. Three days after the assassination, all the opposition parties decided to abstain from further parliamentary action until those responsible for the crime were apprehended and punished. Several weeks later, when it became known that the crime was instigated by the fascist government, the opposition parties "seceded" from parliament and declared that they would not return until Mussolini's private Militia was disbanded and until there was a restoration of legal, constitutional government in Italy. Almost immediately, Amendola became the most forceful spokesman for the "Aventine secessionists." Under his guidance, in the fall of 1924, various members of the opposition parties— liberals, Christian democracts, republicans, socialists—founded the "National Union of Liberal and Democratic Forces," which Luigi Salvatorelli aptly describes as "A distant foreshadowing of the interparty committees of national liberation that will take shape after the fall of the fascist regime" [10] in July 1943.

Amendola also used the pages of *Il Mondo* to publish several documents that contained irrefutable evidence of Mussolini's complicity in the murder of Matteotti, the most important of which, a "memorandum" written by Cesare Rossi, appeared in the December 27, 1924, issue. The fascists had sought to blame Rossi, the former head of Mussolini's Press Office, for the Matteotti murder. Rossi admitted his part in the plot, but stated in his memorandum that "everything that has happened has always happened either through the direct will or through the approval or complicity of the Duce." [11] Amendola's campaign in 1924 to undermine Mussolini's power, although unsuccessful at the time, established a precedent for the moral opposition to fascism that later proved to be of decisive importance to the Resistance Movement of the years 1943 to 1945.

Amendola was not of course the only anti-fascist journalist who in 1924 challenged the moral legitimacy of Mussolini's regime after the assassination of Matteotti. He was assisted in this effort by—among many others—Ferdinando Schiavetti, the chief editor of *La Voce Repubblicana,* Luigi Salvatorelli of *La Stampa,* Giuseppe Canepa of the socialist newspaper *Il Lavoro* in Genoa, Francesco Luigi Ferrari of *Il Domani*

[9] Matteotti's articles in *La Giustizia* in 1923 and 1924 are collected in Giacomo Matteotti, *Reliquie,* edited by Mario Guarnieri and Claudio Treves.
[10] Salvatorelli and Mira, *Storia d'Italia nel periodo fascista,* p. 317.
[11] Rossi's memorandum is cited by Salvatorelli and Mira, *ibid.,* p. 329.

d'Italia in Milan, and, in particular, Giuseppe Donati of *Il Popolo* in Rome.

III
Guiseppe Donati and Il Popolo

The history of anti-fascism during the period 1919 to 1926 includes the names of many Catholic journalists [12] who upheld the principle of a free press and who refused to accept the fait accompli of the fascist revolution.

Among the most courageous and eloquent Catholic opponents of the regime was Giuseppe Donati, who in Rome was managing editor of the newspaper *Il Popolo,* the official organ of the *Partito Popolare,* from February 1923 to June 1925. Although subjected to constant ridicule and threats of physical violence, Donati devoted many of his writings in *Il Popolo* to demonstrating the fundamental incompatibility of Christian teachings with the anti-democratic methods and aims of Mussolini's regime. By 1924 it had become clear to Donati that whenever nonviolent methods of persuasion proved inadequate the fascists resorted inevitably to beatings and killings. The assassination of Matteotti aroused the most bitter feelings of contempt and indignation in Donati, as evidenced in an article he published in *Il Popolo* as soon as it became known that the crime had been committed by persons closely associated with the fascist hierarchy in Rome. "By now it is clear," wrote Donati, "that Matteotti

---

[12] One of the strongest voices against fascism, particularly after the Matteotti murder, was that of the Catholic journalist Francesco Luigi Ferrari, who was chief editor of *Il Domani d'Italia* in Milan from December 1922 to 1925, when he emigrated to Belgium. On June 29, 1924, Ferrari published an article in *Il Domani d'Italia* significantly entitled "Resistere," whose prophetic message of protest deserves to be cited here in this study of the Italian anti-fascist press: "What agitated and disturbed the Italian soul and the conscience of the world . . . after the fascist assassination of Matteotti will be, by others, isolated and evaluated as the most heinous of political crimes. For us, this crime is the culmination of the inevitable and inexorable reality of the entire fascist regime, as we have predicted and judged it to be for several years. Very few persons can feel as morally serene as we do in affirming that they have given nothing of their spirit or action to fascism from its first appearance in the turbulent postwar years of Italian life. Not by reason of sectarianism, nor of reaction; but out of the clear and sure conviction that the ideas, the methods, the men and works of fascism would produce nothing of value and that gradually or rapidly fascism would instead be led to every vile form of degeneration and abomination. We refused the promised "normalization" of fascism, we denied its boast of "moralization." The chain that led to the assassination in Rome, link by link, crime by crime, was clear to us from our objective and precise study of what fascism does, of what it is and will continue to be unless the powerful storm of national and universal indignation strikes it and destroys it forever." Ferrari's article is reprinted in *L'antifascismo italiano,* edited by Paolo Alatri, vol. 1, pp. 317–19.

has been suppressed for reasons connected with his exercise of his political mandate. . . . We have only two requests to make of the guardians of the law: that light be shed on the crime and that justice be meted out to those responsible for it. We do not ask this—let it be known—to give satisfaction to one side or the other; we ask it simply for the honor of Italy." [13] Donati was in fact responsible for bringing formal charges, on December 6, 1924, against General Emilio De Bono, the commander of Mussolini's private fascist militia. General De Bono's guilt in organizing the assault and murder of Matteotti was an open secret. Nevertheless he was later acquitted of the crime.[14]

Donati's repudiation of fascism was based in part on the same liberal and democratic convictions that inspired Albertini and Amendola but derived in an even more fundamental sense from his interpretation of Catholic doctrine. On June 23, 1923, he wrote an editorial in which he explained that, as a Catholic, he could never accept fascism's "deification of the state," its exaltation of nationalism, its contempt for the dignity of the individual.[15] A week later he reiterated his reasons for opposing fascism. Certain of the regime's proposals for social and economic construction, he said, were acceptable. But, he noted, "we are aware of two important characteristics of fascism: the theory of violence and the conception, as 'absolute,' of the nation, common to the nationalists. Now these two principles are in opposition to the doctrine of the Catholic Church and are therefore incompatible with Catholicism." [16]

Donati was a militant defender of freedom of the press. His most significant article on this question, entitled "Arbitrary Power, the Law, and Freedom of the Press," [17] appeared in *Il Popolo* on July 13, 1923, in response to the decree reinforcing the punitive potential of the edict of 1848 (the decree had already been announced, though it would be formally signed by the King on July 15). The fascist governent, Donati said, regarded the free expression of political opinions as "intolerable, an act of hostility, a threat against the state." The reason for this attitude lay in the fact that the fascists did not conceive of the state as "the political organization of social forces whose end was the synthesis of various interests, and the ethical expression of associated minds" but rather as an absolute power that controls its subjects and treats them as "adolescents

---

[13] Donati's article is cited textually by Giuseppe Rossini, *Il fascismo e la Resistenza*, p. 37.

[14] See Salvatorelli and Mira, *Storia d'Italia nel periodo fascista*, pp. 329, 334.

[15] This article is reprinted in Lorenzo Bedeschi, *Giuseppe Donati*, pp. 153–54.

[16] This article is reprinted in Bedeschi, *ibid.*, pp. 155–56.

[17] This article is reprinted in Giuseppe Donati, *Scritti politici*, edited by Giuseppe Rossini, pp. 85–91.

in need of correction." He then proceeded to show how the new decree had violated established constitutional principles and had brought the press, which ought to be free and autonomous, under the arbitrary control of a governing political party. He branded the decree "a very serious and dangerous precedent for the confusion of powers and for demagogic despotism."

In June 1925, Donati chose the path of exile to Paris. *Il Popolo* was suppressed in November 1925 and did not reappear again until the latter part of 1943, when Alcide De Gasperi, Guido Gonella, Giuseppe Spataro, and other Catholic anti-fascists collaborated in publishing the first clandestine issue of the newspaper in Rome during the German occupation.

IV
Piero Gobetti and Rivoluzione Liberale

The weekly political review *Rivoluzione Liberale* was founded by Piero Gobetti in Turin in February 1922. From that date to the day of its suppression—November 25, 1925—Gobetti carried on an uninterrupted campaign against the undemocratic methods of the fascist regime and published a whole series of articles on social, economic, and political problems that fascist authorities invariably found to be subversive in intent. An injunction of October 23, 1925, cited as subversive the review's "tendentious and irreverent attitude toward the Monarchy," its "injurious abuse of the Catholic Church," its "defamatory writings directed against the authority of the state," and its "anti-patriotic interpretation of the Fiume enterprise." [18]

The Prefect in Turin who issued this injunction was substantially correct in his charges, since most of the contributors to *Rivoluzione Liberale,* and particularly Gobetti, did not limit themselves to attacking the fascist government alone but instead sought to identify the causes of and seek the remedies for the deficiencies in Italian life that had allowed fascism to gain power in the first place. With few exceptions, Gobetti's colleagues had two traits in common: intransigent opposition to fascism and a capacity for making precise analyses of sociopolitical problems. Among the contributors to *Rivoluzione Liberale* were the historian Gaetano Salvemini, whose pragmatic, incisive mind exerted a profound influence on Gobetti; the liberal economist and future president of Italy Luigi Einaudi; the

---

[18] As indicated in note 41 of Chapter I, the text of this injunction is displayed at the *Centro Gobetti* in Turin.

historian Luigi Salvatorelli; the *liceo* professor Augusto Monti, whose example and teaching inspired a whole generation of Turinese anti-fascist intellectuals; Max Ascoli, now publisher of *The Reporter,* who left Italy in 1929 to take up his career as a university professor in the United States; Don Luigi Sturzo, the founder of the Catholic *Partito Popolare,* who continued his opposition to fascism as an exile in London and, during World War II, in the United States; and other eminent anti-fascists such as Riccardo Bauer, Carlo Rosselli, Guido De Ruggiero, Mario Grieco, and Rodolfo Morandi.

Piero Gobetti was a liberal but a liberal of a special sort. For him, liberalism signified the dynamic, ongoing struggle of men to "liberate" themselves from every form of oppression and paternalism and to achieve a free, thoroughly democratic social and political order. For Gobetti, liberals were not worthy of their name unless they collaborated in the task of bringing the masses of people into active, direct participation in government. Although he was never a Marxist, or even a socialist in any accepted sense of the word, he attributed a liberal, that is, a "liberating" value to the Bolshevik Revolution in that it was the product of a popular mass struggle against a paternalistic, autocratic regime that had created an ever-widening gulf between the rulers and the ruled of Russia.[19] For the same reason, he admired the work of Antonio Gramsci and other Italian communist leaders who in 1920 and 1921 had attempted to establish democratically elected workers' councils in the factories of Turin.[20]

Gobetti regarded fascism as the inevitable outcome of certain deficiencies in the Italian character and in Italian historical development. He belived that the Risorgimento had failed to free Italy from the burdens of monarchical paternalism, Catholic traditionalism, and the conventional, hide-bound conservatism of the country's business and industrial leaders. Nearly every established institution and custom of Italian life was repudiated by Gobetti. Fascism was merely the latest and worst form of a type of political corruption to which the Italian people had allowed itself to be subjected for centuries. What segments of Italian society had supported fascism? Gobetti asked in one of the first numbers of *Rivoluzione Liberale.* His answer was unambiguous: the supporters of fascism were the tycoons of heavy industry, the large landowners, the "ex-liberals," and "ex-Catholics" who had converted to fascism to protect

[19] Piero Gobetti, in a review of Trotsky's *Terrorism and Communism,* reprinted in *Le riviste di Gobetti,* edited by Lelio Basso and Luigi Anderlini, p. 134.

[20] For an excellent analysis of Gobetti's point of view with regard to the communist-led workers' councils in Turin, see Lelio Basso's introduction to *Le riviste di Gobetti.*

their power and privilege.[21] His attitude toward King Victor Emmanuel III was one of utter contempt, since the King had approved Mussolini's assumption of power on October 31, 1922, and had subsequently rubber-stamped every illiberal decree and law initiated by the fascist government.

By reason of his moral intransigence, his belief in the liberating function of the working classes, his conception of democracy as a sociopolitical order in which all segments of society participate actively in the processes of government, and his contempt for every form of paternalism, Gobetti placed himself at the vanguard of a political movement that was to play a decisive role in the struggle against fascism in the 1930's and then during the period of armed Resistance. This movement, which in 1929 took the name of "Justice and Freedom" and numbered among its members many of Italy's outstanding liberal and socialist intellectuals, formed the basis of the Action Party founded in 1942. As we shall see, there is an unbroken link of continuity between the political thought of Gobetti and the radical anti-fascism of the actionists.

On November 25, 1925, because of his defiance of the injunction of October 27, Gobetti was ordered by police authorities in Turin to resign from his position as editor of *Rivoluzione Liberale*. He almost immediately went into exile in Paris, where he died of influenza on February 16, 1926, at the age of twenty-four. His friends in Turin did not fail to publicize the fact that the persecution and beatings to which Gobetti had been subjected during the preceding two years had undoubtedly undermined his power of resistance to the disease that killed him.

V
Pietro Nenni and Avanti!

Pietro Nenni assumed the editorship of the newspaper *Avanti!* [22] in April 1923, at the time the Italian Socialist Party was passing through the gravest crisis of its thirty-one-year history. In the first place, in January 1921 and in October 1922, two segments of the formerly unified socialists had broken with the party and had formed autonomous political parties of their own. In January 1921, a group of left-wing socialists withdrew from the Socialist Party and, under the leadership of Amadeo

[21] Almost all of Gobetti's articles and editorials in *Rivoluzione Liberale*, especially those of 1923 and 1924, place the blame for the triumph of fascism on these elements of Italian society. However, Gobetti also spoke frequently in derisive tones of the political immaturity and impressionability of the Italian people in general.
[22] The information on *Avanti!* and on the political problems of the Italian Socialist Party during the years 1921 to 1923 has been drawn mainly from Gaetano Arfé, *Storia dell'Avanti! 1896–1926*.

Bordiga and Antonio Gramsci, founded the Italian Communist Party. Then in early October 1922, the reformist wing of the Socialist Party was expelled for advocating continued parliamentary collaboration with Italy's bourgeois liberal government. The immediate result of this expulsion was the founding of a reformist Socialist Party, led by the venerable Filippo Turati, that called itself the *Partito Socialista Unitario.* Thus by the beginning of 1923 the majority of socialists who had remained within the fold of the party was faced with the determined opposition of two small but powerful groups that both claimed to be the legitimate heirs to the tradition of the Italian and international socialist movement. Second, in 1922 and 1923, the Italian Socialist Party was one of the principal targets of fascist violence. Raids on rural socialist cooperatives, numerous assassinations of rank-and-file party organizers, and frequent devastating assaults on the offices and presses of *Avanti!* had succeeded in demoralizing and intimidating thousands of persons who had theretofore given their unqualified support to the party's directives and campaigns. Third, on the international scene the Italian Socialist Party had incurred the wrath of the world communist movement by its reluctance to endorse all the theses of the Third International founded in Moscow in 1919. By April 1923, the Soviet government, through its own emissaries and Italian communist spokesmen, had declared the Italian Socialist Party to be beyond the pale of revolutionary salvation. The Soviet leaders took this position despite the fact that many Italian socialists had since 1917 been among the most militant supporters of the Russian Revolution.

Nenni himself, after a brief flirtation in 1919 with the "revolutionary" ideas of the nascent fascist movement and an equally brief affiliation with the Republican Party, had worked as a Socialist Party organizer in 1921 and 1922, during which time he also contributed occasional articles to *Avanti!* He rose to sudden prominence, however, in January 1923, when he took a strong position against those Socialist Party leaders who, like *Avanti!*'s chief editor, Giacinto Menotti Serrati, advocated the immediate fusion of the Italian Socialist and Communist Parties and the consequent entrance of the Italian socialists into the ranks of the Third International. Nenni argued that a step of such grave import should only be taken after the party membership had weighed all the consequences and, in accordance with democratic procedure, had voted either to accept or to reject Serrati's proposals.[23]

Nenni's rebellion against the "fusionists" was approved by the great

---

[23] Nenni's editorial of January 3, 1923, opposing the immediate fusion of the Italian Socialist and Communist Parties is cited in part and discussed by Arfé, pp. 193–95.

majority of the party's members, and for the next two and one-half years, as managing editor of *Avanti!*, he engaged in constant polemical debate with the communists on the left and the reformist socialists on the right. At the same time he confronted the difficult task of articulating his party's ambivalent attitude toward the methods and aims of the new Soviet state. Although he never tired of expressing his solidarity with the Bolshevik Revolution, Nenni was much influenced by the liberal socialism and constitutionalism of Filippo Turati, as well as by the writings of Leon Trotsky. As a consequence, in 1923 and 1924 *Avanti!* began to speak more and more frequently about the dangers of a bureaucratic degeneration of Soviet political life and published articles criticizing the undemocratic, dogmatic mentality of the Soviet leadership.

But in 1923 and 1924, the main problem faced by Nenni remained that of the fascist phenomenon, which he saw as the reaction of Italy's bourgeois class—led by industrialists and landowners—against its traditional class enemy, the urban and agricultural proletariat. Yet he also recognized that not all bourgeois regimes are identical, that the fascist government, although representing capitalist interests, was substantially different from the bourgeois liberal governments that had preceded it.[24] He therefore called for a united anti-fascist front, a maneuver that was promptly rejected by the communists as collaborationist and by the reformists as inopportune.

During the months just prior to the elections of April 1924, Nenni became increasingly aware of the need for cooperation between the socialists and all other anti-fascist parties in the struggle to restore the political freedoms already largely suppressed by the fascist regime. After the fascists' electoral victory, and especially after the murder of Matteotti, he intensified his campaign in the pages of *Avanti!* for a united front against fascism and subsequently announced his party's complete solidarity with the Aventine secessionists. But the Aventine opposition parties moved too slowly to suit the Socialist Party, so that by the middle of 1925 most of the party's members followed Nenni's lead and again retreated into their traditional and rigidly "autonomist" position. Nenni subsequently tried to find a middle way between the extremes of collaboration with the liberal anti-fascists and revolutionary intransigence, and on December 12, 1925, published a letter in *Avanti!* in which he called for the reunification of the Italian Socialist Party and the *Partito Socialista Unitario*.[25] The party's leadership immediately repudiated reunification, and as a result Nenni resigned from his position as managing editor of *Avanti!*

[24] *Ibid.*, p. 202.
[25] *Ibid.*, pp. 219–20.

The position was filled by Riccardo Modigliani, who directed the newspaper until its suppression on October 31, 1926.

Nenni was discouraged but not defeated by the frustrations and struggles of the preceding three years. From March to October 1926, he worked together with Carlo Rosselli in publishing the magazine *Il Quarto Stato* in Milan. Following its demise, he left Italy for a period of prolonged exile in France, where he continued his career as an organizer and propagandist for the embattled, perenially faction-ridden Italian Socialist Party.

VI
Antonio Gramsci and L'Ordine Nuovo

The first issue of *L'Ordine Nuovo,* a "weekly review of socialist culture," appeared in Turin on May 1, 1919. The review was created by four dedicated and intellectually gifted left-wing socialists who, in January 1921, were to found the Italian Communist Party: Antonio Gramsci, Palmiro Togliatti, Angelo Tasca, and Umberto Terracini. Gramsci was the leader and principal spokesman for the *L'Ordine Nuovo* group. He was a sickly, hunchbacked man, but his exceptionally lucid mind and tenacious will more than compensated for his physical disabilities. Gramsci had left his native Sardinia in 1911 to pursue a course of literary studies at the University of Turin. During World War I, he resumed his early interests in politics and economics, and by the beginning of 1917 he was named secretary of the Turinese section of the Socialist Party. From that point on he devoted himself to the task of building a militant socialist movement in Italy.[26]

The weekly *L'Ordine Nuovo* of the years 1919 and 1920 reflected the experiences and thought of those Italian socialists who, like Gramsci and his colleagues, were dissatisfied with what they regarded as the excessively cautious and opportunistic policies of their party's leadership and who aspired to place the Italian Socialist Party at the vanguard of a genuinely national and revolutionary movement capable of rebuilding all of Italian society on a new foundation. The review constantly spurred on the Turinese workers in their struggle against the paternalism of the city's industrial and managerial class and elaborated a carefully planned program for the creation of workers' councils that were, in fact, successfully if only temporarily established in many of the factories of Turin.

In January 1921, coincident with the founding of the Italian Com-

[26] For a thorough and readable account of Gramsci's life and political thought, see John Cammett, *Antonio Gramsci and the Origins of Italian Communism.*

munist Party, *L'Ordine Nuovo* was transformed from a weekly into a daily newspaper whose motto, borrowed from Lassalle, was "To tell the truth is revolutionary." But Lenin, not Lassalle, was the guiding spirit behind the new communist daily. Nearly all of Gramsci's articles in *L'Ordine Nuovo* during the years 1921 and 1922, although bearing the mark of an independent and creative mind, were inspired by the teachings of Lenin. The most painful "truth" to be told, according to Gramsci, was that in Russia a workers' state had been founded on the principle of the dictatorship of the proletariat, while in Italy the Italian Socialist Party, despite its mass following and many opportunities for concrete revolutionary action, had indulged in idle propaganda and had allowed itself to be overwhelmed by the assault of fascist and other reactionary forces. Since the Italian Socialist Party had proved itself incapable of leading the Italian proletariat toward the acquisition of effective state power, it was clear that only a truly revolutionary Communist Party, functioning within the framework of the Third International, could mobilize the energies of the working class in its struggle to overthrow the capitalist system.[27] Gramsci never deviated from this position. As fascist violence increased and as it became more and more evident that the Fascist Party would eventually seize total power in Italy, his point of view acquired an undeniable relevance for Italians who looked to the Soviet Union as a model for the revolutionary transformation of their own society.

Throughout the year 1921, Gramsci grappled with the phenomenon of Italian fascism. Fascism was, for him, the ideology and political movement of a disaffected petty bourgeoisie which, by reason of its lack of working class consciousness and *arrivisme,* its cult of nationalism and fear of socialism, had allowed itself to be used by the cynical financiers and industrialists who actually ruled Italy. The petty bourgeoisie provided the men and ideas for the movement; they were the organizers of the "punitive expeditions" against socialist and democratic institutions; they spoke most vociferously of Italian national greatness. But they were essentially puppets in the hands of Italian capitalists, who with fascism were attempting to resolve the problem of capitalist production and trade resulting from World War I through the establishment of a dictatorship able to safeguard their economic interests.[28] Yet like Lenin in *Imperialism: The Highest Stage of Capitalism,* Gramsci also saw the crisis of Italian society following World War I as part of the general crisis

[27] Gramsci, "Lo stato operaio," *L'Ordine Nuovo,* January 1, 1921, reprinted in *2000 pagine di Gramsci,* vol. I, pp. 547–50.

[28] Gramsci, "Italia e Spagna," *L'Ordine Nuovo,* March 10, 1921, reprinted in *2000 pagine di Gramsci,* vol. I, pp. 563–65.

of international finance capital, which had brought unprecedented misery and suffering to the peoples of the world in its lust for territorial expansion and profit.[29]

As for Mussolini, Gramsci regarded him as the very incarnation of the worst Italian petty bourgeois traits. The fascist leader was a "subversive reactionary," an "illogical, inflated, grotesque, superficial" man who sooner or later would bring catastrophic ruin upon the Italian people.[30] Indeed, in his judgment of Mussolini and analyses of the fascist phenomenon in general, Gramsci was often profound and prophetic.

In June 1922, Gramsci left Italy, and for the next two years he worked in Moscow and Vienna as a propagandist for the Third International. He returned to Italy several weeks before the assassination of Matteotti in June 1924, following his election as a communist deputy to the Italian Parliament. On March 1, 1924, *L'Ordine Nuovo* had been refounded as a bi-monthly review in which Gramsci sought to outline new proposals and goals for the Italian Communist Party. Fascism was now in power; the entire Italian working class was demoralized and disoriented. In response to this situation, Gramsci said, Italian communists had to lay the groundwork for a future revolutionary organization. He called for the independent political action of the working class and for the mobilization of small, thoroughly disciplined groups of communist labor organizers, advocated a strengthening of ties with the Third International, and proposed the formation of special cells and schools to train party propagandists.[31] Gramsci's program already reflected the imminent need for the kind of clandestine, conspiratorial apparatus that the Italian communists did in fact create during the next several years.

Because of fascist violence, censorship, and other harassments, only six issues of *L'Ordine Nuovo* appeared in 1924 and only two in 1925. Yet the review provided Gramsci with the means to continue his analyses of fascism and to rally the party faithful to renewed action. Had it not been for his example and thought, it is doubtful that the Italian Communist Party would have been able to function as effectively as it did during the next eighteen years and to play a predominant role in the Resistance from 1943 to 1945. Gramsci himself did not live to see the end of Mussolini's regime. He died in a Rome clinic in 1937, after serving

[29] Gramsci, "Chi deve pagare," *L'Ordine Nuovo*, March 20, 1921, reprinted in *2000 pagine di Gramsci*, vol. I, pp. 576–78.

[30] Gramsci, "Sovversivismo reazionario," *L'Ordine Nuovo*, June 22, 1921, reprinted in *2000 pagine di Gramsci*, vol. I, pp. 592–94.

[31] Gramsci, "Il Progamma dell'Ordine Nuovo," *L'Ordine Nuovo*, April 1–15, 1924, reprinted in *2000 pagine di Gramsci*, vol. I, pp. 720–25.

nine years of a twenty-year sentence imposed on him in 1928 by the Fascist Special Tribunal.

Gramsci's contribution to the Italian communist movement was not limited to his activities as a political strategist and spokesman for the Third International. As noted by Aldo Garosci, if on the one hand the Italian Communist Party "was born through the direct intervention of the Communist International, which was already [in 1921] dominated by the overpowering weight of the effective power and 'myth' of the Russian revolution," it is also true that the party "had native roots" and was from its inception an authentic "representative of certain historical traditions of the Italian working class . . ."[32] Gramsci was primarily responsible for imparting this "national" character to Italian communism, since from the first years of his involvement in the Italian working class movement one of his chief concerns was "to translate the Mazzinian tradition into socialist terms."[33] In both his early writings and his *Prison Notebooks,* which he wrote from 1927 to 1935, Gramsci expressed a constant conviction that a thoroughgoing socialist revolution in Italy was the only way of fulfilling the promises and struggles of the Risorgimento. His analysis of the economic and social problems that plagued the southern Italian peasantry, whom he saw as the chief potential ally of the country's industrial proletariat, also "imparted a 'national' character to the [projected] socialist revolution in Italy, since only such a revolution could complete the unification of the country by ending the 'colonial' subjection of the South."[34]

Another natively Italian aspect of Gramsci's thought was his lifelong indebtedness to the neoidealist philosopher Benedetto Croce, whose influence at the University of Turin was spread through the appointment in 1913 of Croce's disciple Umberto Cosmo as professor of Italian literature. From his study of Croce, Gramsci developed a strongly voluntaristic and subjectivistic approach to history that led him to repudiate the element of historical determinism that characterizes many Marxist thinkers.[35] It

[32] Aldo Garosci, "The Italian Communist Party," *Communism in Western Europe,* edited by Mario Einaudi, p. 159.

[33] Gramsci used this expression in a short treatise written in 1917 entitled *La città futura.* See Cammett, *Antonio Gramsci and the Origins of Italian Communism,* p. 43.

[34] Cammett, *Antonio Gramsci and the Origins of Italian Communism,* p. 177. For Gramsci's views on the relationship between the southern question, the Risorgimento, and the development of Italian socialism, see Antonio Gramsci, *Il Risorgimento.*

[35] Gramsci's reflections on Croce's philosophy and view of history are collected in the volume *Il materialismo storico e la filosofia di Benedetto Croce.* Among the works in which the relationship between the thought of Croce and that of Gramsci is discussed are Eugenio Garin, *Cronache di filosofia italiana,* and Michele Abbate, *La filosofia di Benedetto Croce e la crisi della società italiana.*

is probable that Croce's influence on Gramsci, Togliatti, and other members of the *L'Ordine Nuovo* group has been responsible for the relative "liberalism" and "autonomy" of the Italian Communist Party during and after World War II, as compared with the rigidly doctrinaire character of other European sections of the communist movement.

CHAPTER THREE

ANTI-FASCIST JOURNALISTS IN THE UNDERGROUND AND IN EXILE (1925–1939)

With the enactment and rigid enforcement of the Special Laws in Defense of the State of November 1926, the fascist government put an end to all legal opposition to its power. From the mid-1920's to the first years of World War II, however, the spirit of active resistance to fascism was kept alive by workers, journalists, intellectuals, and political leaders who either chose the path of exile—chiefly to France, Belgium, Switzerland, England, the United States, and the Soviet Union—in order to reestablish the anti-fascist newspapers and political movements that had been outlawed by Mussolini's regime or who remained in Italy and engaged in various forms of conspiratorial activity, among the most important of which was the printing and distributing of underground newspapers.

I
The Concentrazione Antifascista and La Libertà

From the early 1920's to the beginning of World War II, all roads led away from Rome for those Italians who refused to accommodate themselves to the triumph of the fascist revolution. A first wave of emigration, composed mainly of industrial and agricultural workers whose lives had been disrupted by the terror of the fascist action squads, began to take shape even before the March on Rome, and continued to grow apace from 1924 to about 1930. These rank-and-file victims of fascist violence formed political groups and associations in widely dispersed European cities, from Brussels to Paris, from Berne to Marseilles. They founded the first anti-fascist émigré newspapers, such as *L'Italie Libre* and *La Voce Socialista* of Paris, *Le Radical* of Marseilles, *Il Mezzogiorno* in Toulouse, most of which were sporadic and short-lived.[1]

---

[1] For a discussion of this first proletarian wave of anti-fascist emigration, see Salvatorelli and Mira, *Storia d'Italia nel periodo fascista*, pp. 551, 552. The names and places of publication of the first working-class émigré newspapers are mentioned in *L'Exposition de la Presse Antifasciste Italienne*, p. 53.

Beginning in 1924 and continuing thereafter until the years just preceding the outbreak of World War II, many of the leading representatives of Italy's intelligentsia followed their proletarian allies into exile. Among the émigrés who left Italy for the United States were the journalist Max Ascoli, the novelist G. A. Borgese, Arturo Toscanini, and Enrico Fermi. From 1924 to 1940, when he emigrated to the United States, Don Luigi Sturzo, the founder of the Catholic *Partitio Popolare,* lived in London, where he published an important cycle of historical studies under the general title *Italy and Fascism.* Other distinguished and internationally known Italian intellectuals who left Italy from 1924 to 1927 included the historian and diplomat Count Carlo Sforza, the jurist Silvio Trentin, the art critic and historian Lionello Venturi, the historian Guglielmo Ferrero, the liberal ex-prime minister Francesco Saverio Nitti, and the historian Gaetano Salvemini.

Like Salvemini, most of the émigré intellectuals and politicians chose Paris as their home and principal center of activity. From the mid-1920's on, Paris was the scene of intense political action on the part of Italian anti-fascists of every possible sort. All of the outlawed opposition parties set up new headquarters there. Almost every organized anti-fascist movement, from the republicans to the communists, began publishing pamphlets, newspapers, and magazines in the French capital.

It was in Paris, on May 1, 1927, that the first issue of the weekly newspaper *La Libertà,* the organ of the *Concentrazione Antifascista,* appeared. It was from Paris that it was subsequently distributed illegally in Italy. The *Concentrazione Antifascista* was a heterogeneous organization composed of political groups united only by their common desire to restore freedom in Italy. This common commitment inspired the revolutionary socialist Pietro Nenni; the reformist socialists Filippo Turati, Giuseppe Emanuele Modigliani, and Claudio Treves; the Catholic Giuseppe Donati; the liberal Alberto Cianca; Luigi Compolonghi of the Italian League for Human Rights; and the republicans Eugenio Chiesa, Mario Bergamo, and Ferdinando Schiavetti, all of whom belonged to the *Concentrazione* and contributed articles to *La Libertà.* Claudio Treves, a former editor of *La Giustizia* and a close friend of Giacomo Matteotti, was managing editor of *La Libertà* until his death in June 1933. In November 1931, the Justice and Freedom Movement, whose ideas and campaigns will be discussed later in this chapter, also joined the *Concentrazione,* so that in effect this alliance in exile included every important anti-fascist group except the Italian Communist Party.

Although *La Libertà* did not make an official declaration of the *Concentrazione's* repudiation of the Italian Monarchy and commitment to a republican form of government until May 1928, the newspaper's

"Program," as announced on May 1, 1927, was decidedly anti-monar-
chical, radical, and socialistic in character. After blaming King Victor
Emmanuel III for his subservience to the dictatorship, the Program
stated that three concepts would underlie the action of the *Concentrazione*
in the following years. The first was that "the conquest of freedom is
the indispensable premise for all political and moral movements committed to a future of political democracy and social justice." Second, the
Program declared that "the masses of workers constitute the principal
nucleus of the anti-fascist forces." Third, it affirmed that "the anti-fascist
battle will be effective to the extent that it becomes united with the
radicalism of the oppressed, frankly socialist and republican masses." [2]

In 1928 and particularly in 1929, following the treaty and Concordat
between the fascist government and the Vatican signed on February 11,
1929, *La Libertà* began attacking not only fascism but also the various
reactionary forces in Italy that were allied with fascism: the Monarchy,
the "capitalist plutocrats," and the pro-fascist segments of the Vatican
hierarchy. A bitterly contemptuous article on March 24, 1929, when
the fascist regime was preparing the Italian people for the forthcoming
national plebiscite, probably expressed the sentiments of the majority of
Concentrazione members when it announced that "In the name of the
most Holy Fascist Trinity, Monarchy, capital, and clergy, the Italian
people, bound and gagged, march to the Plebiscite." The article asserted
that in a moral sense, the memory of fascism would be forever associated
in the minds of its enemies with the ordeals of anti-fascist martyrs and,
politically, "with this Concordat, which restores in Rome the temporal
power of the Popes and the absolute confessional dominance of the
Catholic religion in the life of the nation." [3]

---

[2] "Il programma della Concentrazione antifascista," *La Libertà*, May 1, 1927, p. 2.
(NY) For a discussion of the background and development of the *Concentrazione*,
see Salvatorelli and Mira, *Storia d'Italia nel periodo fascista*, pp. 568–70, and
Charles Delzell, *Mussolini's Enemies: The Italian Anti-Fascist Resistance*, pp. 56–60,
81–82.

[3] "In nome della Santissima Trinità fascista," *La Libertà*, March 24, 1929, p. 1.
(NY) In *The Cross and the Fasces*, a study of the relations between the Catholic
Church and the fascist state from 1922 to 1943, Richard Webster reaches con-
clusions regarding the effect of the Concordat that substantiate the charge made by
La Libertà in March of 1929. In a chapter entitled "The Catholic Church and the
Fascist Regime," Webster writes as follows (pp. 109, 110):

> On 11 February 1929 a treaty and a concordat signed at the Lateran Palace
> resolved the Roman Question and regulated relations between the Church and the
> Italian State.
> The treaty, which affirmed the sovereignty and independence of Vatican City
> as well as the extraterritoriality of papal palaces and basilicas, generously
> indemnifying the Holy See and guaranteeing its communications with the Catholic
> world, raised few problems. The first article, which declared Catholicism to be

During the early 1930's, which witnessed the strengthening of Italian fascism and the advent of the nazi regime in Germany, *La Libertà* was noteworthy for the many articles in which it espoused the cause of European unity based on the principles of liberalism, federalism, and democracy. These principles alone, the newspaper repeatedly said, were capable of offering the people of Europe a lasting alternative to fascism and nazism.[4] It was on the basis of these principles that *La Libertà* greeted the birth of the Spanish Republic in April 1931 with unrestrained enthusiasm; the Spanish Republic had set an example that would "intensify the desire for combat of all those who are oppressed by monarchical and fascist tyranny." [5]

But the editors of *La Libertà* did not limit themselves to general declarations of principle. The newspaper performed the practical functions of documenting fascist crimes, of listing the names of persons tried and sentenced by the Special Tribunal, and of carrying on fund-raising campaigns to help the victims of fascist persecution. A concerted effort was also made to mail the newspaper to selected individuals in Italy who were then expected to distribute it as widely as possible. The fascist political police, however, soon discovered the plot, with the help of spies in Paris and informers in Italy, and as a consequence the newspaper was subsequently mailed from other cities, mainly from Lyons, Marseilles, Brussels, and Geneva. This strategem was also foiled rapidly by the fascist police.[6]

The inevitable disputes over both tactical and ideological questions

---

"the sole religion of the State," merely echoed the Statute of 1848, the basis of Italian constitutional law.

The Concordat was another matter. In addition to securing the status of the clergy and regulating the appointment of bishops, the Concordat gave to the Church wide powers in areas of direct concern to any modern state. Article 34 guaranteed "civil effects" for any Catholic sacramental marriage performed in accordance with canon law. Article 35 guaranteed equal accrediting, through a state examination, of graduates of Church and state schools. Article 36 declared that "Italy considers as the foundation and crown of public instruction the teaching of Christian doctrine according to the form received by Catholic tradition." Teaching of religion was introduced into secondary as well as elementary schools, with teachers and textbooks approved by Church authorities. In short, *Italy became a confessional state, unique among the great powers of contemporary Europe.* [Italics mine.]

[4] "Dichiarazione della Concentrazione Antifascista alle democrazie del mondo," *La Libertà*, May 31, 1930, p. 1. (NY)

[5] "La Repubblica spagnola," *La Libertà*, April 16, p. 1. (NY)

[6] For a description of the efforts made by the *Concentrazione* to distribute their publications in Italy, and of the successful methods used by the fascist secret police to suppress such distribution, see Guido Leto, *Ovra, fascismo, anti-fascismo*, pp. 42–44.

that plague political exile groups eventually led to the newspaper's demise in 1934 and to the dissolution of the *Concentrazione*. Nevertheless, during the eight years of its existence, *La Libertà* fulfilled the purpose of most émigré newspapers as defined by a group of anti-fascist Italian journalists who participated in an international Press Exposition in Cologne, Germany on June 12, 1928. The motto of the "Giovanni Amendola" Union of Italian Anti-Fascist Journalists in Cologne—"The voice of the Italian émigrés is unanimous: against fascism, the enemy of civilization"—was given concrete expression by *La Libertà*. In addition, *La Libertà* established a precedent for interparty cooperation against fascism that was to prove valuable to the organizers of the underground press during the Resistance of the years 1943–45.

II
Mario Vinciguerra and the National Alliance

The "Giovanni Amendola" Union of Italian Anti-Fascist Journalists had its clandestine counterpart in Italy in the National Alliance founded by Mario Vinciguerra in 1929. Vinciguerra, a liberal scholar and journalist, had been among the approximately one hundred Italian intellectuals who in November 1924 endorsed Giovanni Amendola's program for a "National Union of Liberal and Democratic Forces." He had also been an occasional contributor to *Il Mondo,* served for a short time as secretary of the Liberal Party, and in 1928 was placed under police surveillance for his "subversive" articles in the Genoese political review *Pietre.*

The spirit and substance of Amendola's resistance to fascism lived on in the National Alliance, which from July to November 1930 succeeded in distributing ten issues of a clandestine one-page bulletin entitled *The National Alliance for Freedom* before Vinciguerra and his closest associate, Renzo Rendi, were arrested on November 28. Vinciguerra and Rendi were assisted in their underground activities by somewhat loosely organized groups of individuals in Rome, Milan, and Verona. They also had the moral and financial support of Lauro De Bosis, whose anti-fascist exploits were to end shortly in tragedy, and of De Bosis' American mother, Irene Vernon.

One of Vinciguerra's principal concerns, as revealed in the first clandestine bulletin of July 1, 1930, was that the Communist Party and other extreme left-wing groups would monopolize the active resistance against fascism. He believed that it was up to the liberal "men of order" to provoke the crisis of fascism and thereby "to save Italy from the opposite threat" of communism.[7] Partly by reason of his strongly anti-communist position, Vinciguerra tried in the following months to encourage leading representatives of Italy's tradition-bound institutions—the Monarchy, the Army, the Church—to dissociate themselves from the dictatorship. In the fifth clandestine bulletin of September 1930, he wrote of the ability with which Mussolini had imposed on both Italians and foreigners "a series of myths which even more than the fascist militia serve to keep the country oppressed. . . . The most false and most dangerous of all these myths is the one according to which communism would be the only alternative left to the Italian people if fascism were to be overthrown." [8] This "myth," Vinciguerra said, lay at the core of Mussolini's demagogic but successful appeals for the support of Italian Catholics and conservatives. Even in his defense before the Special Tribunal, Vinciguerra denied any intent to undertake revolutionary action against the regime and spoke of his hopes to rally "the traditional forces of the State, the Church, the Monarchy, and the Army, in order to eliminate the dangers to which fascism exposes us." [9]

On December 28, 1930, the Special Tribunal sentenced Vinciguerra and Rendi to fifteen years in prison for attempting "to provoke the fall of fascism and to assure that the former constitutional parties would succeed fascism in power." [10] Vinciguerra served six years of his sentence and was then amnestied. Rendi died in prison.

III
Militant Catholic Anti-Fascists

The disconcerting ease with which the Catholic Church hierarchy accommodated itself to the fascist revolution was a matter of deep concern to the *Concentrazione Antifascista* and to the National Alliance. Yet the hierarchy's accommodation to the regime did not eradicate all Catholic opposition. In fact, despite the large number of powerful Catholic clergymen and laymen who allied themselves with the fascist government, many Catholic anti-fascists distinguished themselves in the arena of political and moral protest during the 1920's and 1930's. It must also be said that Pope Pius XI, notwithstanding his oft-expressed admiration for Mussolini, made several significant pronouncements denouncing fascist

[7] This section of Vinciguerra's first clandestine bulletin is cited textually by Salvatorelli and Mira, *Storia d'Italia nel periodo fascista*, p. 615.
[8] This bulletin is cited textually by Cesare Rossi, *Il Tribunale Speciale*, p. 300.
[9] Vinciguerra's defense is cited textually by Rossi, *Il Tribunale Speciale*, p. 304.
[10] This accusation is contained in the Rome Prefect's report to the Special Tribunal after Vinciguerra's capture, and is cited textually by Rossi, *ibid.*, p. 301.

violence and state idolatry which indicated that his accommodation to the regime did not signify his unqualified approval of it. Don Luigi Sturzo, the founder of the Catholic *Partito Popolare,* Alcide De Gasperi, Francesco Luigi Ferrari, Giuseppe Donati, as well as numerous lesser known persons who belonged to Catholic Action and to the Guelf Action Movement upheld the dignity of their faith by resolutely refusing to acquiesce in the dictatorship.[11]

As previously noted, Giuseppe Donati, the former managing editor of *Il Popolo,* left Italy for Paris in June 1925 after being repeatedly threatened with death unless he desisted from his denunciations of the fascist regime. Upon his arrival in Paris, Donati immediately joined forces with a disparate group of émigré journalists, including the reformist socialists Carlo a Prato and Francesco Frola, Ernesto Caporali of the Italian General Confederation of Labor, and the republican Mario Pistocchi. Led by Donati, these men collaborated in publishing one of the most important émigré newspapers in Paris, *Il Corriere degli Italiani,* the first issue of which appeared on January 28, 1926. Prominently displayed on the top of the newspaper's front page was the sentence: "This newspaper is published in Paris, because fascism has suppressed freedom of the press in Italy."

During the three years he was chief editor of *Il Corriere degli Italiani,* Donati stressed in particular the need for a moral repudiation of fascism on the part of the Italian people. This problem was paramount, he believed, for unless the Italian people challenged the moral legitimacy of Mussolini's regime, the sacrifices of men such as Piero Gobetti and Giacomo Matteotti would never be completely vindicated. Opposition based on tactical or grossly political motives alone would never suffice to restore the good name of the Italian people and nation.[12]

Donati also maintained that fascism would never be overthrown unless all anti-fascists, regardless of differences in political philosophy and strategy, united in a supreme and "heroic" revolutionary effort. He was offended by most of the propaganda of the Italian communists, who frequently branded him a "betrayer of the proletariat" and an opportunist. In an article published on March 15, 1926, Donati prophetically espoused the kind of united anti-fascist action that was later, during the Resistance of the years 1943 to 1945, to assume concrete form in the interparty Committees of National Liberation. "For us," Donati wrote, "anti-

---

[11] For an acute and thorough analysis of lay Catholic opposition to fascism during the 1920's and 1930's, see Richard Webster, *The Cross and the Fasces.* Another useful study of this subject is Giuseppe Rossini, *Il fascismo e la Resistenza.*

[12] Donati, "Ragioni e propositi," *Il Corriere degli Italiani,* January 28, 1926. The article is reprinted in Lorenzo Bedeschi, *Giuseppe Donati,* pp. 267–68.

fascism is a unitary movement that arises from the consciousness of men who share a minimum common denominator of idealism and will directed toward the achievement of civil rights. The struggle for civil rights is the basis of anti-fascism; without this common basis, the life and therefore the propaganda, the organization and the struggle of parties, from the liberals to the anarchists, will never be possible in Italy, as it is not possible now. . . . For us, whoever struggles against fascism, even if outside our ideological and tactical framework, is not a competitior, but an ally." [13]

In the newspaper *Il Pungolo*, founded in December 1928 by Donati and the socialist Dandolo Lemmi, the combative ex-editor of *Il Popolo* returned again to the moral problem raised by fascism. Anticipating the position taken in 1943 by Alcide De Gasperi and other writers for the Catholic underground press, Donati described fascism as "the organic, and therefore the fatal product" of the spiritual degeneration of "Italian public life." A moral renewal of the Italian people, led and educated by an intellectual elite, was the precondition for the recovery of lasting political freedom.[14]

Like most other Italians in exile who engaged in anti-fascist propaganda warfare, Donati was deprived of his citizenship and suffered terribly because of his separation from his wife and children who had remained in Italy. His health declined rapidly, and in July 1931, Donati died in Paris an impoverished, lonely man.

Within Italy, the treaty and Concordat signed by the fascist government and the Vatican on February 11, 1929, tended to discourage organized anti-fascist activity on the part of Catholic workers and intellectuals. Nevertheless, various student and professional groups associated with Catholic Action and the Guelf Action Movement continued tenaciously to take an independent, often frankly oppositional stand against fascism. The suppression in 1934 of the newspaper *Il Giovane Piemonte*,[15] the organ of a youth group in Turin associated with Catholic Action, was but one of numerous examples of the mistrust and hostility with which the fascist government viewed the work of dissident Catholics. Inspired chiefly by Pope Pius XI's encyclical "Non abbiamo bisogno" ("We have

---

[13] Donati, "Per l'unità antifascista: polemiche oziose e punti fermi," *Il Corriere degli Italiani,* March 15, 1926. The article is reprinted in Lorenzo Bedeschi, *Giuseppe Donati,* pp. 277–79.

[14] Donati, "Programma," *Il Pungolo,* December 15, 1928. The article is reprinted in Lorenzo Bedeschi, *Giuseppe Donati,* pp. 341–43.

[15] For an account of the Catholic clandestine press during the period 1929 to 1943, see Giuseppe Rossini, *Il fascismo e la Resistenza,* pp. 47–63, and Adriano Dal Pont, Alfonso Leonetti, Massimo Massara, *Giornali fuori legge,* pp. 195–99.

no need") of June 29, 1931, which had implicitly condemned fascism's totalitarian conception of the state and persecution of its Catholic opposition, Catholic Action played a significant role in the history of anti-fascism throughout the 1930's. The testimony of Don Roberto Angeli, an anti-fascist priest from Livorno who was deported to Dachau in 1944, indicates that even in the late 1930's various centers of Catholic Action were still carrying on an ideological campaign against fascism in the form of discussion groups and clandestine publications whose purpose was to condemn "the totalitarian, racist, and anti-Christian doctrine" contained in fascist and nazi textbooks.[16]

The Guelf Action Movement was more militant and radical than Catholic Action. Founded in Milan in early 1925 by Piero Malvestiti, Gioacchino Malavasi, and other members of the Lombard League of World War Veterans, the guelfs maintained regular contact with the Justice and Freedom Movement in Paris and formented rebellion against fascism in a series of clandestine manifestoes and newspapers entitled "Christ the King and the People," which were circulated in Italy from 1928 to 1932. In asserting that fascism was "the declared enemy of the Church, of peace, of freedom and of Italy," [17] the Guelf Movement intended to register its support for any and all forms of anti-fascist ferment, although it refused to endorse the use of violence as a means of overthrowing the dictatorship. The Guelf Movement did not exclude a priori the possibility or desirability of revolutionary violence. According to the retrospective testimony of Piero Malvestiti, they believed that the indispensable prerequisite for revolt—the Italian people's willingness to take up arms against the regime—was lacking in the early 1930's. To advocate active resistance without the consent of the people, Malvestiti wrote in 1945, "which would have led to the sacrifice of only a few generous individuals, was not possible for conscious Christians." [18] Therefore, the Guelf Movement limited itself to disseminating underground propaganda that denounced the political tyranny of Mussolini and summoned all Catholics to dissociate themselves from the fascist regime.

As a result of their illegal activities, Malvestiti and Malavasi were arrested in March 1933 and sentenced on January 30, 1934, to five years in prison by the Special Tribunal. They were imprisoned for having written, printed, and distributed pamphlets "inciting the commission of acts directed toward changing the constitution of the state and the form

[16] Don Roberto Angeli, *poi l'Italia è risorta*, p. 16.
[17] This clandestine manifesto of 1933 is cited textually in Dal Pont, Leonetti, Massara, *Giornali fuori legge*, p. 197.
[18] Piero Malvestiti, *Parte Guelfa in Europa*, pp. 186, 187.

of government by means not allowed by the constitutional order of the state." [19]

IV
Socialist Propagandists in Paris and Milan

One left-wing segment of the Guelf Action Movement was in close touch with members of the Italian Socialist Party who had succeeded in eluding the fascist police and who continued to function on a more or less organized basis in Paris and in Milan. The main center of socialist activity was Paris, where in December 1926 Ugo Coccia took over the editorship of *Avanti!* after the newspaper's suppression in Italy in October of that year.

From 1927 to 1934,[20] the year that marked the beginning of close cooperation between the Italian Communist and Socialist Parties within a single "united front" officially sanctioned by Stalin, the Italian socialists, though riddled by internal factional strife, were committed essentially to the concepts of revolutionary socialism and working class autonomy. They were opposed to the gradualist and reformist position of the Unitary Socialist Party led by Filippo Turati and to the involutional, anti-democratic tendencies shown by the Italian Communist Party in its subservient relationship to the Soviet Union. Appeals for the reunification of all movements and parties genuinely devoted to the cause of the independence and freedom of the Italian working class, along with constant denunciations of the anti-proletarian character of the fascist regime, formed the basis of the political line taken by *Avanti!* and other socialist émigré newspapers during those years.

In the early months of 1934, following a series of disputes with the Justice and Freedom Movement and with the republicans and reformist socialists who gravitated around the *Concentrazione Antifascista,* the socialists began publishing *Nuovo Avanti* in Paris. At the same time, various nuclei of party workers, most notably a group in Milan headed by Rodolfo Morandi, attended to the task of distributing the newspaper illegally in Italy.

Nuovo Avanti was the work mainly of Pietro Nenni, Giuseppe Saragat, who is now President of Italy, and Angelo Tasca, a former editor of

---

[19] Richard Webster, *The Cross and the Fasces,* p. 150.

[20] The history of the Italian Socialist Party and of the Socialist press during the period 1926 to 1940 is described in considerable detail by Gaetano Arfé in volume II of his *Storia dell'Avanti!,* from which I have drawn most of the information on *Avanti!* and *Nuovo Avanti.* For an account of the socialist clandestine press during this period, see Dal Pont, Leonetti, Massara, *Giornali fuori legge,* pp. 163–76.

L'Ordine Nuovo, who was expelled from the Italian Communist Party in 1929 for—among other deviations—his refusal to endorse the party's branding of most non-communist enemies of Mussolini as "social fascists" and "semi-fascists." [21] All three of these men, though in profound disagreement with what they regarded as the undemocratic, authoritarian nature of the communist movement, were nevertheless receptive to the possibility of an anti-fascist unity of action pact with the Italian communists. The defeat of democracy in Italy and the triumph of Hitler in Germany had convinced the three editors of *Nuovo Avanti* that Italian socialists should work together with any and all political forces capable of combating their principal enemy, fascism.

On August 25, 1934, *Nuovo Avanti* published the text of the first unity of action pact, which called for a common effort on the part of the Italian Socialist and Communist Parties to struggle against all threats of war, to initiate an international campaign for the liberation of the victims of fascism and nazism, to support the right of Italian workers to independent labor unions, and finally to agitate against the fascist corporative system. [22]

With the establishment of a Popular Front government in France in July 1935, the Italian socialists further strengthened their ties to the Communist Party. In effect, it was largely on the basis of the pact of August 1934 and other subsequent tactical agreements reached by the Socialist and Communist Parties that the Italian anti-fascist movement as a whole was able to act decisively in the Spanish Civil War and later during the period of the Resistance.

As already noted, the message of *Avanti!* and of *Nuovo Avanti* reached Italy mainly through the efforts of a group of socialists headed by Rodolfo Morandi in Milan, which from 1932 to 1937 maintained fairly steady contact with Nenni, Saragat, and other party leaders in Paris. Like so many of the men and women who later worked for the underground press during the Resistance, Morandi and his colleagues paid heavily for their conspiratorial activities. Arrested in April 1937 on the charge of spreading anti-fascist propaganda, Morandi, Aligi Sassu, Alfredo Testa, Vittorio Ravazzoli, and Mario Veneziani were sentenced on October 13 to ten years in prison. [23]

---

[21] Even Antonio Gramsci, generally regarded as liberal and moderate in his judgments of the non-communist enemies of fascism, was not above using the epithet "semi-fascist" to characterize such men as Giovanni Amendola, Don Luigi Sturzo, and Filippo Turati. See Antonio Gramsci, "Il destino di Matteotti," *Lo Stato Operaio,* August 28, 1924, reprinted in *2000 pagine di Gramsci* vol. I, pp. 729–41. The characterization of Amendola, Sturzo, and Turati as "semi-fascists" is on p. 740.

[22] Arfé, *Storia dell'Avanti!,* vol. II, pp. 111, 112.

[23] Dal Pont, Leonetti, Massara, *Giornali fuori legge,* p. 173.

V
Bruno Buozzi and L'Operaio Italiano

Among the Italians closely associated in Paris with the *Concentrazione Antifascista* and with the reformist Socialists was a group of labor organizers who had been affiliated with the Italian General Confederation of Labor and who had rejected Mussolini's "corporative" solution for the "integration" of Italian workers within a totalitarian state apparatus. The ideological orientation of most of these men was similar to that of many American union leaders in that they believed in the efficacy of collective bargaining and leaned toward certain socialistic reforms but repudiated the doctrine of the dictatorship of the proletariat and were in fact strongly anti-communist.

The outstanding representative of the Italian anti-fascist labor movement in Paris was Bruno Buozzi,[24] who before leaving Italy in November of 1926 had had a distinguished career as head of the Italian Federation of Metallurgical Workers and, beginning in January 1926, as secretary general of the Italian General Confederation of Labor. In 1922 and 1923, Buozzi espoused a policy of provisional collaboration with the fascist regime and on several occasions had private talks with Mussolini in which he sought to persuade the Italian dictator to guarantee the autonomy of the non-fascist unions organized within the Confederation of Labor. He of course failed in these efforts and was later rewarded for his conciliatory gestures with a severe beating administered to him in Turin on February 27, 1924, by fifteen blackshirts. In late November 1926, he went to Zurich to attend an international labor conference. At the conclusion of the conference, he decided to emigrate permanently to Paris. With the help of Pallante Rugginenti, Giuseppe Sardelli, Felice Quaglia, and other former labor leaders, he immediately began to reconstitute the General Confederation of Labor in Paris in opposition to those members of the Confederation in Italy who had decided to coexist with Mussolini's regime. The Paris branch of the Confederation headed by Buozzi represented some two hundred thousand Italian workers who had emigrated to France during the preceding ten to fifteen years.

From 1928 to the mid-1930's, Buozzi's main link with the Italian émigré workers in France was the newspaper *L'Operaio Italiano,* which he edited together with Pallante Rugginenti. Through his writings for *L'Operaio Italiano,* Buozzi defended his concept of independent unionism as the only legitimate alternative to the fascist corporative system and to the communist doctrine of proletarian dictatorship.

Buozzi's most important contribution to the cause of anti-fascism was

---

[24] For an account of Buozzi's life, see Gino Castagno, *Bruno Buozzi.*

the campaign he waged in *L'Operaio Italiano* against the fascist labor syndicates. These syndicates, Buozzi asserted in June 1931,[25] were a mockery of authentic labor unions, a travesty of the ideals of the Italian labor movement. The fascist regime had deprived Italian workers of their autonomy by integrating them within a totalitarian police state. Government spies and informers had infiltrated Italian labor organizations and issued regular reports on the activities of all defectors and on every manifestation of disloyalty to the regime. Policies affecting the daily lives and welfare of the workers were no longer arrived at democratically, by consulting the unions' membership, but were instead promulgated by the unions' leaders, all of whom were chosen on the basis of their loyalty to fascism. Fascist syndicalists, Buozzi never tired of reiterating in his articles in *L'Operaio Italiano,* were nothing but instruments in the hands of the élite who controlled the fascist state and the Fascist Party.

During the mid-1930's, Buozzi was an active, articulate opponent of the fascist regime's aggression against Ethiopia and intervention on the side of the falangists in the Spanish Civil War. In the latter years of the 1930's, he joined the Italian Socialist Party and, as a representative of the anti-fascist segment of the Confederation of Labor, returned to Italy in August 1943 immediately after the coup of July 25 that ousted Mussolini from power. From August 1943 to March 1944, he worked assiduously in Rome to rebuild the Confederation of Labor. But he did not live to enjoy the fruits of his efforts. Buozzi was assassinated by the nazis on June 3, 1944, during the course of the German Army's retreat from Rome on the day before Allied forces arrived to liberate the Italian capital.

VI
The Justice and Freedom Movement

The development of the Justice and Freedom Movement forms one of the most interesting and complex chapters in the history of Italian anti-fascism during the 1920's and 1930's. Founded in Paris in 1929, the Justice and Freedom Movement brought together a group of persons who shared a common hatred for fascism and, even more importantly, a common antagonism toward all of the other anti-fascist parties and movements because of their failure to oppose fascism vigor-

---

[25] Bruno Buozzi, "L'annuale processo al sindacalismo fascista," *L'Operaio Italiano,* June 13, 1931. The article is reprinted in Bruno Buozzi, *Scritti dell'esilio,* edited by Alessandro Schiavi, pp. 86–112. For further information concerning Buozzi's views on the fascist labor syndicates, see Bruno Buozzi and Vincenzo Nitti, *Fascisme et sindacalisme.*

ously enough. The members of the Justice and Freedom Movement were also in agreement as to the organic deficiencies of Italian political and social life that gave fascism a reason for being and an undeniable appeal for large numbers of their fellow countrymen. They were angered by the passivity and conformism of Italy's liberal intelligentsia. They felt utter contempt for the Monarchy in the person of King Victor Emmanuel III, whose indecisive character and acquiescence in the dictatorship had deprived the forces of anti-fascism of a potentially powerful ally. They were hostile to the Catholic Church because of its paternalistic attitude toward the Italian people, a paternalism that had reenforced the age-old tendency of the masses of Italians to accept social inequities and injustices as ineradicable components of human life. As for the left-wing parties, the socialists and communists, the Justice and Freedom Movement found both to be anachronistic and sterile. The Italian Socialist Party was tied to a form of puerile class loyalty and to a kind of messianic faith in the inevitable triumph of socialism that precluded any possibility of taking concrete revolutionary action against fascism. Italian socialists were, in the main, romantic dreamers, admirable but irremediably inefficient idealists. As for the communists, they embraced a totalitarian ideology that was profoundly repugnant to most members of the Justice and Freedom Movement. For the *giellisti*—a term applied to members of the Movement that was derived from the two initial letters of the words *Giustizia* and *Libertà*—to substitute one dictatorship for another, to vanquish fascism only to be dominated by a communist bureaucracy, was unthinkable.

The *giellisti* were in general agreement, then, as to what was wrong about Italian political life. They knew what they were against. Like many political movements composed mainly of individualists and intellectuals, they had to struggle much harder to agree on what they were for. Certain commonly accepted ideas and programs, however, did emerge from their efforts during the 1930's and were articulated mainly in the newspaper *Giustizia e Libertà* and in the magazine *Quaderni di Giustizia e Libertà,* both of which were published in Paris.

The original nuclei of the Justice and Freedom Movement were formed around Piero Gobetti's *Rivoluzione Liberale* and in Florence around the *Italia Libera* circle founded in June 1924. From 1922 to 1925, Gobetti published the writings of the publicist and economist Riccardo Bauer, Carlo Rosselli, destined to become one of the titans of the anti-fascist struggle, the liberal philosopher Guido de Ruggiero, the historian Gaetano Salvemini, and the sociologist Tommaso Fiore, all of whom were later affiliated with the Justice and Freedom Movement.

The *Italia Libera* circle[26] in Florence had a hard-core membership of about fifty persons representing nearly every segment of Florentine society. The circle included postal clerks, professors, electricians, lawyers, railroad workers, students, and businessmen. It was founded in June 1924 by a group of World War I veterans—Raffaele Cristofani, Luigi Piani, Nello Traquandi, and several others—who had become disgusted by the pro-fascist collaborationism of the National War Veterans Association and who wanted to perpetuate the democratic values for which they believed Italy had intervened in the war. Their initiative quickly won the approval and active support of Gaetano Salvemini, professor of history at the University of Florence; Piero Calamandrei, a distinguished professor of jurisprudence; Carlo and Nello Rosselli, who were at that time studying political science and history under Salvemini's tutelage; Enrico Bocci, a lawyer; and Ernesto Rossi, a political economist who during the following five years was to become one of the most intrepid underground conspirators against fascism.

The men of the *Italia Libera* circle were all activists, and throughout the year 1924 they issued manifestoes denouncing the fascist regime and the political immaturity of the Italian people, staged demonstrations in the city's main squares (most of which were quickly broken up by the police), leveled accusations against Mussolini and the whole fascist hierarchy for the murder of Matteotti, and on frequent occasions covered the walls and billboards of Florence with anti-fascist slogans. But their most significant enterprise was the publication of one of the first underground newspapers to appear in Italy after the decrees of 1923 and 1924 had effectively destroyed freedom of the press.[27] The name of the newspaper, *Non Mollare!* ("Don't give in"), symbolized the intransigent combativeness of the *Italia Libera* circle.

An editorial in the first number of the clandestine *Non Mollare!*, dated January 1925, made effective use of the verb "to resist" which, during

---

[26] For an excellent, firsthand account of the origin and development of the *Italia Libera* circle, see Ernesto Rossi's chapter "L'Italia Libera" in the volume *No al fascismo*.

[27] Although *Non Mollare!* is often spoken of as the first clandestine newspaper to appear in fascist Italy, at least one other newspaper, *Il Comunista*, preceded it into the underground. *Il Comunista*, which was published clandestinely in Rome from November 1923 to the early months of 1925, was the work of five prominent members of the Italian Communist Party: Palmiro Togliatti, Ruggiero Grieco, Carlo Farini, Felice Platone, and Giuseppe Di Vittorio. These men collaborated with an obscure and courageous printer from the quarter of Trastevere, Ettore Anzaloni. For further background information on both *Non Mollare!* and *Il Comunista*, see the articles by Carlo Farini and Gaetano Salvemini, "Giornali Clandestini," *L'antifascismo italiano*, edited by Paolo Alatri, vol. I, pp. 159–99.

World War II, was to become the watchword of anti-fascists throughout Europe. The editorial summoned the Italian people "to resist those who constantly attempt to intimidate us with threats of violence, who buy off witnesses and judges to condemn us, who burn our meeting places, who confiscate our newspapers. It is necessary to resist despite the guns of the police, despite the pardons granted to criminals, despite all the decrees that can be signed by the King." [28] In the issue of May 23, 1925, a concisely worded affirmation of faith in the value of *Non Mollare!* as a means of combating the dictatorship stated: "This is the point: *Non Mollare!* keeps us together shoulder to shoulder. Each group of readers spontaneously forms a nucleus of resistance for the great hour and of political action for the period following liberation." [29]

Resistance, then, was the watchword of *Non Mollare!*, resistance designed not only to spark opposition to certain of the most anti-democratic aspects of Mussolini's regime but inspired by the determination to foment rebellion against the entire structure of the fascist system itself. From January to October 1925, twenty-three issues of *Non Mollare!* were published. Each issue methodically documented the abuses and crimes of which the regime in general, and particularly fascist authorities in Florence, were guilty. Indeed, *Non Mollare!* was forced to suspend publication in October 1925 as a consequence of fascist violence in Florence that culminated in the assassination on October 5 of Gaetano Pilati and Gaetano Consolo, both of whom had been among the active supporters of the *Italia Libera* circle.[30]

Nearly all the leading figures of *Italia Libera* paid dearly for their anti-fascist activities. Nello Traquandi, Enrico Bocci, and Piero Calamandrei were placed under police surveillance. Carlo Rosselli's home was ransacked and burned by a gang of fascist hoodlums who were searching for incriminating evidence against him. Gaetano Salvemini was arrested in Rome on June 8, 1925, and soon after lost his professorship at the University of Florence when he refused to abjure his anti-fascist convictions.[31] Ernesto Rossi left Florence secretly after being placed under close surveillance for his role in printing and distributing *Non Mollare!*

---

[28] "Nel titolo è il nostro programma," *Non Mollare!*, January, 1925, p. 1. (ISRT) All but a few issues of this newspaper have been reprinted in their entirety in the volume *Non Mollare!*, edited by Raffaele Ramat.

[29] "A che serve?" *Non Mollare!*, May 23, 1925, p. 2. (ISRT)

[30] Gætano Consolo was a prominent Florentine lawyer. Gætano Pilati was a retired socialist deputy.

[31] For the circumstances surrounding Salvemini's dismissal from the University of Florence, see Gaetano Salvemini, *Memorie di un fuoruscito*.

The campaign waged by *Non Mollare!* was continued and amplified four years later by groups of liberal, republican, and socialist intellectuals who in 1929 worked together in Paris and in various Italian cities to form the Justice and Freedom Movement. The founding members of the Movement in Paris included first of all three veterans of the *Italia Libera* circle in Florence—Salvemini, Rossi, and Carlo Rosselli, who maintained regular clandestine contact with Nello Traquandi, a railroad employee, and Dino Vannucci, a physician, two members of the *Italia Libera* circle who had remained in Florence. Second, the Movement numbered among its charter members a group of men who had militantly defended the principle of a free press in Italy during the first years of the fascist era, some of whom were also destined to make decisive contributions to the underground press during the Resistance from 1943 to 1945: the republican Fausto Nitti; Emilio Lussu, a fiery socialist and leader of the Sardinian Action Party; Riccardo Bauer, who with Ferruccio Parri established an underground apparatus in Milan; Alberto Tarchiani, a former editorial writer for *Il Corriere della Sera;* and Alberto Cianca, who had worked closely with Giovanni Amendola on the staff of the newspaper *Il Mondo* in Rome. Before arriving in Paris in the summer of 1929, Nitti and Lussu had both been imprisoned on the island of Lipari along with Carlo Rosselli. All three men reached Paris after a daring escape by boat from Lipari on July 27, one of a series of storybook adventures that became a characteristic feature of the *giellisti*. Third, in addition to its already mentioned Florentine and Milanese contingents, the Movement attracted small groups of individuals in Italy headed by Gino Luzzatto, Ercole Miani, Egidio Meneghetti, and Francesco Fancello, who organized conspiratorial centers of activity in Venice, Trieste, Padua, and Rome, respectively. There was also an active section of the Movement in Turin, composed mainly of university students and professors. Among the Turinese *giellisti* were the lawyer Piero Zanetti, the writer Carlo Levi, the university student and future historian Aldo Garosci, and the *liceo* professor Augusto Monti. Other Turinese intellectuals who joined the Movement somewhat later, in 1933 and 1934, included Leone Ginzburg, Vittorio Foa, Renzo Giua, Massimo Mila, and Franco Venturi, all of whom, like most of the *giellisti,* were to become affiliated with the Action Party in 1942.[32]

The newspaper *Giustizia e Libertà,* which was published in Paris from

[32] For information on the men who founded the Justice and Freedom Movement in 1929, see Salvatorelli and Mira, *Storia d'Italia nel periodo fascista,* pp. 588–91, and Charles Delzell, *Mussolini's Enemies: The Italian Anti-Fascist Resistance,* pp. 60–67, 71–75.

November of 1929 to May of 1940, took an even more intransigent position against fascism than had *Non Mollare!* In fact, in calling themselves members of a "revolutionary anti-fascist movement," the authors of the paper's first statement of purpose declared that the time for "constitutional and moral campaigns" had ended, that only a revolutionary uprising of the Italian people could bring about the end of the dictatorship. Revolutionary violence, said the editors of *Giustizia e Libertà,* though dangerous and destructive, was far less evil than political dictatorship that imposed on its victims a servile, ignoble existence.[33]

In 1930 and 1931, the Justice and Freedom Movement in Paris began making a determined effort to organize the clandestine distribution of their publications in Italy.[34] They had some success in this endeavor, principally due to the labors of two indefatigable conspirators, Ernesto Rossi and Riccardo Bauer, who in an issue of *Giustizia e Libertà* dated 1930 published a jointly written article entitled "Advice on Tactics." [35] Among the various forms of active resistance recommended by Rossi and Bauer was the distribution of clandestine newspapers, through which enemies of the regime could "strengthen their faith, demonstrate the usefulness of individual efforts and sacrifices because they form part of the general anti-fascist movement, and define more clearly the reasons for our struggle and the objectives toward which it must be directed." But what counted most, said Rossi and Bauer, was that the sense of solidarity engendered by the human contacts required to create and distribute underground newspapers would eventually lead to the development of an organized base of operations for further revolutionary action.

In November 1931, the Justice and Freedom Movement joined the *Concentrazione Antifascista* but continued to take positions and advocate courses of action that were far to the left of those generally approved by the *Concentrazione.* The accord reached by the *giellisti* and the *Concentrazione* was based in large measure on their common belief that the overthrow of fascism necessarily involved also the overthrow of the Savoy Monarchy.

The republican position taken by the members of the Justice and Freedom Movement was motivated essentially by their philosophical opposition to all forms of hierarchical and hereditary privilege but was also determined to some extent by a tactical consideration of no little impor-

[33] "La libertà," *Giustizia e Libertà,* November 1929, p. 2. (CG)

[34] The methods used by the *giellisti* to introduce their propaganda into Italy are described by Cesare Rossi, *Il Tribunale Speciale,* pp. 265–73, and by Guido Leto in *Ovra, fascismo, antifascismo.*

[35] Ernesto Rossi and Riccardo Bauer, "Consigli sulla tattica," *Giustizia e Libertà,* 1930, p. 1. (CG)

tance. They reasoned that since the fascist regime owed much of its prestige among the masses of Italians to the cooperation it received from the Monarchy, the monarchical institution itself and in particular the person of King Victor Emmanuel III had to be unequivocally repudiated. Thus when they spoke in the newspaper *Giustizia e Libertà* of the need to overthrow the fascist dictatorship and to create "a free, democratic, republican regime," [36] they did so in order to emphasize the fact that fascist power depended on the subservience and complicity of the King and that freedom and democracy could no longer coexist in Italy with the Savoy Monarchy.

One of the ideological factors that set the Justice and Freedom Movement somewhat apart from the *Concentrazione* was its much keener awareness of the international character of both fascism and anti-fascism. The year 1932 marked the end of the first decade of fascist power, and the regime therefore organized a series of celebrations whose purpose was to convince the Italian people and the world at large that it was indisputably in control of Italy's national destiny. The *giellisti* took advantage of these celebrations to remind their followers that the struggle between fascism and anti-fascism was not merely a civil war between two opposed factions in Italy but reflected more essentially a political conflict of worldwide proportions:

> The furious campaign [waged by the fascist government] against the political émigrés associated with the *Concentrazione Antifascista* remains ineffective because the émigrés represent the real people of Italy. They are poor, they rely only on small legions of persecuted men to sustain themselves; nevertheless, in response to the command and will of the Italians, they exist, struggle, and are invincible. Every day they speak to the world of anti-fascism: through denunciations, criticism, protests, they warn the peoples of other nations of the common danger that threatens them. The struggle for the Italian people is a struggle for all peoples because either freedom is universal or it is a lie for everyone. In fact, fascism too tends toward universality. The saying that fascism "is not an article for exportation" is false. It is not exportable only to those countries that refuse to accept it. Wherever it succeeds in going it weaves its dark conspiracies and agitates those passions on which the success of its operations depends.[37]

The years 1935 and 1936 witnessed the fascist conquest of Ethiopia and the outbreak of civil war in Spain, two events that further intensified

---

[36] The republicanism of the Justice and Freedom Movement was most forcefully expressed in a small 124-page booklet it published in 1932 in collaboration with the *Concentrazione*. The booklet is entitled *Contro il decennale e per l'azione*. (CG)

[37] This statement was published in the afore-mentioned booklet *Control il decennale e per l'azione*, p. 8. (CG)

the revolutionary commitment of the Justice and Freedom Movement. Many of its members, most notably Carlo Rosselli, fought with the Spanish republicans against the insurgency led by General Franco and militarily supported even from the outset of the war by the nazi and fascist regimes. Yet, those were trying and anguished years for the *giellisti,* and the pessimistic tone of many of their writings in *Giustizia e Libertà* reflected their discouragement and sense of moral isolation. To advocate revolutionary anti-fascist action was one thing, but to effect a change in the policies of the world's most powerful states was another. They were temporarily buoyed up when the League of Nations imposed economic sanctions on Italy after the fascist invasion of Ethiopia, but they were plunged into despair when in July 1936 both England and the Popular Front government of France decided to revoke those sanctions after the Italian conquest of Ethiopia had been completed.

Even more demoralizing to the *giellisti* was the policy of neutrality adopted by the Western democracies with regard to the Spanish Civil War. On October 2, 1936, *Giustizia e Libertà* carried an article entitled "The War of Fascisms" that again revealed a keen awareness of the international character of both fascism and anti-fascism and that condemned the Western democracies for their failure to rally to the defense of the Spanish Republic. "Alvarez del Vayo's speech in Geneva," the article noted, "contains two irrefutable assertions: the first, that the civil war in Spain is a phase of a larger war between irreconcilably conflicting ideologies and interests; the second, that the neutrality adopted and maintained by the so-called democratic powers is a crime against the Spanish people, against their own peoples, and against peace." [38]

One of the distinguishing features of the Justice and Freedom Movement, in contrast with the *Concentrazione Antifascista,* was that its members were not content merely to carry on propaganda warfare against fascism but also attempted to formulate a political program for the renewal of Italian life after the overthrow of the regime. Sharp differences of opinion existed within the Movement since, as already indicated, its individualistic members were rarely unanimous on what they were for. Three groups coexisted uneasily in the Movement: a liberal faction, of which Alberto Tarchiani, the former editorial writer for *Il Corriere della Sera,* was a leading representative; a republican faction, for whom the establishment of a republican Italy was the foremost goal of their struggles; and a socialist faction, headed by the fiery Sardinian Emilio Lussu. Carlo Rosselli was at once a republican and a revolutionary democratic socialist,

---

[38] "La guerra dei fascismi," *Giustizia e Libertà,* October 2, 1936, p. 1. (NY)

and his ideological position proved to be the dominant one in the Movement.

The "Program" [39] of the Justice and Freedom Movement, as announced in the magazine *Quaderni di Giustizia e Libertà* in January 1932, was presented as "activist" in method, "republican" in principle, and "revolutionary" in aim. It repudiated "conservatives, monarchists, and papists" and declared that all modern revolutions must have a social as well as political content. After the overthrow of fascism, the Program stated, Italian democracy would be based primarily on the autonomous organizations of the working class, which would exercise their control democratically over socialized industries and thereby protect the population in general from the dangers of a bureaucratic, centralized state. With regard to the political structure of the nation, a regional federation would replace the totalitarian apparatus of fascism. A vast agrarian reform would give the land to those who work it by expropriating and redistributing the property owned by idle landlords. A new educational concept, aiming chiefly to inculcate into Italian youth a strong sense of democratic and civic consciousness, would replace the "priest-ridden, authoritarian, paternalistic" system created by fascism. This Program was offered by the *giellisti* as the only alternative to stodgy conservatism, anarchic individualism, and dictatorial communism.

The *giellisti* rejected the Soviet model for a socialist state as a matter of principle but also on the basis of their evaluation of the realities of Italian society. In March 1932, in an article entitled "Dictatorship and Democracy," [40] the editors of *Quaderni di Giustizia e Libertà* stated that any objective analysis of Italian society would reveal a preponderance of small landowners and businessmen, of merchants and artisans. The industrial and agrarian proletariat were simply a large minority of a people in whom the tradition of small individual enterprise was deeply rooted. Therefore, the establishment of communism in Italy could be accomplished only by imitating the methods of the fascists. The answer to the Italian problem lay in a predominantly socialized, cooperative system that would nonetheless provide ample opportunity to individuals to function economically outside the framework of that system.

In his political thought and action during the 1930's, Carlo Rosselli was the very embodiment of the Justice and Freedom Movement's commitment to activism, republicanism, and revolution. A dynamic, articu-

---

[39] "Il programma rivoluzionario di Giustizia e Libertà," *Quaaerni di Giustizia e Libertà,* January 1932, pp. 1–5. (NY)

[40] "Dittatura e democrazia," *Quaderni di Giustizia e Libertà,* March 1932, pp. 2–8. (NY)

late, highly intelligent man, Rosselli also had the advantage of possessing considerable wealth with which he financed all kinds of anti-fascist enterprises. He was among the organizers and financers of two Icarian exploits: a flight over Milan by Giovanni Bassanesi on July 9, 1930, during which Bassanesi succeeded in dropping thousands of GL propaganda leaflets over the city's main square; and a second flight over Rome by Lauro De Bosis on the afternoon of October 3, 1931, during which De Bosis also succeeded in dropping leaflets that urged King Victor Emmanuel III to turn against Mussolini and exhorted the Italian people to rise up against the regime. Bassanesi crashed in Switzerland on his return flight and was subsequently tried by the Swiss government, along with Rosselli and Alberto Tarchiani, for having violated Swiss territorial sovereignty.[41] The three men were convicted but were then amnestied after they had served a short prison term. De Bosis presumably ran out of fuel on his return flight and fell into the Mediterranean. In any case, no trace of his body or of the airplane he flew to Rome has ever been found.[42]

Rosselli was also among the first Italians to volunteer his services to the Spanish Republic in 1936. He led a small brigade of Italian volunteers in several of the initial battles and was wounded twice. On November 13, 1936, he made an urgent appeal to the Italian people over Radio Barcelona. In this broadcast, entitled "Today in Spain, Tomorrow in Italy," [43] Rosselli spoke in the name of the anti-fascist Italians who were fighting for the Spanish Republic. He recalled the sacrifices and struggles of Italian patriots in the nineteenth century and urged his countrymen to emulate Garibaldi and Mazzini and to liberate their country from their fascist oppressors. The fight in Spain, he said, if brought to a victorious conclusion by the Republic, would lead eventually to the reconquest of political freedom in Italy.

As a political thinker, Rosselli undertook the arduous task of recon-

[41] The events leading to Bassanesi's flight and to the trial of Bassanesi, Rosselli, and Tarchiani by the Swiss government are described in Carlo Rosselli, *Scritti politici e autobiografici,* in an article by Rosselli entitled "Il diritto dei popoli ad insorgere contro la tirannia," pp. 53–57. This article, which is an account of the trial and the three mens' defense, appeared originally in the newspaper *La Libertà,* November 8, 1930. (NY) The best biographical study of Rosselli is Aldo Garosci, *Vita di Carlo Rosselli.*

[42] For the circumstances leading to De Bosis' flight, and the full text in English translation of the leaflets he dropped over Rome, see Lauro De Bosis, *The Story of my Death,* edited by Ruth Draper. Among the best biographical studies of De Bosis is Silvio Trentin, *Lauro De Bosis.* See also the pages on De Bosis in Salvatorelli and Mira, *Storia d'Italia nel periodo fascista.*

[43] This broadcast has been reprinted in Carlo Rosselli, *Scritti politici e autobiografici,* pp. 166–72.

ciling and fusing the tenets of liberalism with those of socialism. His efforts in this intellectual enterprise ran parallel to those of many of the *giellisti,* but in particular of Silvio Trentin, a professor of law who left Italy in February 1926, settled in Toulouse in southern France, and in 1934 became an active member of the Justice and Freedom Movement. Rosselli and Trentin became close friends during the mid-1930's; indeed, their ideas on the question of liberalism and socialism were remarkably similar and, in fact, formed the ideological basis on which the Action Party was to function from 1942 to 1945.

Rosselli was strongly influenced by Piero Gobetti, whose emphasis on the dynamic aspect of liberalism as a "liberating" force formed one of the cornerstones of Rosselli's philosophy in *Liberal Socialism,*[44] a work he wrote during his confinement on the island of Lipari in 1929. In this book, Rosselli presented himself as a Marxist revisionist. He accepted the substance of Marx's analysis of the development and contradictions of capitalism but rejected the "deterministic" component in Marx's thought. He also found inadequate Marx's blueprint for working-class revolution leading to the dictatorship of the proletariat. What was lacking in Marxist theory, he said, was any understanding or appreciation of the problem of human freedom. A new synthesis of socialism, resting on the foundations of Marxist theory and modern liberalism, was therefore needed. "The neo-Marxism of the revisionists," Rosselli wrote, "and the working-class movement constitute the theoretical aspect and the practical aspect of a new liberal socialist conception in which the problem of social justice and of collective life can and must be confronted simultaneously with the problem of freedom and of individual life. Socialism must tend toward liberalism; liberalism must derive its strength from the proletarian struggle."[45] The struggle of the proletariat for complete emancipation formed part of an ongoing historical process, while the practice and philosophy of liberalism guaranteed the progressive transformation of society by protecting opposing interests and classes from the oppression of an all-powerful state.

---

[44] I have been unable to locate the original Italian edition of this work. Consequently, I have relied on the presumably reliable French translation by Stefan Priacel: Carlo Rosselli, *Socialisme Libéral.* One of Rosselli's first attempts to define the meaning of liberalsocialism was his article "Liberalismo socialista," published in *Rivoluzione Liberale* in March 1924 and reprinted in *Le riviste di Gobetti,* pp. 227–33. Another of his significant writings on this question, signed "Curzio," Rosselli's "nom de guerre," is "Liberalismo rivoluzionario," in *Quaderni di Giustizia e Libertà,* January 1932, pp. 25–27. Gobetti's influence is very much in evidence in all these writings.

[45] Carlo Rosselli, *Socialisme Libéral,* pp. 120, 121.

The central idea of *Liberal Socialism* was articulated repeatedly by Rosselli during the following years, although he gradually became more and more skeptical about the "progressive" character of liberalism and therefore tended at times to treat "bourgeois liberalism" and "proletarian struggle" as antithetical rather than reconcilable phenomena. But the general direction of his thought remained constant, toward a synthesis of liberalism and socialism.

Like Rosselli, Silvio Trentin was a firm believer in the methodology and ideal of liberalism. From the time of his departure from Italy in 1926 to 1931, he ardently defended the accomplishments of the Italian liberal constitutional Monarchy created by the Risorgimento.[46] But the years 1932 and 1933, which witnessed the depression, the strengthening of fascism in Italy, the beginning of the nazi era in Germany, and the rise of proto-fascist movements in many areas of eastern Europe, provoked an ideological crisis in Trentin from which he emerged with a new system of political ideas. Although still devoted to the ideal of liberalism, he concluded that monopoly capitalism, combined with the most reactionary form of nationalism, had been principally responsible for the triumph of fascism, and that the solution of the world's crisis lay in the establishment of socialist economies within the framework of decentralized, federally organized states.[47]

Trentin's opposition to capitalism was based on a historical analysis that owed much to the doctrines of Marx, but it derived also from his conviction that the capitalist system was inherently unethical and undemocratic. Complete socialization of the means of production, which would prevent illegitimate concentrations of wealth and power, was therefore the best method of protecting the economic and social rights of all members of society. At the same time, he consistently opposed the bureaucratic authoritarianism of the Soviet state. Like Rosselli and most other *giellisti*, he believed that Western political thinkers had much to learn from the Soviet Union, particularly in the areas of economic planning and mass education, but rejected the doctrines of proletarian dictatorship and "democratic centralism" expounded by Lenin and Stalin.[48]

The liberal socialism of the Justice and Freedom Movement, as for-

---

[46] Trentin articulated his defense of liberalism as a political ideology and of the accomplishments of the Risorgimento in *L'aventure italienne,* and in *Aux sources du fascisme.*

[47] These ideas were developed most fully by Trentin in a work written from 1937 to 1939 and published posthumously with the title *Stato-Nazione-Federalismo.*

[48] Opposition to the doctrine of proletarian dictatorship and to the Leninist concept of democratic centralism is a leit-motif of all of Trentin's political and historical writings from 1926 to the time of his death in 1944.

mulated by such thinkers as Rosselli and Trentin, attracted many young anti-fascist intellectuals in Italy and even won small groups of converts during the mid- and late 1930's despite the ever-watchful eyes of the fascist political police. The most important of these latter groups of converts was the semi-clandestine "Liberalsocialist" Movement founded in 1936 by Guido Calogero and Aldo Capitini, who were then teachers of political science at the *Scuola Normale Superiore* in Pisa. Inspired by the writings of the *giellisti,* Calogero and Capitini strove to reconcile the liberal tradition of the Risorgimento with the aspiration for social justice embodied in Christian teachings and in socialist thought. Within a year, the two young men had gained the support of students, teachers, and professional men in many of the principal Italian cities. Among the movement's members were Carlo Ragghianti in Bologna, Piero Calamandrei and Enzo Enriques-Agnoletti in Florence, Mario Delle Piane in Siena, Guido De Ruggiero in Naples, and Tommaso Fiore in Bari. Ragghianti, an art critic and historian, was to become President of the Florentine Committee of National Liberation in 1943. Agnoletti, a lawyer, and Calamandrei, a professor of jurisprudence, also played important roles in the Florentine Resistance Movement from 1943 to 1945, as representatives of the Action Party. Delle Piane was to become an Action Party propagandist and organizer in Siena. Capitini was a pacifist and a reverent admirer of Saint Francis of Assisi and therefore did not take an active part in the armed Resistance. Calogero, however, like most of the liberal-socialists, joined the Action Party in 1942 and became a contributor to the party's underground newspaper *L'Italia Libera.*[49]

But the activist revolutionary ideology of the *giellisti* was not the only significant influence on the thought of Calogero and his comrades. Of equal importance to their development was the teaching of the idealist philosopher Benedetto Croce. Croce's writings in the magazine *La Critica,* his *History of Italy from 1871 to 1914* (1928), and other historical and philosophical works he published during the 1930's, embodied the tradition of conservative but enlightened liberalism that the fascist regime had sought to eradicate entirely from Italian political life.

Croce's influence on these young liberalsocialists cannot be measured in terms of the direct impact of his political ideas, which Calogero's group found inadequate in many respects, but rather should be gauged in terms of the example of moral rectitude and uncompromising devotion to freedom that the Neapolitan philosopher set for them. In a retrospective

---

[49] For an account of the development of the liberalsocialist movement founded by Calogero and Capitini, see Ruggero Zangrandi, *Lungo viaggio attraverso il fascismo,* pp. 234–38, and Charles Delzell, *Mussolini's Enemies: The Italian Anti-Fascist Resistance,* pp. 169–71.

chapter of his *Difesa del Liberalsocialismo,* published originally in the magazine *Mercurio* in October 1944, Calogero explained the influence of Croce in the following manner:

> The reading of Croce had decisive importance [for the young people of the liberalsocialist movement]. There was a period in which Croce was the *livre de chevet,* the secret book of the best Italian youth. The heavy Crocean volumes published by Laterza had the same fascination for us which in other times a forbidden novel might have had. On their part, many professors did as much as they could to awaken and strengthen the taste for such readings in the young people. . . . The study of Croce was so intense and widespread that Gentile, having neither the courage to prohibit it nor the courage to allow it, resorted on one occasion to the device of changing the title of a professor's course from "Studies in the History of Philosophy" to "Studies in the History of Ancient Philosophy," in order to prevent him from continuing his lectures on Crocean texts.
>
> For these young men, Croce opened up the world of freedom. He revealed to them a new horizon, from which they were never again to allow themselves to be excluded. In this way, they placed themselves in opposition to other young people who were moving, to be sure, beyond the "corporative solution," but who, because of their failure to absorb and to understand the profoundest elements of Croce's teaching, were continuing to see the problem of reconciling individual freedom with the need for social reforms in exclusively economic terms. These young men remained fascists or semi-fascists (and, among this group, many have passed, and others will pass, to the old Marxism of traditional socialism and communism). Those, on the other hand, who had studied and understood Croce, were protected against this type of contagion.[50]

Calogero and his followers were dissatisfied with Croce's tendency "to see in any future whatever a providential epiphany of freedom," an attitude that encouraged "the lazy and the timorous to accept every accomplished fact," [51] and also criticized their preceptor's lack of interest in the social and economic aspects of the problem of human freedom. Nevertheless, as the passage quoted above demonstrates, Croce's teaching was at the ideological core of their rebellion against fascism. As for Calogero's stricture of the "traditional socialism and communism" of Italian Marxists, it should be remembered that Croce had also exerted an important influence on Antonio Gramsci and his colleagues on *L'Ordine Nuovo.* But Calogero's judgment that the majority of Italian communists, especially those who embraced communism after defecting from fascism, had "failed to understand the profoundest elements of Croce's teaching," is, in my opinion, sound.

Most of the *giellisti* in exile, though hounded by spies, managed to

---

[50] Guido Calogero, *Difesa del Liberalsocialismo,* pp. 193, 194.
[51] *Ibid.,* p. 194.

stay out of prison and to continue their work in relative safety until the fall of Mussolini in July 1943 allowed them to return to Italy. Most of those who remained in Italy, however, paid heavily for their conspiratorial activities. On October 30, 1930, practically all of the leading members of the Movement in Milan were arrested by the fascist political police. Several months later, following a trial before the Special Tribunal, Ernesto Rossi and Riccardo Bauer were sentenced to twenty years in prison. Rossi was released in 1939 and sent to the island of Ventotene, where he remained until July 1943, at which time he resumed his anti-fascist activity as a member of the newly founded Action Party. The other members of the Milanese group—including Ferruccio Parri, who was to become a leading organizer of the Italian Resistance Movement in 1943; the accountants Raffaele Cantoni and Vincenzo Calace; Pietro Zari, a professor of history; the socialist Dino Roberto; Umberto Ceva, a chemist; Francesco Fancello, a lawyer and journalist; and Mario Damiani, an engineer were given sentences ranging from five to fifteen years imprisonment. Ceva committed suicide in prison because he was afraid that, if tortured, he might reveal information about the Movement.[52] All of these men were charged with having supported a movement whose purpose, as revealed in its clandestine propaganda, "constituted a crime, because from an initial generic anti-fascism this new group had affiliated with a revolutionary, republican, and anti-dynastic movement that placed the responsibility for the advent and permanence of the fascist regime on the King and the Monarchy." [53]

The Turinese members of the Justice and Freedom Movement also fell afoul of the secret police. Mario Andreis and Luigi Scala were sentenced on April 29, 1932, to eight years in prison. On February 28, 1936, four other Turinese *giellisti*—Renzo Giua, Augusto Monti, Vittorio Foa, and Massimo Mila—were sentenced by the Special Tribunal to five years imprisonment. Leone Ginzburg served a short prison sentence and lost his assistantship at the University of Turin because of his refusal to sign an oath of loyalty to the regime.

In the latter part of 1942, the various groups in France and in Italy that comprised the Justice and Freedom Movement collaborated to form the Action Party. As we shall see, many of the persons mentioned in the preceding pages were among the party's chief organizers and propagandists

---

[52] The capture and trial of the Justice and Freedom members in Milan is described by Cesare Rossi, *Il Tribunale Speciale,* pp. 267–73. Ceva's career as an anti-fascist conspirator, and the reasons underlying his suicide in prison, are discussed by his sister Bianca Ceva, *1930: Retroscena di un dramma.*

[53] Cesare Rossi, *Il Tribunale Speciale,* p. 276. The quote are the words of Rossi, not those of the prosecuting attorney of the Special Tribunal.

and made important contributions to its clandestine organ, *L'Italia Libera,* which began to appear in Rome on January 1, 1943.

VII
The Communist Press: L'Unità and Lo Stato Operaio

In 1926, the Italian Communist Party rapidly began to apply the directives for conspiratorial anti-fascist action formulated by Antonio Gramsci in *L'Ordine Nuovo.* Indeed, it has generally been recognized by Italian historians of the Resistance that, of all the movements and parties that fought against fascism during the 1920's and 1930's, the Italian Communist Party paid most heavily in terms of personal sacifice,[54] waged the most relentless propaganda campaign, and possessed the most efficient conspiratorial organization. A strong spirit of self-sacrifice and discipline, deriving from a sense of belonging to a movement whose ultimate victory forms part of a progressive and inevitable historical process, was characteristic of the Italian communists from the outset of the fascist epoch and enabled the party to function on an efficient basis even under the most difficult conditions imaginable.

From 1926 to the beginning of the "united front" era in 1934, the Italian communists operated on an autonomous, self-contained basis. They refused to collaborate with the other anti-fascist parties and persisted in denouncing the non-communist opposition to fascism with such epithets as lackey, opportunist, traitor, social-fascist, and semi-fascist. This immoderate, rigidly sectarian position separated them from the other anti-fascist parties. But on the other hand, this very isolation allowed them to create an underground apparatus that remained intact despite the massive assault of the fascist political police.

From an organizational point of view, the Italian communists enjoyed the advantage of having a numerically small but well-disciplined and dedicated following among workers and party functionaries in many areas of the country. It was for this reason that many of the clandestine newspapers published during the fascist era by labor unions owed their existence to the initiative of communist workers.[55] Communist workers

---

[54] According to Cesare Rossi in *Il Tribunale Speciale,* pp. 23, 24, four-fifths of the 5,072 sentences imposed by the Special Tribunal on political enemies of the regime were against Italian communists. The volume *Lettere di antifascisti dal carcere e dal confino,* a collection of personal correspondence of imprisoned anti-fascists during the 1920's and 1930's, contains an extremely high percentage of letters written by both prominent and rank-and-file Italian communists.

[55] For an account of the communist clandestine press during the years 1926 to 1939, see Dal Pont, Leonetti, Massara, *Giornali fuori legge,* pp. 105–61.

and labor organizers were among the principal contributors to the clandestine newspaper *Battaglie Sindacali* which, from 1927 to the late 1930's, waged a continuous campaign in defense of independent unionism and working-class solidarity as the official organ of the anti-fascist segment of the General Confederation of Labor. Other clandestine newspapers that were either completely or in large part the result of the initiative taken by communists include *La Riscossa* and *Il Giovane Operaio* in Trieste, *Bandiera Rossa* in Turin, *La Fiaccola* in Genoa, and *La Scintilla* in Milan, all of which grew out of the efforts of organized groups of factory workers.

Particular attention must be given to the Communist Party's clandestine organ *L'Unità,* since during the fascist period this newspaper confronted many of the larger national and international problems that were later to occupy the attention of Resistance leaders.

L'Unità was founded on February 12, 1924, and for the next two years, despite threats, censorship, and other forms of harassment imposed on the Communist Party by the fascist regime, managed to appear fairly regularly in the major Italian cities. Following the repression of all organized anti-fascist movements that resulted from the Laws in Defense of the State of November 1926, and the subsequent trials and imprisonment of Antonio Gramsci, Umberto Terracini, Mauro Scoccimarro, and many other prominent Italian communists, a small group of party propagandists and functionaries who had succeeded in avoiding arrest immediately began to prepare the first clandestine issue of *L'Unità*, which was dated January 1, 1927.[56]

During the first seven months of 1927, the newspaper's beleaguered staff, headed by Camilla Ravera, Alfonso Leonetti—who was later expelled from the party for "left sectarianism"—and Felice Platone, worked in rapidly improvised headquarters in a house on the outskirts of Genoa. In August of that year, the house was wisely abandoned in favor of safer headquarters in Lugano, where there was less danger of being observed by informers than in Genoa. The first "Genoese" issues of *L'Unità,* dated January 1, January 21, and February 5, 1927, set the basic tone and policy that remained characteristic of the newspaper up to the outset of World War II in 1939. Its fundamental message was directed, of course, to the working class, which was told that fascism represented the

---

[56] The information in these pages concerning the clandestine *L'Unità* has been drawn mainly from Dal Pont, Leonetti, Massara, pp. 114–26, and from Velio Spano, "Grande come un frazzoletto l'Unità minava il fascismo," *L'Unità,* January 21, 1951, p. 3. Much useful information on the clandestine operations of printers and distributors of *L'Unità* in Italy from 1927 to 1934 can be found in the section entitled "Cronache del mese," a regular feature of the monthly magazine *Lo Stato Operaio,* a theoretical organ of the Italian Communist Party published in Paris.

interests of Italian industrialists and large landowners in league with the tycoons of international finance capital, that fascism would inevitably plunge the Italian people into war, that only through constant strikes, protests, demonstrations, and eventual armed struggle could the Italian working class hope to regain its autonomy and power.

The clandestine *L'Unità* fulfilled the important function of providing its scattered and intrepid readers[57] with information, reports and analyses of events both in Italy and in the world at large that the fascist press either ignored entirely or interpreted in accordance with the directives issued by the Ministry of the Press and Propaganda in Rome. Whereas the official fascist press told its readers that the fascist state was invulnerable to the kind of economic chaos which afflicted the capitalist world in 1929 and 1930, *L'Unità* spoke of the millions of unemployed in Italy, of the inadequate wages and working conditions that condemned Italian workers to hunger and sickness. In 1933, the year of Hitler's assumption of power, *L'Unità* made an accurate analysis of the reactionary and aggressive character of the nazi movement. In 1936 and 1937, while the Italian people were being told of Italy's "civilizing mission" in Africa and Italian industry was supplying Franco's insurgents with planes, tanks, guns, and "volunteers," *L'Unità* branded the invasion of Ethiopia as an imperialist adventure and summoned all Italians loyal to the cause of democracy and working-class solidarity to support the Spanish Republic with every possible means at their disposal.

The "Popular Front" approved by the Seventh Congress of the Comintern in the summer of 1935 brought the Italian Communist Party out of the isolation in which it had functioned during the preceding ten years. The rapprochement that the Soviet Union sought to effect between Western communist parties and other anti-fascist movements—a policy whose articulation was actively promoted and in some small measure initiated by the Italian Communist Party[58]—was reflected in particular

---

[57] The aforementioned section "Cronache del mese" in *Lo Stato Operaio* from 1927 to 1934 lists over one hundred incidents of Italian communists being caught in the act of reading or distributing the clandestine *L'Unità,* and of receiving sentences ranging usually from two to five years imprisonment. One particularly dramatic example of the courage required to be an underground distributor of *L'Unità* is described by Cesare Rossi in *Il Tribunale Speciale.* The story concerns a textile worker named Adele Bei, who in October 1933 returned from exile in Paris to Rome in order to reorganize the propaganda apparatus of the Communist Party. After establishing contact with various groups of couriers and workers, she was caught on November 25, 1933, and was sentenced in March 1934 to eighteen years in prison. Mrs. Bei remained in prison until July 1943, when she was amnestied by the Badoglio Government following the ouster of Mussolini.

[58] There is some evidence that the Italian Communist Party, although fundamentally subservient to the dictates of the Comintern, did in fact elaborate independently

in the position adopted by *L'Unità* with regard to the Spanish Civil War. In 1936 and 1937, instead of denouncing liberals, socialists, and social democrats as traitors to the working class, the communist newspaper acknowledged that fascism was a threat to the democratic civilizations of the world, that the falangist uprising in Spain was a phase of a general campaign on the part of fascist or militantly rightist groups everywhere in Europe to destroy utterly their liberal, socialist, and communist opposition. In the early part of 1937, *L'Unità* expressed the following judgments on the events in Spain:

> Each passing day allows the Italian people to understand more and more clearly that its own cause is identical with the cause for which the Republicans are fighting and dying. . .
>
> It is necessary that every militant opponent of the fascist regime, every anti-fascist, every worker and citizen who is dissatisfied with the present situation realize that the victory of the Spanish Republic will make possible an uprising of the Italian people against the regime that has oppressed our country for fourteen years and that the Republic's defeat will plunge Italy into a new bloodbath.
>
> This is why we have said and repeat again and again that the front along which men have been fighting in Spain for eight months extends to our country, because the organizers, the allies, the supporters of the reaction that has provoked the rebels' uprising in Spain are the profiteers, the hierarchy, and government of fascism that exploits and oppresses our people. The front extends to our country because Italian workers and the Italian people know

---

some of the first ideological criteria for a frontist policy of collaboration with certain other anti-fascist groups. One section of the "Lyons Theses," issued by the Italian Communist Party's Third Congress in Lyons, France, in January 1926, anticipates the policy of interparty anti-fascist solidarity in its acknowledgment that certain segments of the Italian bourgeoisie had remained consistently opposed to fascism, thereby forcing Mussolini's regime to struggle against them as well as against the communists. With respect to this fact, the communist document asserted that "This struggle, which is, whether one wants it or not, the indication of a split in the block of conservative and anti-proletarian forces, can in certain circumstances favor the development and the affirmation of the proletariat as the third and decisive factor of a political situation." *L'antifascismo italiano*, edited by Paolo Alatri, vol. I, p. 427. And in April 1933, the central committee of the Italian Communist Party published an appeal in Paris entitled "Single Front of Struggle to Break the Offensive of Capital and of Fascism": "Following the call to action of the Communist International, the Communist Party of Italy has sent an open letter to all socialist, maximalist, and republican workers, to the leadership of these parties and to that of the Justice and Freedom Movement and to all other political groups of anti-fascist workers, proposing as a basis of common action a series of immediate economic and political grievances." Nevertheless, this same document repudiated collaboration "with the so-called anti-fascist bourgeoisie, with the Nittis and the Sforzas of any type whatever," and was therefore still a far cry from the attitude the party assumed during the Popular Front era. The above-mentioned appeal of April 1933 was published in the *Bollettino del Partito Comunista d'Italia* and is reprinted in *L'antifascismo italiano*, edited by Paolo Alatri, pp. 265–72.

that those who want to strangle the Spanish Republic are also their own internal enemies, those same forces from which the Italian people wishes to free itself.

Therefore just as there exists a close solidarity between the fascist oppressors of our country and the criminal Generals Franco, Mola, and Queipo de Llano, so in the same way there must be a close solidarity between the Spanish and Italian peoples.[59]

The Italian communists were again forced to make a major readjustment in their attitude toward non-communist anti-fascists following the Nazi-Soviet non-aggression pact of August 23, 1939. Palmiro Togliatti, the head of the Italian Communist Party from 1927 until his death in 1964, made various attempts in the postwar years to deny what he called "the ridiculous calumny that we were against the war of Hitler and Mussolini only in the interests of the Soviet Union and after the USSR was attacked." [60] But most of the available evidence belies Togliatti's denial. The announcement of the pact itself, even before its full meaning and implications became known, threw the Italian Communist Party into a temporary state of utter confusion, indicating that the transition from the policy of a Popular Front to one of proletarian anti-war solidarity— which lumped together the nazi-fascists and the British and French governments into one vast, undifferentiated "imperialistic" block—was not as smooth as Togliatti suggests. Two prominent Italian communists, Leo Valiani and Romano Cocchi, general secretary of the Italian Peoples Union, resigned from the party.[61] The historian Aldo Garosci notes that, although the Italian Communist Party finally weathered the storm of the Nazi-Soviet pact, "young party militants like Lombardo-Radice, Natoli, Buffalini, as well as old-timers like Umberto Terracini and Girolami Li Causi, took positions at this time which carried them nearly outside the party or even beyond it. But once the critical moment had been surmounted, they were taken back into the fold." [62]

[59] "L'ora dell'eroismo," *L'Unità*, N. 3, 1937, p. 1. (CG)

[60] Togliatti, *Il Partito Comunista Italiano*, p. 92.

[61] Fulvio Bellini and Giorgio Galli, *Storia del Partito Comunista Italiano*, p. 352.

[62] Aldo Garosci, "The Italian Communist Party," *Communism in Western Europe*, edited by Mario Einaudi, p. 176. For a well-documented account of the nazi-Soviet pacts of August and September 1939, and of the impact of these pacts on the Communist Parties of western Europe and the United States, see Angelo Tasca (A. Rossi), *Le Pacte Germano-Soviétique*. Tasca, it will be remembered, had been a colleague of Gramsci on *L'Ordine Nuovo*, but was expelled from the Italian Communist Party in 1929. Later, during the 1930's, he joined the French Socialist Party and took a particularly strong stand against the Italian and French sections of the Communist International at the time of the Nazi-Soviet pact. For this act of political ingratitude, he was vilified in truly repulsive fashion by the propagandists of the Communist International, which no doubt explains the ill-concealed pleasure with which he documented the most unsavory aspects of the 1939 pact in his study of 1954.

To be taken back into the fold after September 1939, Italian communists, like party members loyal to the Soviet Union throughout the world, had to accept and to promulgate the idea that the conflict between the nazi-fascists and the Western bourgeois democracies was one of rival imperialistic forces, both equally guilty for war and territorial expansionism, while only the Soviet Union was genuinely interested in peace and freedom. As articulated in March 1940 by the Italian communist magazine *Lo Stato Operaio*—which was published in New York from 1940 to 1943 as a result of the French government's suppression of the Paris branches of the French and Italian Communist Parties in September 1939—the outbreak of hostilities had clearly shown that:

> In reality the longer the war goes on the more the people understand it, in the sense that the people are becoming more and more aware that this is a war of brigands provoked, on both sides, by imperialistic rivalries.
> The longer the war goes on the more the people are aware that the phrases about "the reparation of suffered injustices" or "living space" (in Germany), like the phrases about "the war for freedom, against Hitlerism" (in France and in England) are lies to push the people to massacre each other for imperialistic interests, by exploiting—in Germany—the feeling of nationalism and—in France and England—the anti-fascist sentiments of the masses.[63]

In early 1941, *Lo Stato Operaio* declared that "we don't want the victory either of English imperialism or of Italian imperialism, but the victory of the English people and of the Italian people against their own imperialist governments." [64]

As is well known, however, the nazi invasion of the Soviet Union necessitated another return to the Popular Front policy that had been in effect from 1935 to 1939. After June 1941, *Lo Stato Operaio* again resumed its appeals for democratic solidarity against the Axis powers. *L'Unità,* too, again took up its propaganda struggle in the name of a united democratic front against Hitlerism and fascism and, in fact, became one of the most important and widely diffused underground newspapers of the Italian Resistance from 1943 to 1945.

During the years 1927 to 1939, the principal theoretical organ of the Italian Communist Party was the monthly magazine *Lo Stato Operaio,* which began to appear in Paris in March 1927. The managing editor of *Lo Stato Operaio* was Palmiro Togliatti, one of the few prominent Italian communists who consistently managed to stay out of fascist prisons. Tog-

---

[63] "Lottiamo per la pace! Resti l'Italia fuori della guerra!", *Lo Stato Operaio,* March 15, 1940, p. 3. (NY)

[64] "La lotta delle masse contro la guerra," *Lo Stato Operaio,* January–February 1941, p. 3. (NY)

liatti took over the reins of the party after Gramsci's imprisonment in 1927. From 1927 to the mid-1930's, he traveled back and forth from Paris to Moscow as the leading Italian member of the Third International. From 1936 to 1939, he worked in Spain as a tactician and propagandist for the Spanish Communist Party. He devoted himself to organizational activities in France and Belgium in 1939 and 1940, when he emigrated to the Soviet Union. Togliatti remained in the Soviet Union until late March 1944, at which time he returned to Italy to direct the activities of the Communist Party in the Resistance.

In many of his articles in *Lo Stato Operaio,* Togliatti continued Gramsci's effort in *L'Ordine Nuovo* to define and interpret the meaning of the fascist phenomenon. One of his most important writings on this question appeared in the first issue of the magazine, in March 1927. This article, entitled "The Workers State," [65] began by belittling the campaign of the Aventine secessionists in 1924 and 1925. An "insurrection" of public opinion and a "moral revolt" would never topple a regime based on force, Togliatti said. The overthrow of fascism would be accomplished only with guns and bayonets, and insofar as the Aventine had limited itself to peaceful tactics it had become counterrevolutionary.

Following this initial barrage against the Aventine, Togliatti proceeded to define the origin and nature of fascism. Fascism, he said, was the force that had "saved the capitalistic regime in Italy from the insurrection of the working masses, of the proletariat and the peasants." It had "furnished the Italian industrial and agrarian bourgeoisie with the means to attempt a stabilization of capitalism in Italy." No accurate historical analysis of fascism, Togliatti asserted, could ever be made unless fascism and capitalism were seen as inextricably interrelated phenomena. He was willing to concede that the economic and political system created by fascism was not "a normal capitalistic regime" and that the men to whom fascism had given supreme power were exceptionally rapacious and exploitative. This fact however, did not belie the equally obvious truth that "what fascism today incarnates and defends is Italian capitalism in the form that it has had, substantially, in all the periods of its development since the formation of the unified Italian state." Thus, Togliatti based his analysis of fascism on a still more primary evaluation of the development of Italian capitalism from the post-Risorgimento era to the end of World War I: Italian capitalism had always been politically reactionary, it had always relied on the state for economic and political support, it had always sought to suppress the struggles of the Italian working class. The crisis of World War I had compelled Italian capitalism to support the

[65] Togliatti, "Lo stato operaio," *Lo Stato Operaio,* March 1927, pp. 1–9. (NY)

fascists in 1922 and 1923, for without an aggressively anti-socialist and anti-democratic regime in power, there would have been "a new, vaster and more decisive insurrection of the masses than had taken place immediately after the end of the war."

Togliatti concluded from his analysis of fascism that there was "a need for the hegemony of the proletariat in the struggle for the liberation of Italy from fascist tyranny." Fascism could be overthrown only by the working class, which alone was capable of leading the other strata of the population in a revolt against the regime. Therefore the only genuine anti-fascist policy was the communist policy. "The struggle to overthrow fascism and to eliminate it entirely from Italian political life coincides with the struggle for the establishment of a workers' state in Italy."

In 1928, Togliatti published a number of articles on fascism, two of which reveal a more subtle and precise understanding of the fascist phenomenon than does the essay discussed above. In his "Observations on the Policy of Our Party," [66] published in *Lo Stato Operaio* in June 1928, Togliatti criticized many of his comrades for having failed, in 1922, to see that capitalism was not always synonymous with fascism. The Italian Communist Party, he said, had grossly underestimated the impact of fascism on the political life of the nation and on the destiny of the Italian working class. The reason for this error in judgement derived from the mistaken assumption that the methods used by the bourgeoisie to hold down the workers were substantially equivalent at all times and in all places. It was necessary, Togliatti said, to examine the concrete situation that had allowed fascist reaction to triumph in Italy.

In August 1928, Togliatti published another article[67] in which he proceeded to examine fascism as it had concretely manifested itself in Italy. Fascism was a specific form of reaction. The formula, as expounded by the Italian communists in the early 1920's, that "fascism was purely and simply capitalist reaction," had proved to be inadequate. The fascist phenomenon was composed of other elements as well, for the fascist movement had been able to rely on the support of the disaffected rural petit-bourgeois masses, had capitalized on the political struggle of certain representatives of the small and middle bourgeoisie against the old liberal ruling class, and in addition created a para-military organization that won the loyalty of thousands of declassed, embittered individuals. Moreover, fascism, unlike bourgeois "formal" democracy, was a thorough reaction that

[66] Togliatti, "Osservazioni sulla politica del nostro Partito," June, 1928; reprinted in *L'antifascismo italiano,* edited by Alatri, vol. II, pp. 83–84.
[67] Togliatti, "A proposito del fascismo," appeared originally in August 1928 in Russian and French editions of the magazine *Communist International;* reprinted in *L'antifascismo italiano,* vol. II, pp. 85–103.

brought about "the total systematic suppression of every autonomous form of mass organization." Thus, although Togliatti still saw the capitalist system as organically related to the rise of fascism, he also recognized that the specific features of Italian capitalism—which was still weak and in an undeveloped stage—had to be taken into account to explain the appeal and the success of the fascist movement in Italy.

As we shall see, during the course of the 1930's and, except for the period of the Nazi-Soviet pact, during the war years, Palmiro Togliatti was to become the principal exponent among the Italian communist leaders of a policy of collaboration with the socialist and anti-fascist bourgeois parties in the struggle against fascism. Gramsci's successor was always a superbly gifted political strategist whose "theoretical" analyses of fascism, of the role of the Italian working class, and of other Italian problems were strongly influenced by the needs and aims of the international communist movement led by the Soviet Union.

PART III

THE UNDERGROUND PRESS OF THE ARMED RESISTANCE (1943–45)

CHAPTER FOUR

THE UNDERGROUND PRESS IN ACTION

I
The Development of the Resistance Movement

In both a military and political sense, the experiences of the more than three thousand Italians who fought on the side of the loyalists in the Spanish Civil War were of inestimable value to the development of the Resistance Movement in Italy. Not only did many future partisan leaders receive their baptism of fire in Spain, but it was in Spain also that Italian anti-fascism first became fully conscious of itself as part of an international rather than only a national conflict. From a purely military point of view, it is important to realize that many veterans of the Spanish Civil War occupied positions of authority in the various partisan units that were formed after September 8, 1943, as well as in the highly effective terrorist units—named GAP (*Gruppi di Azione Patriottica*)—whose functions were to attack and kill isolated groups of German and fascist soliders, seize weapons from police stations, disrupt and sabotage railway and urban communications systems, and support all other forms of anti-fascist activity—strikes, street demonstrations, distribution of clandestine manifestoes and newspapers—that could be of help to the Resistance Movement. Luigi Longo, who became commander-in-chief of the communist-led "Garibaldi" partisan brigades and a leading organizer of the *Corpo Volontari della Libertà* (Corps of Freedom Volunteers) during the Resistance, acquired his first military experience as inspector general of the International Brigades in Spain; the first partisan units that operated in the region of Belluno were led by two veterans of Spain, Manlio Silvestri and Raveane Rizzieri; Giovanni Pesce, Ilio Barontini, and Vittorio Mallozzi, all of whom had fought in Spain, were the principal organizers of GAP units in Turin, Bologna, and Rome; numerous Italians of lesser renown who participated in the defense of Madrid in November 1936 and in the battles of Guadalajara, Huesca, and the Aragon front in 1937 were destined in 1943 to provide military leadership for partisan units throughout northern and central Italy.[1]

In the more essential realm of political and ideological warfare, the Spanish Civil War was of crucial importance in that it helped to forge a sense of unity of purpose among the diverse anti-fascist movements in Italy and in exile. The slogan "Today in Spain, tomorrow in Italy," created by Carlo Rosselli in November 1936, became the battle cry of the entire Garibaldi brigade in Spain, which was composed, like other volunteer units belonging to the International Brigades, of communists, socialists, liberals, anarchists, republicans, as well as of many men who were not affiiliated with any political movement. This sense of unity was further strengthened when it became known that the fascist government, despite promises to the contrary, was supporting Franco's insurgents with "volunteers" and massive quantities of planes, tanks, and guns.[2] It should also be noted that certain key political leaders of the Resistance acquired valuable organizational experience in Spain. For example, Palmiro Togliatti, the principal spokesman for the Italian Communist Party during the Resistance, worked in Spain as a tactician and propagandist for the Spanish Communist Party in 1936 and 1937, and Pietro Nenni, who headed the Socialist Party's ideological campaign from 1943 to 1945, helped organize Spanish socialist workers prior to the defense of Madrid.

The Spanish Civil War also helped forge a sense of solidarity and *esprit de corps* among the beleaguered opponents of fascism in Italy itself. Symbolic of this solidarity was the almost simultaneous departure for Spain, in the latter part of 1936, of four Turinese anti-fascists affiliated with four diverse political movements: the communist Vitale Giambone, the socialist Fernando de Rosa, Renzo Giua—who belonged to the Justice and Freedom Movement—and the anarchist Vittorio Ortore.[3] All four men were among the close to six hundred members of the Garibaldi brigade who died on the battlefields of Spain. Danilo Masi, who organized

[1] Luigi Longo's role in the Spanish Civil War is described by Hugh Thomas in *The Spanish Civil War,* passim; Roberto Cessi makes mention of the contribution of Silvestri and Rizzieri to the GAP organization in *La Resistenza nel Bellunese,* p. 39; Giovanni Pesce's activities as a GAP organizer are described at the beginning of his *Un garibaldino in Spagna;* the crucial role played by Barontini and Mallozzi in the GAP is referred to in many works dealing with the Italian Resistance Movement.

[2] Hugh Thomas cites precise facts and figures on the military aid given by the fascist government to Franco in *The Spanish Civil War,* pp. 634, 635. On the basis of documents released by the Italian government after World War II, the historian Leo Valiani estimates that "fascist intervention in Spain cost fourteen billion lire, that is, almost two-thirds of the income of the Italian state as reflected in the budget of 1936–1937." See Leo Valiani, "L'intervento in Spagna," *Trent'anni di storia italiana,* p. 229.

[3] Raimondo Luraghi, *Il movimento operaio torinese durante la Resistenza,* p. 22.

an anti-fascist circle in Florence in 1937 that numbered about three hundred and fifty members, was inspired by the reports of Radio Barcelona and Radio Madrid to found a clandestine newspaper named *Il Notiziario Settimanale della Giovane Italia,* with which he and a few friends "gave their readers a true picture of the war in Spain." [4] The novelist Elio Vittorini, who in the mid-1930's belonged to a group of revisionist, "left-wing" fascists in Florence, speaks in his preface to *Il Garofano Rosso* (Verona, 1948) of the tremendous impact that the Spanish Civil War had on him and on many of his young colleagues. It was this event, Vittorini says, that precipitated his definitive and irreversible break with fascism.

Following the defeat of the Spanish Republic, the fascist government sought to consolidate its already *de facto* alliance with Nazi Germany through military and political pacts designed to buttress nazi-fascist unity against both the Western democracies and the Soviet Union. Among the first consequences of this alliance was a series of "racial laws" promulgated in the latter part of 1938 by the fascist government in subservience to Hitlerian doctrines. Italian Jews, many of whom had attained high positions under fascism in business, in the professions, in the universities, and even in the armed forces, were suddenly told that they belonged to an inferior, corrupt race of people whose presence in the upper echelons of fascist society could no longer be tolerated. Jewish professors lost their teaching positions, business firms owned by Jews were boycotted, Jewish high school and university students were ostracized, Jewish army and navy officers were stripped of their rank and dismissed.[5] Since anti-Semitism had never been widespread in Italy, and since thousands of Italian Catholics had intermarried with Jews, the racial laws were greeted with a mixture of startled dismay, ridicule, and contempt by the great majority of Italians. It was precisely the racist elements of the nazi and fascist mentalities that brought thousands of ordinary Italians into the ranks of the Resistance in 1943.

But the gravest consequence of Mussolini's alliance with Hitler was that it brought the Italian people into a war for which it was militarily and psychologically unprepared. Despite the warnings of his closest advisers, who told him that Italy would not be capable of undertaking a full-scale war effort until the latter part of 1943, Mussolini decided to gamble on a quick German victory and on a rapidly negotiated peace between the

---

[4] Danilo Masi, "Documenti: storia di un antifascista," *Società,* April 1953, p. 257.

[5] For a concise description and analysis of the legislation of 1938 affecting Italian Jews, see Armando Gavagnin, *Vent'anni di Resistenza al fascismo,* pp. 377–82. See also Renzo DeFelice, *Storia degli ebrei sotto il fascismo.*

Axis powers and England. Thus by declaring war on England and France on June 10, 1940, the Italian dictator hoped to gain maximum advantage with a minimum investment of manpower and money. In June 1940 Mussolini's hopes were not entirely unfounded. The Nazi-Soviet pact of August 1939 was a guarantee of Russian neutrality. The United States had remained neutral during the Spanish Civil War, and there was little indication in June 1940 of America's intention to intervene militarily in the war that had begun in September 1939. England seemed to be incapable of withstanding the German onslaught, which within a period of nine months had conquered almost all of western Europe. Four days after Italy's declaration of war, German troops occupied Paris, while at the same time Italian troops marched across the French border to complete the conquest of an already prostrate France.

Mussolini, however, had also gambled with the imponderables of history, which in this case assumed the form of English determination to continue the war at all costs and the rapid growth of resistance movements in all of the nazi-occupied countries. Encouraged by a series of easy victories in Africa, the Italian dictator embarked on the conquest of Greece in October 1940, and immediately encountered another unpredictable event, namely, the stubborn resistance of the Greek Army against Italian troops whose military performance left much to be desired. But it was the year 1941 that revealed the errors and contradictions of Mussolini's strategy. The German invasion of the Soviet Union in June 1941, of which Mussolini knew nothing until it was an accomplished fact, and, six months later, the entrance of the United States into the war, following the Japanese attack on Pearl Harbor, completely upset the balance of forces that had heretofore favored the Axis powers.

For the next two years, except for sporadic and temporary victories in North Africa, Italian armed forces met with one defeat after the other. The Italian Navy was in relatively good fighting condition, but the Army and Air Force were completely unprepared to wage modern warfare. Inadequately fed, clothed, and armed, Italian soldiers were hurled into the Russian campaign in 1942, where starvation and cold were more fearful enemies even than the Red Army. Relations between German and Italian troops in Russia were strained from the beginning and quickly degenerated into openly expressed contempt on the part of the Germans, and widespread rancor and resentment on the part of the Italians. Frederick Deakin notes in this regard that the first successful Soviet counteroffensive "was a turning point in the relations between [Italy and Germany] and the decisive psychological failure in 'Fascist' warfare. The lack of comradeship with the Germans of course was widely felt throughout the Italian armed forces, in particular after the North African campaign of Rommel, but the situation on the Eastern Front was more deep and grave than that. The Germans were fighting a fanatical crusade against Bolshevism, a concept which never really penetrated the Italian military mentality, and the lasting effect of contact between the Italian troops and the Russians was both to give the former a marked respect for the industrial potential of a society with which they were not familiar, and, as the Italian Consul-General in Innsbruck put it (in a dispatch of April 7) 'a feeling of increased consideration for the (Russian) army and possibly even for Russia.' " [6]

The attitude of Italian troops during the winter of 1943, following the final phases of the Soviet victory at Stalingrad on February 2 of that year, was characterized by a mixture of despair and furious resentment. As revealed by the testimony of many men who participated in the Russian campaign, thousands[7] of Italian soldiers began to question the legitimacy of the fascist war, others openly expressed their admiration of the Soviet Union and their hatred of the Germans, still others retreated into embittered silence, unable to comprehend the tragedy through which they were living. At the same time, the situation in Italy was disastrous. Discontent among the masses of Italian workers, who were suffering ever more intolerable privations of food and clothing as a result of the war, began to spread to other strata of Italian society, particularly intellectuals, professionals, and small businessmen. Protests against the fascist regime and demands that Italy withdraw from the war proliferated throughout the country. Then on March 5, 1943, an event occurred that can be legitimately called the beginning of a vast mass movement destined to culminate in the organized Resistance of September 1943 to April 1945. On that day almost one hundred thousand workers at the Fiat Mirafiori plant in Turin went on strike and for a week remained on strike until some of their main economic demands were satisfied. During the following weeks the agitation spread rapidly to other industrial centers of northern Italy, especially to Milan. But the real significance of these strikes and protests does not lie so much in the immediate economic demands of the Italian workers as in the political content of their struggle. To strike meant to

[6] Frederick W. Deakin, *The Brutal Friendship*, pp. 206, 207.

[7] Nuto Revelli explains the psychological and moral factors underlying the hatred felt by Italian soldiers for the Germans during the Russian campaign in *La guerra dei poveri*, as does Enzo Collotti in *L'amministrazione tedesca dell'Italia occupata*. In *Russia at War*, p. 507, Alexander Werth cites a passage from the official Soviet *History of the Second World War* that states that "a large number of Italians who had survived the Don battle were murdered by the Germans, particularly at Lwow in 1943, after they had refused—this was after the fall of Mussolini—to swear allegiance to Hitler."

show defiance of the fascist regime. This defiance was expressed in hundreds of clandestine manifestoes that circulated in Turin and Milan in March and April 1943. Historian Giorgio Vaccarino, who has made an exhaustive study of the strikes of March 1943, indicates that in addition to economic protests, these clandestine manifestoes also demanded, in the words of the manifestoes themselves, "the liberation of our comrades who have been arrested," "the expulsion of police guards from the factories," "the right to have and to elect real workers' representatives." Most of the manifestoes ended with the appeal: "Working men and women of Turin! Reason, number and strength are on our side. We shall win if we remain determined and united. Long live peace and freedom!" [8] Both Vaccarino and Raimondo Luraghi, who has also devoted himself to the recent history of the working class in Turin, stress the fact that these strikes and protests were not organized entirely by the Communist Party, which in March 1943 was still not in a sufficiently strong position to exert its authority over large numbers of Italian workers. Some preparatory work had been done, to be sure, by Umberto Massola, Leo Lanfranchi, and several other communist labor organizers who had begun to lay the groundwork for the strikes in the latter part of 1942.[9] But the force and compactness of the agitation came directly from the ranks of the workers themselves. Luraghi summarizes the significance of the strikes of March 1943 as follows: "The direct struggle against fascist domination . . . had begun. The workers had shown the way to the entire nation; they had shown that it was possible to fight against fascism and to win; they had revealed to free peoples another Italy that had nothing to do with the crimes of fascism and that was ready and determined to struggle for its own freedom and for the freedom of the entire world." [10]

Indeed, "another Italy" radically different from that known by the victims of fascist aggression was emerging from the struggles of March 1943. The events of the following five months, which witnessed the Allied landing in Sicily on July 10, the downfall of Mussolini on July 25 as a result of a coup staged by members of the Fascist Grand Council in concert with the King and with elements of the Italian Army, the peace negotiations between representatives of the new Italian government headed by Marshal Pietro Badoglio and Allied military authorities in Portugal, and the announcement of an Italian-Allied armistice on Sep-

[8] Giorgio Vaccarino, "Gli scioperi del marzo 1943—contributo per una storia del movimento operaio a Torino," *Aspetti della Resistenza in Piemonte,* p. 15.

[9] The role played by communist labor organizers in the strikes of March 1943 is described by Umberto Massola in *Marzo 1943 ore dieci.*

[10] Luraghi, *Il movimento operaio torinese durante la Resistenza,* pp. 59, 60.

tember 8, served to give official diplomatic and political sanction to the sentiments of the majority of the Italian people.

During the forty-five days that had intervened between the fall of Mussolini on July 25 and the announcement of the armistice on September 8, Italian anti-fascists who had been in exile began to return to Italy in ever-increasing numbers and to undertake the task of reorganizing the political parties with which they were variously affiliated. In late August the Badoglio government granted amnesty to political prisoners, which further swelled the ranks of anti-fascists in Italy. Since the early months of 1943, the newly founded Action Party had been waging an effective ideological campaign in its clandestine organ *L'Italia Libera* and had succeeded in gaining the support of intellectuals and workers in many areas of the country. All of these factors, combined with the collapse of the Italian Army, which resulted in the dispersion of thousands of embittered soldiers sustained only by a desire for revenge against a regime that they believed had betrayed them, contributed to the rapid development of an organized Resistance Movement after September 8.

The German military occupation of Italy, which was accomplished within a week after the armistice, immediately clarified the situation for those Italians who before September 8 had entertained the illusion that Italy would be spared further violence. But even after the German occupation, it is probable that most Italians did not support the idea of opposing armed resistance to the nazis and to the segments of the Italian army and police that remained loyal to the cause of the nazi-fascist alliance. The task of convincing them that resistance was necessary and just fell to the men who organized the Committees of National Liberation after September 8, and in particular to the underground press.

II
The Methodology of Underground Journalism

With the exception of France, in no country in which there existed organized Resistance Movements was the underground press as large and various as in Italy.[11] Clandestine journalism was already a tradition in

[11] From 1940 to 1945, according to statistics furnished by the Bibliothèque Nationale, 1,034 clandestine newspapers were published in France: Mme. Granet, "La presse clandestine en France," *European Resistance Movements 1939–1945*, p. 183; during four years and four months of occupation, the Belgian Resistance produced about 500 clandestine newspapers: F. Demany, "La presse clandestine en Belgique," *European Resistance Movements 1939–1945*, p. 164; about 225 clandestine newspapers and periodicals were published in Denmark during the occupation: *Denmark during the German Occupation;* more than 300 underground newspapers appeared in Norway: Ronald Seth, *The Undaunted*, p. 26. The figure for Italy is 581 clandes-

Italy at the time the anti-fascist parties began laying the groundwork for the Resistance in 1943. Many veterans of the clandestine press during the 1920's and 1930's merely continued their activities in 1943, while others who had been in contact with democratic movements in exile, particularly in Paris and later in Spain, joined forces with the new generation of anti-fascists that had come into maturity during the latter half of the 1930's. Among the most important representatives of this new generation were the young men and women of the "liberalsocialist" movement founded by Guido Calogero and Aldo Capitini in 1936 and a group of students at the University of Rome—including Mario Alicata, Pietro Ingrao, and Carlo Salinari—who in 1938 and 1939 had taken a political direction that led them into the Communist Party in 1943. Many young and enthusiastic participants in the Resistance also emerged from the ranks of labor unions, from diverse professional groups and associations, and from segments of both the lay and clerical branches of the Catholic Church, of which the most active and best organized was the Catholic Action Movement. In addition, a significant number of former young "left-wing" fascists who had been associated in the late 1930's and early 1940's with various dissident political and literary coteries, such as the *Campo di Marte* group in Florence and the intellectuals who gravitated around the review *Corrente* in Milan, were compelled at long last by the rush of events to translate into action the ideas that had led them to repudiate many aspects of fascist society. Among these former "left-wing" fascists who made important contributions to the Resistance as political organizers and propagandists were the novelists Vasco Pratolini and Elio Vittorini, the promising young Germanist Giaime Pintor, and the journalist and critic Davide Lajolo.[12]

But there are two other reasons for the exceptional development of the underground press in Italy. In the first place, whereas the peoples of other occupied countries rose up against a foreign invader with whose methods

---

tine publications, as tabulated by Laura Conti and Giampaolo Pansa in *La Resistenza in Italia,* a bibliographical guide to the names, dates, and places of publication of Italian underground newspapers, magazines, pamphlets, and manifestoes of the period July 25, 1943, to April 25, 1945.

12 Vasco Pratolini describes his experiences as a member of the Italian Communist Party's propaganda and organizational apparatus in Rome during the German occupation in *Il mio cuore a Ponte Milvio;* Elio Vittorini's largely autobiographical novel *Uomini e no* is an account of the Resistance in Milan; some of Giaime Pintor's literary and political writings dealing with fascism and with the motives that led him to abandon his career as a German scholar in order to participate in the Resistance have been collected in the volume *Il sangue d'Europa.* Pintor was killed on December 1, 1943, while going from Naples to Rome to help organize an underground in the Italian capital.

and ideology they had never been collectively associated, the Italian people was forced not only to rebuild a sense of national integrity in reaction to the massive fact of German occupation but also to explain the causes that had originally led Italy to fascism and subsequently to a political and military alliance with nazism. Many Italians who in a clearer psychological and moral atmosphere might have limited themselves to military action felt the need to explain, above all to themselves, the sentiments and ideas that had motivated their decision to join the Resistance. Widespread among Italians of all classes and walks of life, this state of mind was particularly characteristic of soldiers who had fought in France, Greece, Yugoslavia, and Russia and who after September 8 became anti-fascist partisans. These men needed a means of expression for their conflicts and aspirations, a need that found its outlet in the pages of numerous partisan newspapers. Second, the large number and variety of clandestine newspapers in Italy was also the result of the country's extraordinarily diversified, polycentric character. Each of the cities and regions of Italy has its own customs and dialect, its own political and cultural traditions. Therefore there was a need for clandestine newspapers which, while establishing the overall national aims of the Resistance Movement, could also frame their messages and appeals in accordance with the local traditions of the city, province, or region in which they were circulated.

From July 25, 1943, to April 25, 1945, according to the bibliographical guide prepared by Laura Conti and Giampaolo Pansa, five hundred eighty-one clandestine newspapers were published by anti-fascist organizations in Italy. But since many Italians own private and as yet unclassified collections of underground newspapers, this figure will within a few years undoubtedly be revised upward to between six hundred and six hundred fifty.

Italian underground newspapers fall into six main categories: (1) those published by the interparty Committees of National Liberation, of which *La Riscossa Italiana* (Turin) and *Fratelli d'Italia* (Padua) are two distinguished examples; (2) the official organs of the five political parties that were chiefly responsible for the organization of the Committees, namely *L'Unità* (Communist Party), *Avanti!* (Socialist Party), *L'Italia Libera* (Action Party), *Il Popolo* (Christian Democratic Party), and *Risorgimento Liberale* (Liberal Party); (3) the official organs of political parties and movements not directly associated with the committees, such as the Republican Party's *La Voce Repubblicana,* the Christian Social Movement's *L'Azione,* the Federalist Movement's *L'Unità Europea,* and the Catholic Communists' *Voce Operaia;* (4) newspapers of partisan units affiliated with one or the other political parties, such as *Il Partigiano Alpino* (Action Party) and *Stella Gari-baldina* (Communist Party), of politically independent partisan groups generally called "autonomist," and of the unified military command of the Resistance, the *Corpo Volontari della Libertà,* whose main organ was *Il Combattente;* (5) newspapers published by national youth movements, the most important of which were the predominantly communist *Fronte della Gioventù,* the Catholic Youth Organization, and the Youth Action Movement associated with the Action Party; (6) newspapers written by and directed primarily to members of politically independent groups of individuals such as labor unions and student, professional, and women's organizations: *Il Grido di Spartaco,* the organ of a group of Turinese industrial workers, *L'Italia degli Studenti,* published by Rome University students, *Noi Donne,* published by a nationally organized women's organization called *Gruppi di difesa della donna,* and *Il Giornale del Medico,* are examples of this latter type of newspaper.

It is necessary to add, however, that some clandestine publications do not fit exactly into any of the categories listed above. A separate classification must be reserved for newspapers and magazines which, although published under the auspices of the various anti-fascist parties, were directed exclusively to specific categories of people such as intellectuals, industrial workers, artisans, and farmers. Among clandestine publications directed to intellectuals and dealing largely with matters of political theory and doctrine, were the Communist Party's theoretical organ *La Nostra Lotta,* the Action Party's *Nuovi Quaderni di Giustizia e Libertà* and *Lo Stato Moderno,* the Liberal Party's *L'Opinione,* and the Socialist Party's *L'Edificazione Socialista.* Other examples of this type of publication directed to specific segments of the population are the Action Party's *Azione Contadina* and *Voci d'Officina,* the Christian Democratic Party's *Il Segno,* and the Socialist Party's *La Compagna.* It is also important to note that representatives of the major anti-fascist parties in some cities took it upon themselves to supplement the work done by the nationally circulated party organ and published newspapers of their own with different names and in some cases with a somewhat different ideological slant. In Florence, for example, in addition to attending to the distribution of *L'Unità* and *L'Italia Libera,* the Florentine communists and actionists had their own separate newspapers, *L'Azione Comunista* and *La Libertà.* Also not included in any of the categories yet mentioned are the newspapers of several dissident, extreme left-wing groups of "international communists" who rebelled against the Italian Communist Party's collaboration with the Allies (including the Soviet Union) and with the other anti-fascist parties in Italy. Their principal organs were *Prometeo* and *Stella Rossa*.

Lack of funds, police surveillance of all known printing works, the omnipresence of paid spies and informers, systematic inquisition of persons suspected of harboring anti-fascist sentiments, were some of the practical obstacles to the successful production and distribution of the underground press. Yet all of these obstacles could be and were often overcome, as long as there were courageous people willing to take the risks involved in spreading anti-nazi and anti-fascist propaganda. Indeed, the consequences of proved association with any phase of clandestine press activities were extremely grave, ranging from long prison terms to torture, deportation, and summary execution.

During the period of forty-five days between the fall of Mussolini on July 25, 1943, and the announcement of the Italian-Allied armistice on September 8, anti-fascists had been able to function in reasonable safety, on a kind of semi-legal basis, despite the police restrictions officially imposed on them by the Badoglio government. Following the German occupation, this ambiguous, semi-legal situation changed to one of extreme danger, for by the end of September, with the help of a residual but particularly fanatical segment of the fascist hierarchy, the Germans had control of the nation's police and administrative apparatus. Nazi military commanders in Italy were able to rely on the support of fascist army and police authorities, whose position had been greatly strengthened as a result of Mussolini's liberation by German parachutists on September 12 and the subsequent establishment of the neo-fascist Republic of Salò on September 23. Carlo Ragghianti, one of the editors of *La Libertà*, the Action Party's clandestine organ in Florence, noted with telegraphic brevity in a letter to Riccardo Bauer on November 26, 1943: "press activities extremely difficult, police surveillance, houses searched."[13] In saying that press activities were extremely difficult, Ragghianti was referring principally to an edict issued by the German commandant in Florence on October 3 that stated: "Anyone who is discovered compiling, printing, distributing, and spreading anti-German propaganda will be punished with immediate execution by firing squad." [14] Similar edicts and warnings were promulgated by nazi military commands in cities and towns throughout Italy in October of 1943. In most cases the Germans let the fascists do the actual work of capturing and punishing persons who defied their

---

[13] *Una lotta nel suo corso,* edited by Sandro Contini Bonacossi and Licia Ragghianti Collobi, p. 15.
[14] Carlo Francovich, *La Resistenza a Firenze,* p. 69.

orders. Disposition of individuals who were unfortunate enough to be captured was, however, usually made after consultation with German military authorities.

The severity of nazi-fascist reprisals against subversive propagandists depended to a large extent on the level of responsibility of the accused individuals. The writers, chief organizers, and printers of the underground press ran the greatest danger of torture and execution, since they were held responsible for the entire apparatus with which the newspapers, pamphlets, and manifestoes were circulated. Distributors, runners, and persons suspected or proved to be in possession of clandestine publications were generally imprisoned.

The martyrs of the underground press belonged to nearly every political movement engaged in the struggle against nazism and fascism. Eugenio Curiel, who in Milan functioned as chief editor of the Communist Party's two principal clandestine organs, *L'Unità* and *La Nostra Lotta,* was assassinated by fascist gunmen on the afternoon of February 24, 1945, a few minutes after he had left the offices of *L'Unità* on his way to an appointment with his sister and mother.[15] Like so many of his fellow workers, Curiel was the victim of an efficient spy network that operated in collaboration with the fascist secret police. As Curiel walked toward Piazzale Baracca, a car approached driven by a man whom Curiel regarded as a trusted friend. Without warning, the man shouted "That's him, Curiel!", after which three men armed with automatic rifles suddenly appeared from behind the corner and opened fire, killing Curiel almost instantly. Eugenio Colorni, the chief editor of *Avanti!* in Rome, and Mario Fioretti, who was also associated with the *Avanti!* staff in Rome, met with the same fate that befell Curiel. And again, in both cases, the assassinations were made possible through information passed to fascist authorities by paid informers. Colorni was murdered by the Caruso-Koch band, which terrorized anti-fascists in Rome by interrogation, torture or sudden assault.[16] On May 28, 1944, Colorni was going from via Salerno to Piazza Bologna to attend a meeting of the Socialist Party's military command when he realized that he was being followed by two men. When the men asked him to show them the contents of his briefcase, Colorni shrugged his shoulders in a gesture of contempt, in response to which his assailants shot him six times. Colorni died a few days later, a little more than a week before the Allies liberated Rome.

---

[15] The events leading to Curiel's assassination are described by Enzo Modica in his introduction to Eugenio Curiel, *Classi e generazioni nel secondo Risorgimento,* p. LXXX.

[16] "Il professor Eugenio Colorni capo-redattore dell'*Avanti!* assassinato dalla banda Caruso-Koch," *Avanti!,* June 5, 1944, p. 1. (INS)

Assassination was less common, however, and in a certain sense a less terrible fate than the kind of torture, both physical and psychological, to which many other men and women were subjected before finally being executed or deported to extermination camps in Germany. On the evening of November 18, 1943, fascist police raided the apartment at via Basento, 55, in Rome where the Action Party's clandestine organ *L'Italia Libera* was being printed.[17] The only persons present at the time of the raid were the printer Manlio Gualerni and a young student named Mario Fiorentino, both of whom were arrested. Several fascists remained on guard, however, and on the morning of the next day arrested practically the entire editorial staff of *L'Italia Libera,* including Manlio Rossi-Doria, Carlo Muscetta, and Leone Ginzburg. Rossi-Doria and Muscetta were able to withstand the following months of imprisonment, beatings, and cross-examinations, but Ginzburg, who suffered from a heart ailment, was not strong enough to endure the torture inflicted on him and died in prison on February 5, 1944. Three other celebrated martyrs of the clandestine press in Rome were Placido Martini, Mario Magri, and Silvio Campanile, who in early August 1943 had founded the National Union of Italian Democracy. On August 26, the three men began publishing a weekly newspaper called *Unione Nazionale,* which continued to appear as a clandestine publication after September 8. Arrested in January 1944, Martini, Magri, and Campanile were brought to a jail on via Tasso reserved for political prisoners. Two months later, on March 25, 1944, after enduring frequent and savage beatings, all three men were executed at the *Fosse Ardeatine* along with three hundred thirty-two other anti-fascists.[18]

Deportation to concentration camps in Germany was a common method of punishing anti-nazi and anti-fascist propagandists. On December 30, 1943, five members of the Committee of National Liberation in Trieste—Gabriele Foschiatti, Zeffirino Pisoni, Edmondo Puecher, Giovanni Tanasco, Fernando Gandusio—were arrested. Foschiatti was chief

---

[17] Carlo Muscetta, "La sventurata Italia Libera," *Mercurio,* December 1944, pp. 212–17.

[18] On March 21, 1944, a truck carrying German policemen was blown up by Roman partisans, resulting in the death of thirty-three German soldiers. In adherence to their ten-for-one policy, which stipulated that ten Italian anti-fascists would die for every one German soldier killed by the partisans, 335 Italian political prisoners were taken to the Ardeatine Caves near St. Paul's Cathedral and executed on March 25. Actually, therefore, the quota was exceeded by five. For information on the background of events and immediate circumstances leading to this massacre, see Renato Perrone Capano, *La Resistenza in Roma,* vol. II, pp. 230–42. See also the recently published study of the Ardeatine Cave massacre by Robert Katz, *Death in Rome.*

editor of the Action Party's clandestine organ in Trieste, *Giustizia e Libertà,* and Pisoni organized the printing and distributing of the communist press, so that they were regarded by fascist authorities as particularly dangerous elements. Both men were deported to Dachau, where they died in the latter part of 1944. In early March 1944, the Milanese staff of *Avanti!* was decimated when five of the newspaper's leading organizers were captured and placed under arrest. Two of the five men, Filippo Acciarini and Andrea Lorenzetti, were deported to the extermination camp at Mauthausen.[19]

Among the many other persons who suffered deportation and death as a result of their association with the underground press was Teresio Olivelli, an ex-fascist Italian Army officer, who in March 1944 founded the partisan newspaper *Il Ribelle.*[20] Olivelli was a profoundly religious person, and it was precisely his faith in God and in the basic goodness of man that allowed him to withstand for more than a year a barbarous example of the cruelty of man. Olivelli's ordeal began on September 9, 1943, when he was deported to a forced labor camp in Germany. In mid-October he escaped and returned to Italy. On October 28, he arrived in Udine, where he began his conspiratorial activity. In the early part of 1944, after establishing contact with the Committee of National Liberation in Milan, he became the leading organizer of the Resistance in the provinces of Cremona and Brescia. The clandestine newspaper he founded, *Il Ribelle,* was widely read by partisans and anti-fascists of all political persuasions. On April 27, 1944, Olivelli was betrayed by an informer and arrested, together with Carlo Bianchi, an engineer who had lent financial aid to *Il Ribelle;* Rolando Pertini, a student who assisted Olivelli; and Franco Rovida, who owned the presses on which the newspaper was printed. Pertini died in a concentration camp at Gusen in January 1945; Rovida met his death in Melch a month later. Olivelli was first imprisoned in San Vittore in Milan, where he was tortured but revealed nothing of his activities. On June 9 he was transferred to a concentration camp at Fossoli, on August 5 to a camp at Bolzano, and on September 4 he was deported to Flossenburg, which the nazis themselves called "an extermination camp." But Olivelli was not to die in Flossenburg. Instead he was transferred on October 1 to Hersbruck, where he was horribly beaten. He finally collapsed, and on January 12, 1945, Olivelli died.

Equal to Olivelli in moral and physical courage were Carlo Tavecchia

---

[19] Ercole Miani, "La Resistenza nella Venezia Giulia," *Il Ponte,* April 1948, pp. 339–45.

[20] Alberto Caracciolo, *Teresio Olivelli,* pp. 101–20.

and Angelo Conca of the *L'Unità* staff in Milan; Walter Perotti, who helped found *La Fabbrica* in Milan; Giovanni Bertora, the printer of *La Voce d'Italia* in Genoa; Anna Maria Enriques, who wrote for the Christian Social Movement's newspaper *Rinascita* in Florence; and Duccio Galimberti, one of the founders in February 1944 of the partisan newspaper *Il Partigiano Alpino,* all of whom were tortured and killed.[21]

The success of the underground press depended heavily on the cooperation of many ordinary and obscure individuals. If the lists of prisoners issued in June and September 1944 by police authorities in Florence and Milan are indicative of the situation in other urban centers, the number of persons imprisoned for clandestine press activities throughout the period of the Resistance must have been extremely high. In June 1944, the Florentine fascist police, headed by the notoriously cruel Mario Carità, arrested seven persons accused of possessing or distributing clandestine newspapers and manifestoes,[22] while the police register issued by the Milanese police in September includes the names of fifteen persons charged with the same crime.[23] The names and occupations of a few of the persons captured by the Milanese police suggest to what a large extent ordinary people contributed to the underground press. Listed at random among the names of thieves and murderers were: Virginio Bianchi, baker, charged with possession of clandestine newspapers; Luigi Bellini, janitor, charged with possession of subversive newspapers; Ercole Bellini, mechanic, charged with membership in the Socialist Party and possession of subversive newspapers; Stefano Carrelli, farmer, charged with distributing subversive newspapers; Carolina Crippa, apartment house superintendent, charged with possession and distribution of subversive newspapers; Luigi and Eugenio Memo, printers, charged with distributing subversive newspapers.

But courage and a spirit of self-sacrifice were not the only qualities necessary for the successful functioning of the underground press. Of equal importance were ingenuity and resourcefulness, without which the practical problems of news-gathering and of financing, producing, and distributing the clandestine newspapers would have been insuperable.

[21] The facts concerning the martyrdom of Tavecchia, Conca, Perotti, Bertora, Anna Enriques, and Galimberti are drawn from the following sources: Giovanni Brambilla, "Gli scioperi del marzo 1943 a Milano," *Fascismo e antifascismo,* pp. 454, 455; *Lettere di antifascisti dal carcere e dal confino* vol. II, p. 85; "Walter Perotti," *La Fabbrica,* December 8, 1944, p. 4 (IG); Renzo Baccino, *Contributo alla storia della Resistenza di Genova,* p. 44; *Anna Maria Enriques,* edited by Lidia Manetti Barbieri, pp. 5, 6 (ISRT); *Duccio Galimberti, eroe nazionale,* pp. 1, 2 (ISRT).

[22] Francovich, *La Resistenza a Firenze,* p. 80.

[23] *Elenco Detenuti* of September 1944. (INS)

The methods used to meet these problems varied greatly, of course, in accordance with the economic means, personal contacts, and type of organization available to individuals engaged in the ideological war against nazism and fascism.[24]

The first obstacle to overcome was that of obtaining sufficient funds to defray printing and paper costs for large, nationally circulated newspapers and, in the case of many locally circulated publications and the majority of partisan newspapers, to meet the expenses involved in acquiring typewriters, copying machines, and small hand presses. The major political parties, the Committees of National Liberation, and nationally organized movements such as the *Fronte della Gioventù* and the *Gruppi di difesa della donna,* were not usually handicapped by lack of funds. They could rely on reserves of capital accumulated through the collection of dues, private contributions donated by industrialists and businessmen in sympathy with their aims, vast fund-raising campaigns, and loans effected through contacts with trustworthy officials of banks and other money-lending agencies. Small, locally organized groups, such as student and professional associations, labor unions, and partisan units, had to depend entirely on the private resources of their members and frequently on the free contributions of printers, storekeepers, and other persons who were in a position to lend material assistance to them. Yet the element of personal contact and loyalty was crucial even for those organizations that generally had adequate funds at their disposal, since there were critical moments when regular sources of income had to be supplemented with a large number of private contributions.

Once sufficient funds were available, organizations and political parties that aspired to publish newspapers with a regional or nationwide circulation were faced with the problem of finding printers willing to take the risks of association with the underground press. Since all known printing works were under more or less constant police surveillance, the best solutions were either to establish contact with one or two trustworthy printers not suspected of anti-fascist sympathies or to persuade printers located in rural and less closely watched areas of the country to allow their presses to be used once or twice a week for clandestine purposes. Printers who wanted to help the underground press but were under more rigorous surveillance than others by reason of their past affiliation with anti-fascist circles, often managed to escape detection by running clandes-

---

[24] For a complete list of books and articles from which I have drawn information regarding news-gathering, and methods of financing, printing, and distributing underground newspapers, see the section of the bibliography entitled "Works on the Underground Press."

tine material through the presses in rapid and successive alternation with newspapers, bulletins, and other publications issued by fascist or at any rate politically acceptable organizations. Another method used with considerable success was to make contact with reliable linotypists employed by the printing works in which the nation's leading fascist or pro-fascist dailies were produced, such as Turin's *La Stampa,* Milan's *Il Corriere della Sera,* and Florence's *La Nazione.* Profiting by the know-how and ingenuity that only the specialized technician possesses, these linotypists were often able to prepare galleys, print, and pack clandestine material with amazing rapidity. Many a plant supervisor was unaware that the workers and presses under his control were simultaneously producing pro-fascist and anti-fascist literature. In some cases, when printers were not readily available, underground organizers hired technicians to dismantle presses, transport the parts to a safe hideout, and there reassemble them. The same technique was often used for type, plates, and galleys, which were brought piece by piece, in separately packed cartons, from town to town, from one hideout to another. Extensive use was also made of hand and pedal-operated presses, which were advantageous in that they could be easily moved from one place to another and were small enough to be hidden quickly when necessary.

All the methods mentioned above were employed at one time or another by the organizers of the regionally and nationally circulated press. For example, the Milanese issue of *L'Unità* was printed for many months by a peasant family in an abandoned farmhouse in Vaprio d'Adda and thence brought by truck to Milan safely buried under crates of vegetables and eggs.[25] A group of Florentine socialists succeeded in printing a local edition of *Avanti!* by transporting separately packed boxes of type and plates to typesetters who prepared the galleys in their homes and then delivered them to previously designated printers, each of whom worked without the knowledge of the others.[26]

Following the assault on the offices of *L'Italia Libera* in Rome on November 18, 1943, it became necessary for party workers who had avoided arrest to create a multiphased system of communication involving writers, typesetters, and printers. The system was organized by three of the Action Party's most prominent members, Francesco Fancello, Emilio Lussu, and Leo Valiani, who describes the system as follows: "Francello needs me, or rather someone able to help him edit *L'Italia Libera.* As for

---

[25] Giovanni Brambilla, "Gli scioperi del marzo 1943 a Milano," *Fascismo e antifascismo,* pp. 454, 455.

[26] Foscolo Lombardi, *Il socialismo fiorentino dall'azione clandestina agli albori della libertà,* pp. 6, 7. (ISRT)

printing the newspaper, it has become very complicated; it is impossible to find a more or less complete printing works. Two times a week Lussu meets us on a corner not far from *ponte Cavour*. The manuscripts are delivered to him, he brings them to a Sardinian typesetter, a friend of his. He prefers to assume all the risks of the operation, and does not want to reveal his friend's address to anyone. He brings the plates and galleys back to us, and we in turn bring them to a small printer, a friend of Cencio Baldazzi, who owns a small flat press." [27] The clandestine magazine *Nuovi Quaderni di Giustizia e Libertà,* although directed to anti-fascist intellectuals in Turin and Milan, was never printed in either city. Instead, beginning in June 1944, the magazine was printed in Torre Pellice, a small town in the foothills of the Italian Alps that had been liberated by the partisans a month earlier. From Torre Pellice, the magazine was brought to Turin and then distributed to Milan and other cities in northern Italy.[28]

In rare cases, writers and organizers of the underground press were lucky enough to find one or two printers with the contacts and technical means necessary to work for long periods of time on an uninterrupted basis. Such was the good fortune of the Committee of National Liberation in Turin, whose organ *La Riscossa Italiana* was printed for a year and a half by the same printing firm. All of the clandestine propaganda of the Action Party and of the Liberation Committee in Trieste was produced without interruption by a single indefatigable printer, Enrico Tenente, and in Padua local communist leaders safely entrusted their clandestine material to the printers Remo Turra and Roberto Schiavon.[29]

Standard printing methods were not available to many of the smaller and locally circulated newspapers. Most of the newspapers published by partisan units were typewritten, mimeographed, and even handwritten by teams of copyists, as were those of student groups and labor unions. Unfortunately, neglect and the passage of time have rendered some of these newspapers almost illegible, especially as the typewriters and mimeograph machines used were generally secondhand and in poor working order.

Before explaining the methods used in distributing the underground

[27] Leo Valiani, *Tutte le strade conducono a Roma,* p. 130.
[28] Franco Venturi, "La stampa clandestine torinese," *Torino* (rivista mensile della città e del Piemonte), April 1955, pp. 82–85.
[29] Ada Gobetti, the widow of Piero Gobetti, supplied me with the information on *La Riscossa Italiana* in an interview in July 1965; Enrico Tenente's work for the clandestine press is mentioned by Carlo Ventura in *La stampa a Trieste 1943–1945,* p. 96; the clandestine printers Remo Turra and Roberto Schiavon are referred to by Giuseppe Gaddi in *Saggio sulla stampa clandestina della Resistenza veneta,* p. 29.

press, it is necessary to indicate briefly the ways in which news was gathered by the newspapers' editors and organizers. Since the majority of underground newspapers were created not only for the purpose of spreading ideological propaganda but also of furnishing their readers with news reports of military, political, and diplomatic events, the job of news-gathering had to be performed with a maximum of efficiency and precision.

The principal sources of news were: (1) the fascist or officially sanctioned newspapers which, although heavily slanted, contained a vast amount of information about the battles in progress in the main theaters of war and world political events as they affected the situation in Italy; (2) the daily broadcasts of Radio London and Radio Moscow, which reached large numbers of people because of the insufficiently powerful jamming transmitters employed by nazi and fascist-controlled radio stations; (3) the propaganda and news branches of the joint Anglo-American Psychological Warfare Bureau and of the Allied Military Command in Italy, which published the newspaper *L'Italia Combatte* two or three times a month from April 1944 to the end of the war; (4) the foreign newspapers and magazines smuggled into Italy from France, Switzerland, and other western European countries; (5) the clandestine radio units in Italy capable of transmitting and receiving news, the most important of which were Radio Cora in Florence and the *Centro X* in Rome operated by Ettore Basevi, who was in daily radio contact with the headquarters of the Badoglio government in Brindisi; (6) the designated individuals who resided in the various quarters of the main cities or who worked in factories, farms, and business offices and in outlying rural areas and were assigned to communicate local news of interest to the Resistance Movement to the clandestine newspapers with which they were associated. It should also be noted that as soon as the Allies liberated a city or region of Italy or partisans succeeded in driving out the German and fascist forces from a particular town or zone, as happened for example in the case of Domodossola in September 1944, radio operators and runners were free to furnish the newspapers with information gathered from the various sources mentioned above.

Most of the news given by underground newspapers concerned military developments in western Europe and in the Soviet Union, since reports of the steady advances made by Allied troops in Italy and France and the successful counteroffensive launched by the Soviet Army in 1943 were effective antidotes to the propaganda of the fascist press. Much attention was also given to the achievements of Italian partisans and of

Resistance Movements elsewhere in Europe, particularly in France and Yugoslavia. The war in the Pacific, on the other hand, did not receive extensive coverage.

The task of distributing the clandestine newspapers was entrusted to small groups of *staffette,* or runners, many of whom were young women who belonged to student organizations, particularly to the *Fronte della Gioventù,* which played an indispensable role in diffusing clandestine propaganda throughout the period of the Resistance. Young women, such as the courageous Maria Luigia Guaita,[30] were chosen for this dangerous work because they were less likely to arouse the suspicions of the police than were men. But in many instances functionaries and workers belonging to the various anti-fascist parties, as well as truckdrivers, tram operators, apartment house superintendents, storekeepers, indeed anyone whose work necessitated travel or brought them into daily contact with the public, were called upon to do their part in seeing that the newspapers were circulated and read. Unfortunately, not all the individuals entrusted with this task were skillful enough to avoid detection, and there were also some who betrayed their fellow workers to the police in return for financial and political rewards.

Franco Venturi, who had direct personal experience with the clandestine press as cofounder of the magazine *Nuovi Quaderni di Giustizia e Libertà,* notes that any house, factory, barn, or attic was a satisfactory place from which to distribute the clandestine press, "providing that the place chosen for this work was surrounded by an invisible and compact network of solidarity that had to include everyone, without exception." [31] Without the assistance of a conspiracy of silence, without the solidarity of everyone involved in the process of distribution, even the most skillful runner was helpless against the omnipresent police. It was because of the risks and difficulties faced by everyone concerned that clandestine newspapers often issued instructions as to the most efficient methods of distribution and exhorted their readers not to destroy the newspapers after reading them but to pass them on to trusted friends or to leave them in places where they might be seen by other persons.

In most cases, the teams of distributors were divided into two groups—those who worked within the confines of a particular city or town and those whose task was to deliver the clandestine newspapers to other neighboring urban or rural centers. Most of the large-scale publishing was done in the major cities, so that most runners were recruited among

---

[30] Maria Luigia Guaita describes her adventures as a clandestine *staffetta* in *La guerra finisce la guerra continua.*
[31] Franco Venturi, *Torino,* p. 82.

persons who lived in the cities and who were intimately familiar with the location of police stations, roadblocks, and the addresses of known spies and informers. But since many clandestine newspapers were printed in remote areas of Piedmont, Lombardy, and other regions and then brought to the cities for distribution, there was also a need for runners who could traverse the countryside and reach the cities without difficulty on foot, whenever the use of automobiles and trains was rendered impossible by periodic police checks of highway and rail traffic. Several of the most important partisan newspapers, such as *Il Partigiano Alpino* and *Quelli della Montagna,* were read regularly by people in the urban centers of Piedmont through the skill and stamina of couriers who went back and forth from partisan units in the mountains to Turin, Cuneo, Asti, and other cities eight and ten times a month. In the same way partisan units operating in areas inaccessible except to the most intrepid and experienced individuals were informed by runners as to the ideas and programs of the anti-fascist parties.

Among the most efficient systems of distribution was that employed by the Communist Party in Florence. Orazio Barbieri, who worked on the staff of the Florentine communists' organ *L'Azione Comunista,* explains that as soon as the printing and packing operations were completed, a team of distributors brought all the newspapers from the printing works to a central storehouse. When this task was accomplished, three other persons, who were unknown to each other in order to make it impossible for a runner who might be captured to reveal the names of his comrades to the police, brought separately packed and cleverly disguised bundles of newspapers to three other widely dispersed distribution storehouses. One storehouse, called a *deposito città,* was the repository of newspapers destined for distribution in Florence itself, and in peripheral quarters of the city such as Rifredi; a second storehouse, called a *deposito circondario,* held newspapers that were to be brought to small towns and villages close to Florence, such as Sesto, Fiesole, Ponte a Ema, and Grassina; a third, called a *deposito provincia e toscana,* was reserved for newspapers that were to be brought to more distant cities and towns in Tuscany, such as Empoli, Siena, and Arezzo.[32] Other political parties employed similar techniques but were rarely as skillful as the communists in eluding the police.

But organized parties were not the only successful creators of distributing methods. In many instances, politically heterogeneous groups of individuals, working together on their own initiative, achieved excellent results. The distribution of the partisan newspaper *Il Ribelle,* after the arrest of Olivelli,

[32] Orazio Barbieri, *Un anno di lotta contro il nazismo e il fascismo.*

was accomplished through the efforts of persons whose only common denominator was their opposition to fascism. In his biographical study of Olivelli, Alberto Caracciolo describes the distributing procedure used by the editors and printers of *Il Ribelle*:

As soon as the newspaper was printed, the printing works were cleaned scrupulously. Then the bundles were delivered to a farmer named Celestino Ferrario and were stored at times in his home, sometimes in his cellar mixed with cheese and butter, or out in the barn, whenever the alarm was sounded. Ferrario's daughters prudently watched over them. Then Piero Reginella brought them from Lecco to Milan and the team of distributors with Reginella in the lead began to function: Lisetta Bighotto, Bona Uselli, Teresa Morino, Alda Cantiello, Giorgio De Martini, Cece and Nene Bonicelli, Dino Del Bo, the lawyer Sola, the brothers of the Collegio Gonzaga, the priests of the Collegio San Carlo. Through the organizational network of the CVL the newspapers reached the regions of Emilia and Veneto, through that of the Christian Democratic Party it was distributed in Lombardy and parts of Piedmont, to the intense annoyance of the fascist police and the S.S. A copy of each issue regularly reached the command of the S.S. through the efforts of Ugo Osteria. The newspaper continued to be headed Brescia, for sentimental reasons. And the various printers in Brescia were frequently molested by the police while in Lecco, almost miraculously, everything remained hidden and calm. Even Celestino Ferrario was able to conceal his activities from his friends right up to the end. Thus amidst various incidents, numbers four through twenty came out up to Christmas of 1944.[33]

The story of *Il Ribelle* is typical of many clandestine newspapers during the Resistance and exemplifies the elements of interpersonal and intergroup solidarity on which the success of the underground press depended.

According to the statistics furnished by Laura Conti's bibliography, the number of separate issues of clandestine newspapers published by anti-fascist parties and movements from July 1943 to April 1945 ranges from a low of two to a high of sixty-eight, achieved by the Milanese edition of *Avanti!*. The figures for the official organs of the five leading anti-fascist parties are as follows: *Avanti!*—Turin, thirty-two, Milan, sixty-eight, Rome, twenty-nine; *L'Italia Libera*—Turin, fourteen, Milan, twenty-nine, Rome, twenty-two; *Il Popolo*—Milan, twelve, Rome, ten; *Risorgimento Liberale*—Milan, twelve, Rome, nine; *L'Unità*—Turin, twenty-seven, Genoa, forty-three, Milan, fifty-six, Rome, forty-three. More modest numbers are characteristic of the organs of the interparty Liberation Committees. For example, *Fratelli d'Italia* of Padua appeared

---

[33] Caracciolo, *Teresio Olivelli*, pp. 202, 203.

fourteen times, *La Riscossa Italiana* of Turin seven times. The newspapers of the various youth groups associated with the *Fronte della Gioventù* range from the six issues of *La Giovane Italia* in Florence to the sixteen issues of *Noi Giovani* in Turin. Among newspapers published by partisan units, the average number of issues was four or five, but in a few cases the figures are much higher: *Il Ribelle, Il Pioniere,* and *Il Combattente* appeared twenty-four, twenty-five, and eighteen times respectively. As for newspapers directed to specific groups or segments of the population, the figures vary widely, from the two issues of *Il Giornale del Medico* to the twenty-five of *La Fabbrica,* from the seven of *Azione Contadina* to the thirty-three of *La Nostra Lotta,* from the five of *L'Edificazione Socialista* to the twelve of *Noi Donne.*

Circulation figures of underground newspapers are difficult to ascertain, since a single copy could conceivably be read by many individuals and estimates of the number of copies produced in each printing vary so widely as to render them less than trustworthy. These estimates, however, provide the only available basis for conjecture, so that it will be useful to cite the figures given by persons who were closely associated with various clandestine newspapers or who have devoted special attention to the subject. Roberto Battaglia, one of the first and most eminent historians of the Italian Resistance, estimates that in Milan the number of copies produced in each printing of *L'Unità* was about thirty thousand, of *L'Italia Libera* and *Avanti!* twenty thousand, and of *Risorgimento Liberale* and *Il Popolo* ten thousand. Laura Conti states that in the major urban centers of Resistance activity, such as Milan, Turin, Genoa, and Rome, the large, nationally circulated newspapers ranged from ten thousand to twenty thousand copies in each printing, while in the smaller cities local editions of these same newspapers ranged from five thousand to ten thousand. Mario Dal Pra and Leo Valiani, both of whom were prominent members of the Action Party, agree that an average printing of the nationally circulated *L'Italia Libera* was between twenty thousand and thirty thousand copies. Franco Venturi gives the figure of ten thousand for the Turinese edition of the same newspaper. Ernesto Caffarelli maintains that in Rome an average printing of *L'Unità* was eight thousand copies, of *L'Italia Libera* thirty thousand and of the smaller newspapers such as *La Voce Repubblicana* and the Christian Social Movement's *L'Azione* between one thousand and two thousand. Enzo Piscitelli claims, however, that the Roman edition of *L'Italia Libera* never exceeded ten thousand copies, and Carlo Muscetta speaks of "several thousand" copies in his article on the history of *L'Italia Libera* in Rome. The only other statistics I have been able to find are those of Alberto Caracciolo, who estimates the average printing of *Il Ribelle* as about fifteen thousand copies, and those of Orazio Barbieri, who claims that the Florentine *L'Azione Comunista* was printed in issues of twenty thousand to twenty-five thousand copies.[34]

None of the estimates mentioned above exceeds thirty thousand, so it is safe to assume that even the largest and best organized clandestine newspapers reached a relatively small segment of the population, while the others were read by extremely restricted groups of people. The impact of the clandestine newspapers cannot be measured primarily in numerical terms, however, for they provided the minority of individuals who led the Resistance with the information and ideas needed to orient the masses of people. No resistance movement can function effectively without enlisting the support of a significantly large sector of the population, and this support depends to a great extent on whether or not the masses of people acquire a certain political and moral awareness. The underground press was one of the basic instruments with which this awareness was achieved. Therefore I do not share the opinion of the historian Franco Catalano, who believes that the influence of the clandestine press was rather limited because "it did not reach those segments of the population that were less politically conscious and that therefore could more easily fall victim to enemy propaganda." [35] Certainly the newspapers did not reach the majority of Italians in a physical sense. Their influence was felt through the mediating agency of the ideologically prepared minority who created and distributed them and who communicated their message of resistance to others.

III
The Functions of the Underground Press

What were the various functions and purposes of the underground newspapers as defined by Resistance leaders themselves? What role did they play in the daily life of partisan units in the mountains of

---

[34] The statistics on printing and circulation are gathered from the following sources: Roberto Battaglia, "La Résistance italienne," *Cahiers Internationaux de la Résistance*, July 1960, pp. 92–105; Laura Conti, "La stampa clandestina della Resistenza in una raccolta documentaria," *Il Movimento di Liberazione in Italia*, January-March 1960, p. 8; Mario Dal Pra, "Venti mesi di stampa clandestina," *Mercurio*, December 1945, p. 227; Franco Venturi, *Torino*, p. 82; Ernesto Vergara Caffarelli, "stampa clandestina," *Mercurio*, December 1944, pp. 241–45; Enzo Piscitelli, "La stampa clandestina," *Capitolium*, June 1964, p. 353; Carlo Muscetta, "La sventurata Italia Libera," *Mercurio*, December 1944, p. 212; Alberto Caracciolo, *Teresio Olivelli*, p. 185; Orazio Barbieri, *Ponti sull'Arno*, p. 272.

[35] Franco Catalano, *Storia del C.L.N.A.I.*, p. 205.

Piedmont and Veneto, of political and student groups in Rome and Milan, of labor unions in the factories of Turin and Genoa? Precise answers to these questions can be found in numerous articles in the clandestine press itself and in the letters and diaries of persons who participated in the Resistance.

The basic purposes of the underground press can be summarized in the words information, agitation, propaganda, and education. The newspapers were created to inform readers of military, political, and diplomatic events in Italy and in the world at large; to transform passive opposition into active resistance by mobilizing all potentially combative sectors of the population; to discredit nazi-fascist ideology through the use of democratically inspired political propaganda; to educate, or better to reeducate, the Italian people as to the values of a free society after twenty years of dictatorship. In its effort to accomplish these aims, the underground press became an indispensable connecting link between the hard core of anti-fascist conspirators and the masses of people.

The sentiments expressed by two representative figures of the Resistance during the most dramatic phase of the war in Italy serve to emphasize the importance of the role played by the clandestine newspapers. By March 1944 the Resistance Movement in Florence had achieved noteworthy results in mobilizing the energies of Florentine workers and intellectuals, but a series of raids on clandestine printers and the savage reprisals of the fascist police against conspiratorial propagandists had temporarily halted the progress thus far made by the Florentine Committee of National Liberation. Carlo Ragghianti noted this fact in a letter to Leo Valiani dated March 10, 1944. After making reference to the general situation in Florence, he spoke of his efforts to reorganize the underground press: "At present we have two presses, type, printers, paper, but no place in which to work. I am making every effort to solve the problem, and am willing to install a press in my home if necessary. Within the next week we shall solve even this extremely serious problem, because without a newspaper our party ceases to live." [36] As a member of the Action Party and as president of the Florentine Liberation Committee, Ragghianti realized that without newspapers the task of maintaining a sense of ideological orientation and solidarity among resisters was almost impossible.

Equally significant is a letter sent on August 12, 1944, by the partisan commander Dante Livio Bianco to his friend Giorgio Agosti in Turin. At the time this letter was written, Bianco had assumed military leadership of all the partisan units in Piedmont that were affiliated with the

[36] *Una lotta nel suo corso*, pp. 59, 60.

Action Party. He was also concerned, however, with the problem of giving political instruction to the partisans, and for this reason complained to Agosti about the failure of his friends in Turin to send him the newspapers he wanted: "Why is it that no newspapers have arrived? In your letter of July 30, you spoke to me about packages that had already been prepared for delivery; but up to now, I repeat, nothing has been seen of them. It is hardly necessary for me to tell you that without newspapers we cannot even begin any type of propaganda work." [37]

In many instances, Bianco and other partisan leaders took it upon themselves to furnish their men with necessary information and political instruction by founding their own newspapers, since communication with centers of conspiratorial activity in the cities was so arduous and irregular.

As opposed to the doctrinaire tone that often characterized the underground press of the political parties, the partisan newspapers are noteworthy for their simple, unadorned style and for their avoidance of sectarian interpretations of the Resistance. The objectives that they set for themselves were similarly concrete and practical and grew out of the daily problems that the partisans encountered during the course of eighteen months of guerrilla warfare in the regions of central and northern Italy.

One of the principal aims of the partisan newspapers was, in fact, to help create a style of life radically antithetical to that in vogue under fascism. The fundamental goal of *Rinascita d'Italia,* for example, the organ of a partisan unit that operated in the southwest area of Piedmont near Cuneo, was to set an example of directness and sobriety as opposed to the "printed matter" that circulated during the fascist epoch, "when systematic deceit, the most inconclusive rhetoric, the persistent distortion of all values, had the effect of undermining the integrity of language itself."[38] *Il Ribelle* declared its unalterable contempt for the high-sounding verbiage typical of fascist newspapers and stated that its aim was to lay the groundwork for "a free, healthy, profound culture" in which men could speak honestly of their problems and aspirations.[39] *La Disfida* intended to give partisans the opportunity to express themselves freely and thereby to begin the process "of building a new democratic society in Italy." [40]

Since Italian partisans often thought of themselves as pioneers, as creators of a new form of life that required initiative and courage, they used their newspapers as a means of recounting the exploits of particularly heroic men who had fallen in combat against nazi and fascist forces.

---

[37] Dante Livio Bianco, *Guerra partigiana,* p. 276.
[38] "Precisazioni," *Rinascita d'Italia,* September 21, 1944, p. 1. (FC)
[39] Caracciolo, *Teresio Olivelli,* pp. 161, 162.
[40] "Lettera ai compagni," *La Disfida,* February 15, 1945, p. 1. (INS)

Biographical sketches of partisans who died in battle, accompanied with brief explanations of the motives that had brought the fallen heroes into the ranks of the Resistance, formed the principal subject matter of many partisan newspapers. But the tone of these newspapers was not always serious. On the contrary, humorous drawings, anecdotes, and episodes of partisan life were interspersed with descriptions of battles and political discussions. Entertainment was as important as instruction, especially since guerrilla warfare consisted of more waiting and tedium than action. Stories based on the friendship between a partisan and his ever-faithful companion, a body louse; Mauldin-type cartoons picturing inexpert young men trying unsuccessfully to manage a rifle or hand grenade; satirical studies of self-styled brave men who had become incontinent under fire; and other such items helped to fortify the *esprit de corps* of men who belonged, after all, to a volunteer army that depended for its cohesion on the good faith and fighting morale of each soldier.

Political instruction was, of course, a primary function of the partisan newspapers. Because many partisans were ex-soldiers of the fascist army who had fought in Africa, Russia, Greece, Yugoslavia, and other fronts, and though they were convinced of the necessity to defeat fascism, they needed explanations for the dilemma in which they had found themselves after September 8. Toward the latter part of 1944, partisan ranks were further swelled by thousands of young men, ranging in age from eighteen to twenty-one, who had chosen to join various guerrilla units not out of a commitment to democracy but rather to avoid deportation to forced labor camps in Germany or to escape being drafted into the fascist army of Mussolini's Republic of Salò. This type of opportunism, even if understandable in terms of the alternatives available to these young men, could not be tolerated by others who had become partisans for political or moral reasons. Therefore partisan newspapers served as instruments of persuasion and propaganda designed to transform opportunistic motives into genuine commitment. Indeed, the price paid by opportunists and traitors whose activities became known by partisan commanders was in many cases a quick trial and execution by firing squad.

One of the main reasons for the rigorous discipline enforced by partisan leaders lay in the necessity of establishing friendly and mutually beneficial relations between partisan units and the civilian population. Without the solidarity of the mountaineers and farmers who inhabited the regions in which guerrilla warfare was waged, the partisans were unable to obtain the food, clothing, and tools they needed to function and survive. Stealing from farmers was almost always punished with summary execution. A partisan guilty of hostile or arrogant behavior in the presence of a civilian was immediately invited to return to his home. It is not surprising, therefore, that among the most frequently announced aims of the partisan newspapers was that of helping to create good relations with the civilian population. This was the principal purpose, for example, of *Avanguardia Garibaldina, Il Pioniere, Il Combattente,* and *Il Garibaldino.* The problem of maintaining the goodwill of the civilian population became particularly acute whenever partisans succeeded in liberating a valley, town, or province. In many cases partisan units collaborated with civilians in forming democratically elected committees responsible for reorganizing the political life of the liberated zone, setting fair prices for essential foods, establishing new schools, and giving financial assistance to the families of soldiers and partisans who had been killed. Under these circumstances, partisan newspapers tried to instill in the rank-and-file members of the units a sense of collective responsibility and an awareness of their role as representatives of a new, democratic Italy.

Some of the partisan units that operated along the Yugoslav and French borders were faced with an especially delicate problem, that of reacquiring the respect and goodwill of two peoples who had suffered the aggression of fascist armies. Consequently, the main objective of *Il Corriere Partigiano,* the organ of a partisan unit attached to a Yugoslav division in Slovenia, was "to contribute to the brotherhood and unity of the Italians and Slovenes who live in the bi-lingual zones along the Adriatic coast," [41] and *Quelli della Montagna,* founded by Dante Livio Bianco, sought to convince French partisans and civilians of the region in southeastern France that Italian partisans wanted nothing more than to reestablish the amity that had traditionally characterized relations between France and Italy before fascism.[42]

Two other indications of the multiple roles played by partisan newspapers are exemplified by *Naja Repubblichina* and *Il Partigiano. Naja Repubblichina,* written by partisans who belonged to the first Alpine "Justice and Freedom" Division, was directed to the soldiers of the fascist Republic of Salò. The fascist republican army was composed essentially of two types of men: those who felt genuine loyalty to Mussolini and to the fascist regime and who had eagerly joined the Salò Army and countless thousands of young men who merely obeyed the call to arms issued by the fascist republic. These latter men knew nothing of a volunteer partisan army until they were sent to the mountains along with nazi troops to undertake *rastrellamenti,* or mop-up operations. These young and inexperienced soldiers were susceptible to the kind of anti-fascist pro-

[41] *Il Corriere Partigiano,* October 10, 1944, p. 1. (INS)
[42] "Di qua e di là delle Alpi," *Quelli della Montagna,* October 1944, p. 1. (CG)

paganda that *Naja Repubblichina* aimed at them. Toward the latter months of 1944, this and other similar newspapers began to have considerable success in inducing "Republican" soldiers to desert and join the partisans.

Il Partigiano was typical of many partisan newspapers in that it devoted special attention to the problem of establishing diplomatic and military liaisons with Anglo-American missions sent to northern and central Italy to assist guerrilla operations against nazi-fascist troops. Beginning in March 1944, special British and American reconnaissance planes began parachuting supplies of food, clothing, guns, and ammunition to pre-designated areas of Piedmont, Lombardy, Liguria, and other regions. Two- and three-men teams of British and American intelligence officers were often sent to these regions to work with the partisans and instruct them in the maintenance and use of the weapons. Some remained with the partisans throughout the duration of the war and lent them valuable aid as strategists and fighters. Friction between the Allied teams and the partisans was inevitable, since the Allies viewed the frankly leftist orientation of many partisan units with suspicion and the partisans resented their dependence on the Allies. It was the function of *Il Partigiano* and other newspapers to interpret the needs of the partisans to the Allies and, conversely, to explain the directives issued by the Allied military command in terms that the partisans could understand and accept.

Certain of the partisan newspapers, particularly those that reflected the ideas of communist or pro-communist instructors, were created exclusively for the purpose of political indoctrination. Some of the communist-oriented newspapers devoted far more attention to the accomplishments of the Soviet Union and the Red Army than to the daily problems of partisan life. In the main, however, the partisan underground press avoided sectarian positions and so contributed to the development of a broadly democratic consciousness among many young men who had originally taken up arms against fascism for reasons—such as a lust for adventure and violence or fear of deportation—that had nothing to do with the ideals of the Resistance Movement.

The underground newspapers of student groups and nationally organized youth movements, such as the *Fronte della Gioventù* and the Catholic Youth Organization, were more uniform in their objectives than was the partisan press. Basically these newspapers aimed to facilitate communication between young people of the fascist generation and men and women who had attained maturity and identified themselves with various democratic movements before the advent of fascism. This was precisely the purpose of the Catholic *Gioventù Democratica,* which sought "to unify these two generations, both equally victimized by fascism," through a return to Christian teachings.[43] Evangelical Christianity, said the editors of *Gioventù Democratica*, represented the only hope for a world devastated by war and terror, and it was this message of hope that the newspapers intended to use as a means of reviving contact between the generations. The Catholic *La Punta,* founded in February 1944 by Giorgio Tupini, also aimed to help young people who had grown up under fascism to become a part of the traditions of democratic life in Italy from which they had been excluded by the dictatorship: *"La Punta* is the seal that definitively marks the beginning of the inclusion of Italian youth in the vital movement of our currents of political thought. The gap created by twenty-one years of obscurantism is being filled, and our newspaper, the first one of its type to be published by an anti-fascist movement, proposes to clarify ideas that might still be confused, to point the way to the disoriented and to those disillusioned persons who perhaps believed in fascism because they never knew the life of free men." [44]

The editors of *Scuola Rivoluzionaria,* the organ of the Italian University Students Association, was similarly concerned with the problem of re-educating Italian youth as to the values of democratic institutions and placed the same emphasis on reestablishing contact between themselves and the preceding generation of anti-fascists. Italian university students, the newspaper declared, had been made indifferent, skeptical, and opportunistic by the fascist regime, which had demanded conformism as the price for political and economic success. The task of the newspaper was therefore "to combat this deplorable moral situation" and to lead Italian youth back into the struggle for democracy.[45]

The newspapers published by various youth groups belonging to the *Fronte della Gioventù* generally took a more combative position than did those of other youth movements. They were interested in moral and ideological problems, to be sure, but tried principally to encourage their readers to take an active part in the Resistance as partisans and saboteurs, runners and political organizers.

Like the partisan press, the underground newspapers of labor unions, farmers' cooperatives, and similarly cohesive groups almost always sought to achieve concrete and realizable objectives. Many newspapers published by labor unions functioned as connecting links between industrial workers and terrorist or partisan units. Workers were instructed on methods of assisting the teams of saboteurs who operated in almost all of the

---

[43] "Due generazioni," *Gioventù Democratica,* April 10, 1945, p. 1. (LC)
[44] "Ai giovani," *La Punta,* February 3, 1944, p. 1. (LC)
[45] *Scuola Rivoluzionaria,* January 9, 1945, p. 1. (MR)

principal Italian cities and were informed about the interdependent relationship that existed between their strikes and protests and the military actions of the partisans. Among the main purposes of labor newspapers was to spur constant protest against factory owners who collaborated with the nazis and fascists and to agitate for better wages and working conditions. The same was true of newspapers published by farmers' cooperatives, such as *La Falce,* which saw the struggle against fascism as the first step toward the complete emancipation of Italian farmers from all forms of economic and political exploitation. Largely communist or socialist in point of view, these newspapers helped mobilize the energies of the Italian labor movement and provided the kind of rudimentary ideological instruction that workers could understand.

Among the main functions performed by the clandestine organs of political parties and of the Committees of National Liberation was that of formulating programs for the reconstruction of Italian political, social, and economic life after the war. Although constantly immersed in the immediate problems and conflicts that occurred during the course of the war, these newspapers tried to see daily events in historical perspective and therefore to determine to what extent the Resistance could provide both a new vantage point from which to examine the causes of fascism and possible solutions for the post-fascist era. Their vision was broader and more firmly rooted in a knowledge of the unfolding of Italian history than the perspective of other clandestine newspapers. The chief editors of the political press and the majority of the members of the Liberation Committees were highly educated men who belonged to the economically and socially privileged segment of the Italian population. They were lawyers, writers, politicians, university professors, businessmen, most of whom had been affiliated with various democratic and anti-fascist movements during the 1920's and 1930's. These men were concerned not only with contributing to the defeat of fascism but also with the future development of Italian society within a framework of fundamental instiiutional reforms. The ideological questions with which this study deals in the following chapters were elaborated in large measure by precisely this intellectual elite, who conceived of the underground newspapers as instruments of political discussion and debate, of doctrinal instruction, and, above all, of moral education.

The newspapers of the political parties and of the Committees of National Liberation also sought more consistently than others to teach their readers in what ways the Italian Resistance Movement formed part of a universal conflict of men and ideas. One of their primary purposes was to establish contact on all levels with the Allies and with Resistance

Movements in other countries of nazi-occupied Europe, for they were produced by men who were aware that groups of resisters in France, Belgium, Yugoslavia, and elsewhere were confronting problems and attempting to achieve purposes analogous or identical to theirs. Indeed, the dominant themes of French clandestine newspapers often parallel those that were of interest to leaders of the Italian Resistance Movement.[46] The concern of Italian resisters with the causes of fascism and the collapse of democratic institutions in Italy was analogous to French anti-fascists' preoccupation with the reasons underlying the fall of the Third Republic and the establishment of a collaborationist regime in Vichy. The ideological questions most often debated by the clandestine newspapers of French political parties, such as whether the Resistance should be essentially revolutionary or reformist in purpose, the relationship between the intellectual élite and the masses in a democratic society, the "patriotic" as opposed to the "international" conception of the Resistance, and, most important, the problem of reconciling individual freedom and social justice, were also typical of the Italian political press.

The purposes of the political press in Yugoslavia were also similar to those of Italian political newspapers. Tito's biographer, Vladimir Dedijer, indicates that the Yugoslav underground newspapers had two main purposes—to mobilize all of the Yugoslav peoples in the struggle against nazi-fascism and to wage an ideological war against the nation's "internal enemies"—those who remained loyal to the royal government-in-exile or who favored any form of collaboration with the German and Italian occupying armies.[47] Similarly, the Italian political and interparty press tried to instill a sense of solidarity into Italians of all classes, regions, and political persuasions and stressed the danger inherent in even the slightest acquiescence in the dictates of the Republic of Salò.

In Denmark, which among the countries of northern Europe developed the most powerful Resistance Movement, opposition to nazism was quickly mobilized by editors of underground newspapers within several months after the nazi invasion in April 1940. Halfdan Lefèvre, who took part in the Danish Resistance, states that the clandestine press in Denmark "formed the whole basis of our fight for liberty" and was "a potent force in moulding public opinion." Lefèvre emphasizes the contribution made by the newspapers "in teaching the people that Denmark had to

46 The best sources on the ideas of the French Resistance are Henri Michel, *Les courants de pensée de la Résistance* and *Les idées politiques et sociales de la Résistance,* edited by Henri Michel and Boris Mirkine-Guetzévitch.

47 Vladimir Dedijer, *Tito parle.*

fight for her own freedom." [48] As we shall see, an analogous role was played in Italy by the underground press of the political parties and of the Liberation Committees, which constantly stressed the fact that only through its own sacrifices could the Italian people regain its integrity and honor.

[48] Halfdan Lefèvre, "The Illegal Press," *Denmark during the German Occupation,* pp. 62–65.

CHAPTER FIVE

THE COMMITTEES OF NATIONAL LIBERATION AND THE QUESTION OF ATTESISMO

I
The Organization of the Committees of National Liberation

The two most pressing issues involved in the day-by-day development of the Resistance Movement concerned the nature and functions of the Committees of National Liberation and the question of *attesismo*. It was vitally important that the anti-fascist parties reach agreement about the character and purposes of the Committees and, in fact, despite certain differences in emphasis and in the extent of their commitment, the parties did concur in their conception of the Committees as the best political means with which to wage their struggle. The same basic agreement with some differences in emphasis and extent of commitment manifested itself in the parties' attitudes toward the question of *attesismo*, on whose resolution hinged the very reason for being of the Committees. Those persons who followed a policy of *attesismo* believed that the Resistance Movement should take no direct military or political action against the nazis until such action was fully sanctioned by the Allies and until it became clear that innocent people would not suffer nazi and fascist retaliation. This attitude had wide support in both politically conservative and Catholic circles. It was argued that immediate armed action against the occupying German forces and their fascist allies would bring greater devastation to Italy than ever before, that the sanctity of life had to take precedence over the admittedly justified desire for revenge. Each of the five major parties comprising the Committees of National Liberation repudiated this position. The communists and the actionists were the first to elaborate a series of ideological criteria in opposition to *attesismo* and to clarify what they regarded as the only possible policy for the Italian Resistance Movement: direct organized action on all fronts—military, political, economic—led by partisan and terrorist units, with mass insurrrection throughout Italy as the ultimate aim. But before examining the arguments advanced in opposition to *attesismo,* it is necessary to explain the background and development of the Committees of National Liberation.

In September and October 1943, that is, during the two months immediately following the armistice of September 8, Committees of National Liberation were organized in every important city of central and northern Italy. Modeled on the French *Conseil de la Résistance* and the Yugoslav *Osvobodilna Fronta* (National Liberation Front), these committees assumed the responsibility of leading the Resistance and established as a fundamental principle the cooperation and unity of purpose of the five anti-fascist parties that comprised them: the Communist Party, the Socialist Party (renamed the Italian Socialist Party of Proletarian Unity in August 1943), the Action Party, the Liberal Party, and the Christian Democratic Party. The first Committee to achieve organizational and political cohesion was formed in Rome, which was the nerve center of Resistance activity prior to the development of a partisan movement in northern Italy in the winter of 1943–44.

In September and October 1943 the central Committee of National Liberation in Rome issued two policy statements that formed the ideological basis of the Italian Resistance Movement until April 1944, when the Committees were compelled to reverse certain of the positions they had taken up to then. On September 9 the Roman Committee announced that its primary aim was "to summon the Italian people to struggle and to resistance in order to allow Italy to regain the place it deserves among free nations," [1] and on October 16, three days after the Badoglio government in Brindisi had declared war on Germany, the Committee asserted its autonomy by declaring that "the war of liberation, the first task and the supreme necessity for national redemption, depends on the sincere and active spiritual unity of the country, and . . . this cannot be achieved under the aegis of the present government constituted by the King and by Badoglio." [2] This latter statement, written by Giovanni Gronchi, was strongly endorsed by all five parties in the anti-fascist coalition. Thus, from the very outset of the Resistance a grave and apparently irreconcilable conflict existed between the Committees of National Liberation in central and northern Italy and the Badoglio government in Brindisi, which was soon to enjoy the official diplomatic recognition of the Allied powers, including the Soviet Union.

The Committees were formed in almost all cases by men who had

[1] Enzo Piscitelli, *Storia della Resistenza romana,* p. 64.
[2] *Ibid.,* p. 115.

distinguished records of anti-fascist activity extending back to the 1920's and 1930's. The Roman Committee was composed, for example, of the communists Mauro Scoccimarro and Giorgio Amendola, the son of the liberal journalist Giovanni Amendola; the socialists Pietro Nenni, Alessandro Pertini, and Giuseppe Saragat; the Actionists Ugo La Malfa, Riccardo Bauer, and Sergio Fenoaltea; the liberals Alessandro Casati and Niccolò Carandini; the Christian democrats Alcide De Gasperi, Giuseppe Spataro, and Giovanni Gronchi; and the labor democrats Ivanoe Bonomi and Meuccio Ruini,[3] all of whom had paid personally for their opposition to fascism either by imprisonment and exile or removal from positions of political authority.

The various regional Committees that were formed in September and October 1943 were similarly composed of outstanding intellectual and political figures. The Tuscan Committee in Florence included the communists Giulio Montelatici and Gianfranco Musco; the socialists Arturo Bruni, Foscolo Lombardi, and Natale Dall'Oppio; the actionists Carlo Ragghianti, Enzo Enriques-Agnoletti, Carlo Furno, and Cesare Fasola; the liberals Aldobrando Medici-Tornaquinci, Eugenio Artom, and Marino Mari; and the Christian democrats Francesco Berti and Mario Martini. The Committee in Turin was under the leadership of the liberals Guido Verzone, Franco Antonicelli, and Paolo Greco; the Christian democrats Andrea Guglielminetti and Eugenio Libois; the actionists Mario Andreis and Alessandro Galante Garrone; the socialists Piero Passoni, Rodolfo Morandi, and Giorgio Montalente; and the communists Amedeo Ugolini and Celeste Negarville. Like their counterparts in other regional Committees, these men could lay claim to an unbroken record of militant struggle against the fascist dictatorship. The three leading activators of the Liberation Committee in Padua, Silvio Trentin, who returned from exile in France to Padua in early September 1943, Concetto Marchesi, and Egidio Meneghetti, were university professors who combined intellectual integrity with rare moral courage, as evidenced by Trentin's eighteen years of self-imposed exile in France, Marchesi's defiance of fascist authorities in his famous inaugural address[4] to the students of the University of Padua on November 9, 1943, and Meneghetti's decision to remain active in the Resistance even after his wife and daughter were killed in an air raid on December 16, 1943. The same qualities were possessed by the men who composed the Committee of National

[3] The Democratic Labor Party was included in the Committees in Southern Italy and in the Central Liberation Committee in Rome, but was not represented on any of the regional Committees of Northern Italy nor on the CLNAI.

[4] Marchesi's address is published in Concetto Marchesi, *Pagíne all'ombra,* pp. 11–17.

Liberation in Trieste prior to their arrest on December 30, 1943: the actionist Gabriele Foschiatti, the communist Zefferino Pisoni, the socialist Edmondo Puecher, the Christian democrat Giovanni Tanasco, and the liberal Fernando Gandusio.

Beginning in November 1943, the work of the Committees functioning in the regions of Liguria (Genoa), Piedmont (Turin), Lombardy (Milan), Veneto (Padua), and Emilia (Bologna) was coordinated by a central Committee in Milan that on January 31, 1944, began to call itself the Committee of National Liberation for Northern Italy (CLNAI). Each of the regional Committees was in turn responsible for the organization of local committees in all of the provinces and towns in which there already existed active or potentially functional centers of conspiracy. The political organization of the Resistance in northern Italy was further extended in the second half of 1944 when, as a result of a directive issued by the CLNAI on June 2, Committees were established in villages and factories, and student, professional, and women's organizations were called upon to collaborate with regional Committees in every aspect of the struggle against fascism and nazism. The CLNAI also assumed the task of coordinating the military activities of the Resistance Movement and was in constant contact with the partisan leaders attached to the General Command of the *Corpo Volontari della Libertà*. The CVL was entrusted with the job of coordinating the military activities of partisan units and was composed of the following branches: a secretarial staff, an information and counterespionage section, a radio section, a counterfeit document center, a transportation section, a press office, and, most important, an agency responsible for maintaining contact with Allied military, diplomatic, and intelligence authorities in Italy, Switzerland, and France. Among the men who served on the CLNAI were the communists Luigi Longo, Girolamo Li Causi, and Giuseppe Dozza; the actionists Ferruccio Parri and Leo Valiani; the liberals Filippo Jacini, Alfredo Pizzoni, and Giovanni Arpesani; the socialists Alessandro Pertini and Rodolfo Morandi; and the Christian democrats Achille Marazza, Enrico Casò, and Giovanni Falck.

II
The Bases of Unity

Serious differences over questions of both ends and means often divided the five parties that led the Italian Resistance Movement. Nevertheless the Italian Resistance Movement achieved a substantial unity notwithstanding the disputes that arose at certain critical moments in its development. The organizational structure of the Committees was itself the expression of a principle shared by the five parties. This principle was that men of goodwill genuinely devoted to democratic methods of solving problems could, on the basis of mutual respect and without surrendering their autonomy, work together to achieve a common goal. In other words, the Committees concretely embodied the determination of all anti-fascists to subordinate their differences to larger and unanimously accepted aims. They operated on the assumption that the defeat of fascism and nazism and the restoration of free political institutions in Italy took precedence over every other issue and that these aims could be accomplished only through the cooperation of the parties that reflected the main currents of anti-fascist thought and action. This principle of interparty solidarity, the groundwork for which was laid during the Spanish Civil War, had been effectively articulated as early as April 1943 by the venerable Ivanoe Bonomi, who in September was elected president of the Committee of National Liberation in Rome. In March 1943, Bonomi and several representatives of other anti-fascist movements who had begun to return secretly to Italy in the latter part of 1942, founded the clandestine newspaper *La Ricostruzione*. The second number of this newspaper, dated April 1943, contained an article written by Bonomi entitled "Single Front," in which the organizational principle underlying the future Committees was precisely enunciated. After declaring that the overthrow of fascism could be accomplished only by the common action of all men devoted to the ideal of freedom, Bonomi stated:

> This task—which is neither brief nor easy—requires the unity of all currents of anti-fascism. The old motto that teaches that in unity there is strength is today more than ever true and necessary. Anti-fascism has been broken up into many movements that are tied to new and old ideals. That is the product of the political inheritance of pre-fascist Italy and of the new currents of thought that have manifested themselves in the world. . . . We are not averse to the future development of parties: a plurality of parties is the bulwark of freedom. . . . But today the necessity of struggle demands that the various parties, currents, and movements be unified. There is a common program that can absorb the activity of everyone: to demolish and to reconstruct. We must demolish the great prison in which the Italian people has been forced to exist, we must build the edifice of a new, free, and democratic Italy. This task takes precedence over every movement and party because it constitutes the necessary foundation for future construction.[5]

The program for anti-fascist action outlined by Bonomi in April 1943 formed the basis on which the Committees of National Liberation func-

[5] Ivanoe Bonomi, "Fronte unico," *La Ricostruzione*, April 1943, p. 1. (CG)

tioned after September 8. The fact that the principle of interparty co-operation and solidarity lay at the core of the Italian Resistance Movement is demonstrated by many relevant articles in the underground press of the five parties. Although expressed in different ways and with different emphases, these articles lend substance to the claim of Resistance leaders that the National Liberation Movement in Italy was essentially unitary in character and that disputes over specific issues were usually resolved successfully.

An issue of the Communist Party's theoretical organ *La Nostra Lotta* in December 1943 contains an article written by Eugenio Curiel that explains the reasons underlying the communists' support of the committees. Curiel began his argument by pointing out that some anti-fascists, particularly among the younger generation, had refused to recognize the authority of the Committees and had initiated movements of an entirely independent and apolitical character. This attitude, Curiel said, derived from a failure to understand the function of the parties organized in the Committees and also possibly from a sense of nostalgic loyalty to certain achievements of the Risorgimento, particularly the *Società Nazionale* of 1857. But, Curiel continued, the differences between the age of the Risorgimento and the present were profound. The political consciousness of most Italians during the nineteenth century was still undeveloped. The Risorgimento was led by an élite, amidst the general passivity of the masses. Currently the situation was vastly different. The level of political and class consciousness among the proletariat was far higher than it had been in the past century. The middle and upper classes were less secure and unified today than in the past, and the reactionary elements of Italian society were stronger than ever before. Italian society could no longer be generically defined as an undifferentiated mass of "people," in the Risorgimento sense of the word. Italy had become not a nation of "people" but a nation of political parties. "Thus the national insurrection that we are preparing is not a vague and imprecise explosion of elementary aspirations on the part of not well-differentiated social strata; it reflects the organized will to independence, unity, and freedom of classes that are socially distinct and aware of this distinction." Therefore, Curiel concluded, "the best instrument with which to wage the present struggle is not the *Società Nazionale* of 1857, but rather the Committees of National Liberation." [6]

The basic point of Curiel's argument was reiterated by the clandestine newspapers of the other parties, but with less emphasis on the element

[6] Eugenio Curiel, "Fronte Nazionale-Società Nazionale-Blocco Nazionale," *La Nostra Lotta,* December 1943, pp. 1, 2. (LC)

of class divisions existing in contemporary Italian society. Of particular importance are the points of view expressed by the Liberal and Action Parties, which were based on the conviction that the Committees provided a training ground for democratic decision-making that could not but exert a positive influence on the development of Italian political life both during and after the war. The liberals adhered consistently to the position taken in November 1943 by the party's principal clandestine organ, *Risorgimento Liberale*. At that time the Liberal Party had taken a strong stand against both the Monarchy and the ultraconservative elements in Italian society that denied the legitimacy of the Liberation Committees and instead supported the continued functioning of the bureaucratic-administrative apparatus in force under fascism. In January 1944, *Risorgimento Liberale* sought to clarify the basic content of the alliance binding the five parties. The newspaper admitted that the negative factors in common were easier to define than the positive ones: all the parties were fighting against fascism and nazism, all wanted to help the Allies drive the German forces out of Italy. The positive common denominator linking five such heterogeneous parties lay in their agreement to respect the freedom of the individual and to accept the democratic method of solving problems: "With a sense of responsibility and with a realistic vision of the tasks facing the nation, the major Italian parties have found their point of contact in this ideal of freedom that is at once a need for order, respect for the ideas of all concerned, and a commitment to civic dignity." [7] In July 1944, the Liberal Party's *L'Opinione* also expressed deep faith in the Committees as working instruments of democratic interparty cooperation: "Through free and wide-ranging discussion," said *L'Opinione,* "it has always been possible for the five parties to find a common denominator on which to reach agreement regarding the policy of the Committees of National Liberation, without any of them having to renounce its own principles." [8]

Like the liberals, the Action Party believed that the essential significance of the committees lay in the fact that, after more than twenty years of dictatorship, they represented the political means through which many Italians could again be actively engaged in shaping the destiny of their country. As expressed by the Action Party's Florentine organ *La Libertà* "The Committees of National Liberation are in fact a series of small parliaments. Political forces of renewal and military forces of resistance collaborate within these organizations in a practical manner. This is a

[7] "La politica del Comitato di Liberazione," *Risorgimento Liberale,* January 5, 1944, p. 1. (CG)
[8] "Noi e il C.L.N.," *L'Opinione,* July 1944, p. 2. (ISRT)

very great event in Italy, one that gives reason for hope in a deepening of our people's democratic consciousness." [9] Similar opinions were expressed by the clandestine press of the Socialist and Christian Democratic Parties, both of which attributed to the Committees the dual functions of leading the struggle against nazism and fascism and of preparing the programs and men necessary for the task of national reconstruction after the war.

The most forceful statement of the purposes and ideals linking the five parties of the anti-fascist coalition was made by the Liberal Paolo Greco in the first issue of *La Riscossa Italiana,* the organ of the Committee of National Liberation in Turin:

The title *La Riscossa Italiana* reflects, in the extreme gravity of the present hour, the unanimity of purpose of the Italian people, which corresponds to the unity of its various parties in whose name we begin the publication of this newspaper. Common tasks link their political action and transcend their particular programs: to drive the invader out of Italy, to eliminate definitively and radically the evils of the invader's ally, fascism, to give back to our country the honorable place that it had in the family of free and civilized nations, and finally to reestablish and safeguard, within the framework of a new constitutional order, and with respect for freedom and law, the essential bases for coexistence without which no moral order worthy of the name, no productive socioeconomic system, no concept of ideological progress is conceivable. With this program the concord and cooperation of the parties are being reaffirmed.[10]

III
Divisive Issues

It is clear, then, that the unity of the five parties comprising the Committees of National Liberation was not based solely on their collective endorsement of an organizational principle. It rested more fundamentally on a common commitment to a social and political order radically different from that which had existed under fascism. The parties succeeded in working together effectively by reason of their conception of the Resistance as a mass movement organized and led by men devoted to the ideals of individual freedom and social justice. The fact that this unity was broken after the war, when increasing conflict between the democratic and communist powers created a profound schism between former allies, does not alter the situation of unity which existed from 1943 to 1945. Yet there can be no doubt that certain of the problems,

---

[9] "Cos'è il C.L.N.," *La Libertà,* July 15, 1944, p. 2. (ISRT)
[10] Paolo Greco, "Riscossa," *La Riscossa Italiana,* October 20, 1943, p. 1. (CG)

tensions, and conflicts of interest that divided the world into two hostile camps after the war were already in evidence during the period of the Resistance in Italy.

In the first place, each of the parties in the anti-fascist coalition had its own particular conception of the functions of the Committees. Filippo Jacini, who in December 1944 replaced Giovanni Arpesani as the liberal delegate to the CLNAI in Milan, sought to clarify the differences of opinion dividing the five parties in an issue of the Liberal Party's clandestine organ *La Libertà* of February 1945. Jacini noted that during the first two or three months of the Resistance none of the parties had been concerned with defining the exact nature and functions of the Committees. But as soon as the partisan movement began to develop in northern Italy and the Committees were confronted with the task of reorganizing political life in the liberated areas of the country, it was inevitable that certain differences in the points of view of the five parties would manifest themselves. Jacini explained these differences as follows:

Divergent opinions became evident as a result of the reading of long reports which the Communist Party gave to the CLNAI concerning the first sporadic experiences of direct self-government [in the liberated zones] and were caused also by the attitude of the Action Party, which, essentially, considered Italy as being divided into two parts: the one north of the Gothic line, where a popular insurrection would ideally create a new and genuinely democratic order to be extended later to the whole of Italy, the other south of the Gothic line where, according to the actionists, the old and moribund liberal state was dragging out the last steps of its existence. The liberals, who were not unmindful of the noble traditions created by the pre-fascist liberal state, and who were concerned constantly with safeguarding the continuity and spiritual unity of the country, always vigorously opposed this distinction between north and south. The Liberal Party believed that the CLNAI and the smaller regional, provincial, and local Committees should continue to receive their mandate from the government of Rome, which was regarded both by the Allies and by the enemy as the only legitimate government of the nation.[11]

In this article Jacini touched on one of the central issues dividing the five parties, namely, the extent of autonomy and the political legitimacy that the various Committees could rightfully claim in relation to the officially constituted government in Rome that had been formed in June 1944 under the leadership of Ivanoe Bonomi. This same issue of legitimacy had been debated by the Committees during the first half of 1944 when

[11] Filippo Jacini, "I compiti e la struttura del CLNAI e dei comitati periferici," *Libertà*, February 1945. The article is cited textually in Filippo Jacini, *Carattere*, p. 90.

the only government in Italy officially recognized by the Allies was that of the King and Marshal Badoglio in Brindisi. The left-wing parties in the anti-fascist coalition, the communists, socialists, and actionists, regarded every residual element of the pre-fascist state with a mixture of distrust and contempt, since they attributed the triumph of Mussolini's regime to the betrayal of the Monarchy and to the insufficiencies of the liberal order that had directly preceded the advent of fascism. The liberals and Christian democrats, on the other hand, were concerned with upholding the liberal tradition and were not prepared to accept the notion that the Committees represented a radical break with the pre-fascist state.

In order to understand the precise nature of this dispute over the question of the powers and political status of the Committees, it is necessary to clarify the positions taken by the five parties both before and after April 1944, which marked a decisive turning point in the history of the Italian Resistance Movement.

Subsequent to the founding of a central Committee of National Liberation in Rome on September 9, 1943, and the rapid development of an organized anti-fascist movement in many regions of Italy, the communists viewed the Committees not only as the sole legitimate representatives of the Italian people during the Resistance but also as prefigurations of the political structure that would take the place of fascism after the war. On September 30, 1943, *L'Unità* made the following assertion: "In leading the people in this struggle for redemption, the Committees of National Liberation already affirm their right to be the legitimate government of the Italy of tomorrow that is rising amidst the sorrowful torment of this new war for national independence." [12] On October 21, the Milanese edition of *L'Unità* spoke of the Committees as constituting "the vital nucleus from which the new government of Italy will arise, the political force on which the destiny of our country depends." [13] In this same issue the Communist Party declared its unalterable opposition to the Badoglio government: "The political opposition between the Committees of National Liberation and the Badoglio government is clear and precise, and such it must remain in order to provide all Italians with a secure political orientation. Every sort of equivocal compromise and deal-making would be harmful to the country and would deceive the masses. Conscious of the tasks and of the functions that it must fulfill in this grave hour, the Committees make legitimate claim to their right to govern the country, because only through their efforts can the unity of

[12] "La costituzione del Comitato di Liberazione Nazionale," *L'Unità*, September 30, 1943, p. 1. (ISRT)

[13] "Il Partitio Comunista nel C.L.N.," *L'Unità*, October 21, 1943, p. 2. (CG)

all healthy and progressive forces in Italy be realized." [14] In December 1943, and in the first three months of 1944, the communist press frequently reiterated this same idea, urging the Committees to take an intransigent stand against the Badoglio regime and reaffirming its conviction that the Committees should consider themselves the nucleus of Italy's postwar government.

But in the latter part of March 1944, Palmiro Togliatti, the head of the Italian Communist Party, returned to Italy after four years of exile in the Soviet Union. Togliatti's first official act, determined in large measure by the Soviet Union's recognition of the Badoglio regime and desire to cooperate with the United States and England, was to reverse previous communist policy by declaring that the Italian communists were ready to work with everyone, including the King and Badoglio, who opposed fascism. In other words, although continuing to support the Committees, the Italian Communist Party no longer looked upon these organizations as the only legitimate political alternative to fascism and to the neo-fascist Republic of Salò. Instead, it now viewed the Committees as merely the advance guard of a vast mass movement that included all people, from monarchists to communists, who wanted to defeat fascism. This new policy was articulated by the Milanese edition of *L'Unità* dated May 10, 1944: "The initiative taken by the head of our party, comrade Togliatti, to create a democratic war government which, although based on the anti-fascist parties also includes monarchists and Badoglio supporters who are willing to struggle against Hitlerian Germany, in alliance with the United Nations, has been crowned with success. The sense of relief that that initiative has produced in all strata of the population, the satisfaction with which the establishment of the new government has been received . . . , are expressed in the votes of confidence and support that have been given by the organizations leading the people's struggle in the parts of Italy occupied by the nazifascists." [15]

It is true that all of the parties in the anti-fascist coalition eventually accepted the communist initiative as a necessary and practical step. It is not true, however, that this acceptance was given willingly. On the contrary, the Action and Socialist Parties' first reaction to the communists' change of policy was one of bitter indignation.

The actionists were the most vigorous exponents of the idea that the Committees should form the basis for a new progressive democracy in

---

[14] "Il fallimento delle classi dirigenti e il C.L.N.," *L'Unità*, October 21, 1943, p. 1. (CG)

[15] "Il nuovo governo democratico di guerra all'opera," *L'Unità*, May 20, 1944, p. 1. (CG)

Italy. They believed in principle that the Committees alone had the right to lead the Resistance and that they should assume as quickly as possible the full constitutional powers of the state. Intensely antagonistic to both the Monarchy and to the conservative political and economic groups that supported the Badoglio government, the actionists viewed the Committees as the creation of a new revolutionary élite composed exclusively of men who had never compromised with fascism. This conception of the Committees lay at the core of the Action Party's ideological position, insofar as it was based on a commitment to republicanism and to progressive democracy and on a categorical refusal to grant the Monarchy in the figure of King Victor Emmanuel III even the most residual claim to legitimacy. On October 4, 1943, the Action Party's clandestine organ in Rome, *L'Italia Libera*, had published a vehement denunciation of the King, a fact that explains why acceptance of Togliatti's initiative was so difficult for the party's leaders in April 1944: "There is not a single destroyed city, not a single destroyed home, not a single piece of national territory lost that cannot be blamed on the Monarchy, not one innocent victim of fascism or nazism who is not on its conscience, there is no corruption, no speculation, no form of sneaky exploitation that the Monarchy has not accepted." [16] A week later *L'Italia Libera* repeated its allegations against the King and spoke of the Committees of National Liberation as the only institution capable of effecting a genuine renewal of political life in Italy. At the end of April 1944, the actionists recognized the political necessity of including supporters of the Monarchy and the forces identified with Badoglio in the anti-fascist coalition but remained opposed to the principle underlying the communist initiative to the end of the war.

The Socialist Party reacted to Togliatti's shift of policy with the same indignation as that expressed by the actionists, although it, too, finally acceded to what it regarded as a necessary and expedient way of assuring national anti-fascist solidarity. Like the actionists, however, the socialists insisted that the Committees should retain leadership of the Resistance, as evidenced by an editorial in *Avanti!* in May 1944: "In answer to the question: what is the position of the Committees of National Liberation with respect to the new Badoglio government?—the Socialist Party replies that the Committees are not purely and simply organs that execute orders given by the government of Bari, nor are they organs of opposition, but rather autonomous institutions that retain the initiative and leadership of the struggle against nazi-fascism and that apply the directives of the war government, while at the same time adhering firmly to the principle that

[16] "Perché la monarchia è finita," *L'Italia Libera,* October 4, 1943, p. 1. (ISRT)

the unity of the nation for victory and reconstruction has its directing center in the Committees of National Liberation themselves." [17]

The liberals and Christian democrats were less reluctant than the actionists and socialists to adopt the new policy of collaboration with the Badoglio government, since they were inclined to endorse any measure designed to heal the schism that had developed as a result of the formerly intransigent radicalism of the left-wing parties. For both the Christian democrats and the liberals, the Committees were fundamentally a means and not an end, an instrument for the attainment of necessary institutional reforms, not a prefiguration of the new Italy that was to emerge from the war. Therefore, with specific regard to the question of the autonomy and status of the Committees, they were less offended by communist *realpolitik* than were the actionists and socialists.

In reality, the crisis of April 1944 reflected a vast international network of interests and power politics over which none of the Italian parties could exercise control. Great Britain was interested in the Committees of National Liberation only insofar as they could lend military assistance to the Allied cause and was unwilling to recognize the authority of any but the most traditional and conservatively oriented government in Italy. This was the attitude of Winston Churchill, as well as of most of Churchill's closest military and political advisors. The American view of the Italian political scene was more flexible and liberal than that of the British. President Roosevelt and Secretary of State Cordell Hull had often publicly expressed their sympathy for the aspirations of the anti-fascist forces in Italy and, unlike their British counterparts, had no liking for or sense of personal identification with the Savoyard Monarchy. American diplomatic, military, and intelligence authorities in Italy were also far more responsive than were the British to the type of strongly individualistic, enterprising Italians who generally led partisan units and the Liberation Committees. The Committees were, after all, experiments in the kind of local self-government that Americans could easily recognize as akin to their own best historical traditions. Nevertheless, despite all these factors that created a certain sense of solidarity between many Americans and Italian anti-fascists, the fact remains that the overall strategy of the United States government was inexorably and necessarily linked with that of Great Britain. Therefore it was expedient for the Americans to encourage as broad a coalition of non- and anti-fascist forces in Italy as possible, and to grant the King and Marshal Badoglio a continued role in shaping the internal affairs of Italy.[18] As far as the

---

[17] "I comitati e il governo di Badoglio," *Avanti!*, May 15, 1944, p. 1. (INS)

[18] Among the many books dealing with various phases and aspects of American policy toward Italy from 1943 to 1945 are: Charles F. Delzell, *Mussolini's Enemies:*

Soviet Union was concerned, recognition of the Badoglio government, which it granted even before the British and the Americans, was an attempt to win the confidence of its Western allies and at the same time a clever maneuver designed to give the Soviets a possible opportunity to play a bigger role in Italy, which was within the Anglo-American sphere of operations.

But there were other areas of controversy that divided the five anti-fascist parties. Some were of relatively minor importance, yet at the same time threatened to undermine the mutual confidence on which the success of the Committees depended. For example, the Committee in Turin, which eventually achieved perhaps the stongest unity among its members of any regional Committee functioning in northern Italy, was riddled with disputes during the early phases of the Resistance, particularly between the actionists and the communists. On December 24, 1943, the Turinese edition of *L'Unità* took issue with several articles in *L'Italia Libera* that had criticized the communists for their "irrational compulsion" to take armed action against the nazi and fascist armies without first preparing an efficient military apparatus. *L'Unità* responded to these articles by accusing the Turinese Committee of *attesismo* and insisted on its right to express its views, for this right, the newspaper said, "is the fundamental principle of Committee democracy." [19] The dispute continued for several months and was further aggravated by each party's contention that the other was trying to monopolize control of the partisan movement.

Somewhat the same situation existed within the ranks of the Committee in Florence. In a letter he sent to Ferruccio Parri on June 2, 1944, Carlo Ragghianti of the Action Party complained of the severely strained relations between actionists and communists in Florence. The problem lay, said Ragghianti, in "the desire of the Communist Party to monopolize the military phase of the Resistance." [20] The actionists' response was to form their own partisan units and to blame the communists for "the campaign of calumny" that they had waged against the other members of the Florentine Committee. On July 24, 1944, Ferruccio Parri, who served in the General Headquarters of the Corps of Freedom Volunteers in Milan and who was one of the leading organizers of the Resistance in northern Italy, wrote to Ugo La Malfa in Rome of the constant haggling between socialists and liberals in Milan over the question of which party had the

---

The Italian Anti-Fascist Resistance; Norman Kogan, *Italy and the Allies;* Eric Linklater, *The Campaign in Italy;* Mark Clark, *Calculated Risk;* Pietro Secchia and Filippo Frassati, *La Resistenza e gli Alleati;* Cordell Hull, *The Memoirs of Cordell Hull;* Robert E. Sherwood, *Roosevelt and Hopkins, an intimate history;* H. Stuart Hughes, *The United States and Italy.*

[19] "Disciplina," *L'Unità*, December 24, 1943, p. 2. (CG)
[20] *Una lotta nel suo corso*, p. 218.

greater right to receive Committee funds for the establishment of partisan units in the region of Lombardy.[21] These disputes were eventually settled amicably, however, and did not represent as serious a threat to the unity of the Committees as another more burning issue: the territorial question in the region of Friuli-Venezia Giulia.

The region of Venezia Giulia lies in the northeast corner of Italy and is contiguous on its northern border with Austria, on the east with Yugoslavia. Its principal inland cities are Udine and Gorizia, its main urban center and port, Trieste. The entire region was incorporated into the Italian state after the end of World War I, along with parts of the province of Dalmatia. Most of the region's cities and towns that lie along the coast of the Istrian Peninsula are inhabited predominantly by Italians. The majority of the population in Trieste, too, is Italian. Slavic peoples are in the majority, however, in the rural and mountainous areas of the region's southeast interior.

The fascist regime carried on an implacable nationalistic campaign in Venezia Giulia and terrorized the Slavic peoples to such an extent that Slavic nationalists, who had never accepted the legitimacy of Italian domination after World War I, found it relatively easy to foment unrest and rebellion among the region's non-Italian population.

Italian anti-fascists in Trieste had always sought to defend Italy's right to Venezia Giulia on the basis of the predominantly Italian contribution to the region's cultural, political, and economic development but at the same time had opposed the fascists' effort to suppress the cultural identity of the Slavs who lived and worked side by side with the Italians. During World War II Italian and Slavic nationalism came into direct conflict as a result of fascist intimidation of the Slavic peoples and Slavic determination to reacquire the region of Venezia Giulia. But with the fall of Mussolini's regime in July 1943, and the development of a massive Resistance movement in Yugoslavia led by Marshal Tito, the problem of rival claims and counterclaims assumed a new character. The Committee of National Liberation in Trieste was composed of men who felt a deep sense of indebtedness to the sacrifices made by Italian soldiers in World War I, which had contributed to the collapse of the Austro-Hungarian Empire and to Italy's acquisition of Trieste. They were committed essentially to the principle of regional autonomy within a decentralized, federated Italian state that would allow the Slavic people of Venezia Giulia to develop their own culture and uphold their own traditions. This principle was affirmed in November 1943 by Gabriele Foschiatti, who served on the Triestine Committee as a representative of the Action Party. In an article

[21] *Ibid.*, pp. 229, 230.

entitled "Unitary Faith," which appeared in his party's clandestine organ *Giustizia e Libertà,* Foschiatti declared that the principle of Italy's right to Trieste was sacred to the Action Party: "For the Action Party, the only path to follow is that of absolute resistance to the very utmost extent of our power against every effort to separate the Italians of Venezia Giulia from the rest of Italy. Our aim is the unity of Italy. On this point the Action Party, which includes the last survivors of the Mazzinian and republican tradition of World War I and safeguards the sacred memory of its dead, cannot tolerate either timorousness or indecisiveness in its ranks." [22]

The position taken by Foschiatti was at first endorsed by all of the other parties in the Triestine Committee. But the Communists' attitude toward the problem of the territorial status of Trieste and of Venezia Giulia soon began to diverge radically from that of the other four parties. The reasons for this divergence have been analyzed by Carlo Ventura, Mario Pacor, and other Italian historians who have studied the ethnic and class structure of the region. Ventura explains that the conflict between Italian and Slavic nationalism was only one feature of the problem in Venezia Giulia. During the years 1941 to 1945, national rivalry was aggravated "by the development of a fairly well-defined social conflict between the forces of the Resistance, which were determined to keep the region of Venezia Giulia as part of the Italian state, and the forces of the Italian and Slovene proletariat, which were united in their support of a solution of the national problem favorable to the demands of Yugoslavia." [23] In the light of this fact, it becomes clear why the Triestine communists soon repudiated Foschiatti's position and tended more and more strongly to back Yugoslavia's right to reacquire Trieste. Since the majority of both Italian and Slovene workers, in reaction to the oppression of the Italian and Slavic ruling class, spontaneously supported the revolutionary program of the Yugoslav Resistance Movement, it was logical and expedient for Italian communist leaders in Trieste to reject the stand taken in November by the Committee of National Liberation. A semblance of unity was maintained by the Triestine Committee until the middle of 1944, at which point the decision of local Communist leaders to integrate their political and partisan forces in the Yugoslav National Liberation Front and the support they gave to the Yugoslav claims to Trieste provoked an open breach between the parties and the withdrawal

---

[22] Gabriele Foschiatti, "Fede unitaria," *Giustizia e Libertà,* November 1943, p. 1. (INS)

[23] Carlo Ventura, *La stampa a Trieste 1943–1945,* pp. 6, 7. See also Mario Pacor, *Confine orientale,* passim.

of the communists from the Committee of National Liberation. The other parties continued to function without the communists and stubbornly adhered to the federative solution originally proposed by Foschiatti, as evidenced by an article in the Committee's organ *Ricostruzione* of January 1945. The solution for Venezia Giulia, said *Ricostruzione,* was administrative autonomy, not annexation to Yugoslavia: "The new authentic federal Italy, no longer the country of accomplished facts and prefects' reports to the Duce, but the nation whose honor and freedom have been redeemed by hundreds of thousands of its most generous sons, this Italy will give to Venezia Guilia the broadest possible political, administrative, and cultural autonomy. In this climate of freedom, and only in this way, Trieste will be able to fulfill its function as an international meeting place open to all flags, in accordance with the role assigned to the city by its fortunate geographical position. . . . Long live an autonomous and free Venezia Giulia within the framework of a democratic, federal Italy." [24]

The rupture of unity within the ranks of the Triestine Committee did not fail to have serious repercussions in centers of Resistance in other areas of Italy. But since the problem was restricted to a specific region and the general policy of the Italian Communist Party was to collaborate in the anti-fascist coalition, a definitive break such as that which took place in Trieste did not develop in any of the other regional Committees. The only analogous situation to that of Venezia Giulia occurred in the region of the Aosta Valley, the basic elements of which will be explained in Chapter IX.

It is necessary to discuss one other issue that tended to divide the Committees, namely, the moral problem concerning the use of terror as a method of combating nazism and fascism. All the parties were in agreement about the necessity of fighting terror with terror, of countering violence with violence. Even the Christian Democratic Party, which in principle was founded on the teachings of Christ, reluctantly accepted the action of terrorist bands such as the *Gappisti* as an integral part of the Resistance struggle. Yet the problem remained of what quality of terror was legitimate and particularly of what type of person might justifiably be designated for assault or assassination. Organized partisan warfare was one matter; sudden acts of violence against isolated individuals were another. If the victim of these attacks was known to be guilty of torturing or murdering anti-fascists, he was considered by all the parties to be a fair target for terrorist assault. But what if the victim, although known to be

---

[24] This article, entitled "Autonomia per Trieste," is cited textually by Guido Botteri in *I cattolici triestini nella Resistenza,* p. 179.

fascist, was not directly associated with police and military authorities who carried on the work of torture and execution? This was precisely the divisive issue within the various Committees of National Liberation, the most dramatic example of which occurred in Florence in connection with the assassination of the fascist philosopher Giovanni Gentile on April 15, 1944.

Although the facts in the case have never been thoroughly verified, it is almost certain that Gentile was assassinated by a group of five communist *gappisti,* members of the terrorist organization *Gruppi di Azione Patriottica.* In any case, the communists in Florence justified and lauded Gentile's assassins on the ground that he had been responsible for inculcating into the youth of Italy the ideology of fascism, which had brought unprecedented horror and tragedy to the world. The Action Party, although concurring with the communists in their estimate of Gentile's guilt, felt that since Gentile was not engaged in repressive action of any sort and had even attempted to moderate the horrendous cruelty of the fascist police chief in Florence, Mario Carità, his assassination could not be morally justified. The other parties in the Florentine Committee also condemned Gentile's assassins. The question was debated by the underground newspapers of the five parties. *L'Azione Comunista* not only defended the assassination but proudly proclaimed its responsibility for it. The Action Party's newspaper *La Libertà* deplored the episode in an article written by Tristano Codignola, a former contributor to the clandestine newspaper *Non Mollare!* in 1925. Codignola's judgment of Gentile was severe. The fascist philosopher, he said, had tacitly approved "the violence, the lies, the ineptitude that had brought Italy to ruin; even worse he had aligned himself, after September 8, with the forces of persecution and tyranny, at the moment in which the Italy of progress and freedom, regardless of the sacrifices, was entering enthusiastically into battle." But despite his guilt, Codignola said, Gentile should not have been murdered: "While thousands of young men are fighting and dying for freedom, while the newly resurrected parties are paying with blood for their right to lead the country, Gentile could not escape from his responsibility and guilt. But in the profound sadness that the vision of so many blood sacrifices arouses in us, we are especially grieved by the thought that his death, instead of being a reminder of justice, has become just another violent episode, devoid of ethical value." [25] Codignola's point of view was shared by the liberals and socialists in Florence. Strangely enough, the Christian Democratic Party's clandestine organ *Il Popolo*

---

[25] Codignola's article is cited textually by Carlo Francovich, *La Resistenza a Firenze,* p. 190.

avoided a direct confrontation with the moral problem inherent in the assassination and limited itself to emphasizing the fact that in recent years Gentile had drawn closer to the Catholic Church and had won the admiration of Catholic circles because of his effort to moderate the hatred and violence generated by the civil war in Italy between fascists and anti-fascists.

Certain segments of the Catholic hierarchy opposed all forms of "terrorist" and "illegal" violence, the terms used by many *attesisti* to condemn the actions of partisans and *gappisti*. The Judaeo-Christian injunction against murder formed the basis of a famous appeal directed to leaders of the Florentine Resistance by Cardinal Elia Della Costa on December 5, 1943. The appeal was issued several days after the execution of five anti-fascists in retaliation for the assassination on December 1 of Gino Gobbi, the commandant of fascist army headquarters in Florence. Part of Cardinal Della Costa's appeal reads as follows:

We exhort, we beg, every citizen to abstain from all forms of violence. In urging that humanity and respect for the German soldiers and commanders be maintained, it is necessary that we point out that insults, vandalism, the use of arms against anyone at all not only cannot improve conditions, but severely aggravates them, since these actions give rise to reactions that must not be provoked.

As for assassinations of a private or treacherous character, we recall to everyone the fifth commandment: Thou shalt not kill! And we implore everyone to reflect that bloodshed can only cause more bloodshed.[26]

The Action Party assigned the task of answering Cardinal Della Costa's appeal to Enzo Enriques-Agnoletti, whose article in *La Libertà* was endorsed by the entire Florentine Committee. Enriques-Agnoletti reminded the Cardinal that he himself had never published or even spoken a word protesting the arrests, torture, and murders of which the fascists and nazis were guilty in Florence. Enriques-Agnoletti then enlarged upon the ethical content of the struggle for freedom and redemption that was being waged by the Resistance Movement, concluding that constant risks and violence were inevitable "in the war against tyranny, injustice, and intolerance." [27]

IV
The Question of Attesismo

The diametrically opposed points of view expressed by Cardinal Della Costa and Enzo Enriques-Agnoletti formed part of a question that

[26] Francovich, *La Resistenza a Firenze*, p. 103.

[27] Enzo Enriques-Agnoletti, "L'intervento del Cardinale Arcivescovo Della Costa e la risposta del Partito d'Azione," *La Libertà,* December 19, 1943, p. 1. (ISRT)

was discussed by underground newspapers from the very outset of the Resistance, the question of *attesismo*. Religiously inspired injunctions against violence, especially indiscriminate violence, were but one of several arguments used by those who opposed direct military and political action on the part of anti-fascist movements. There were many Italians, particularly among politically conservative circles, who maintained that armed intervention by partisan and terrorist units would merely provoke the nazis to retaliate against innocent persons and that these retaliations were unnecessary since the Allies would eventually win the war with or without the help of the Italian people. These arguments had to be answered, for the attitude of *attesismo* represented one of the gravest threats to the effective functioning of the Resistance Movement in that it appealed to millions of ordinary persons who sought to avoid involvement in conflicts they only imperfectly understood.

The moral necessity of redeeming the national honor of Italy constituted the fundamental argument used by opponents of *attesismo*. Italian Resistance leaders stressed their conviction that only through armed action could the Italian people regain the respect of the democratic world, that freedom had enduring value only when it was fought for and won by the people itself. Resistance leaders were aware, of course, that the military situation as of September 1943 foreshadowed eventual victory for the Allies. Yet they also knew that passive reliance on the Allies to liberate Italy from fascism would place the Italian people in an irremediably weak moral position. They concluded, therefore, that only in the measure in which the Italian people collaborated actively in the struggle to drive the Germans out of Italy, to defeat nazism and fascism, would it be able to win back its independence and freedom.

Among the most determined exponents of this morally based argument against *attesismo* were the men who published the clandestine newspapers of the various Committees of National Liberation. *La Riscossa Italiana,* the organ of the Turinese Committee, addressed itself directly to the problem of the moral redemption of Italy in the first issue of October 20, 1943. Paolo Greco, one of the Liberal Party members of the Committee in Turin, spoke of the supreme task facing the Italian people: "It is necessary to reawaken our conscience, to free ourselves from idolatries and fetishisms based on obedience to the supposed incarnation of the superman, to reacquire, through dignity of character, a critical sense and the courage of our ideas; it is necessary above all that we persuade ourselves that freedom, before constituting a political doctrine, must be an intellectual and moral conviction." [28] The substance of Greco's appeal lay in the challenge it presented to the moral energies of the Italian

[28] Paolo Greco, "Riscossa," *La Riscossa Italiana,* October 20, 1943, p. 1. (CG)

people, in its explicit denunciation of the conformism and passivity on which the autarchic power of Mussolini's regime had depended. This same appeal was echoed by *Fratelli d'Italia,* the organ of the Liberation Committee in Padua. In an issue dated March 15, 1944, Professor Egidio Meneghetti directed a message to the people of the region of Veneto in which he said that too few persons had heeded the Committee's call for action, that too many Italians "had remained indifferent, passive, mistrustful, and selfish." Fortunately, Meneghetti added, "there are some Italians who have committed themselves to battle, and they are the ones who will redeem Italy." [29] *Liberazione,* published by the Committee of National Liberation in Domodossola, stressed the fact that no foreign power, even the most benevolent, can bestow freedom on a people that refused to fight for itself. Reliance on the Allies to deliver Italy from tyranny, the newspaper declared, signified "a failure to derive any benefit from the tragic experience of fascism." [30]

In October 1944, the CLNAI in Milan issued a decree to all regional and provincial Committees in which the same ideas expressed by the newspapers referred to above were placed in a larger international perspective. The decree stated that "in order that the events of the coming months culminate in . . . a national insurrection which, along with the operations of the regular army, must furnish the historical proof of the Italian people's opposition to nazi-fascism and constitute its rehabilitation in the eyes of the entire world, it is necessary that a vast majority of the people participate in the struggle." [31] Thus the Committees of National Liberation themselves established the moral and political basis of Resistance and led the struggle against *attesismo.*

Among the clandestine newspapers of the five leading anti-fascist parties, the communist organ *L'Unità* was most consistently active in combatting *attesismo. L'Unità* did not fail to emphasize the moral necessity of armed resistance. On November 15, 1943, for example, the newspaper asserted that "through armed resistance against nazism we shall regain our independence, against fascism we shall regain our freedom. And in the eyes of the world we shall regain our dignity and the respect of free peoples, thereby redeeming ourselves from the infamy and crimes of fascism." [32] But of equal importance to the Italian Communist Party was the problem of mobilizing the energies of Italian workers against

[29] Egidio Meneghetti, "Ai veneti," *Fratelli d'Italia,* March 15, 1944, p. 1. (LC)

[30] "La vera opinione," *Liberazione,* September 23, 1944, p. 1. (MR)

[31] Decree dated October 1944 and entitled "A tutti i comitati regionali e comitati provinciali di liberazione nazionale." (CG)

[32] "Per la vittoria del popolo italiano nella guerra contro la Germania nazista," *L'Unità,* November 15, 1943, p. 1. (ISRT)

the capitalist ruling class, which the communists blamed for the rise and triumph of fascism and, when Mussolini's regime fell, for the attitude of *attesismo* and passive reliance on the Allies. The communists did not believe in the efficacy of "spontaneous" or "instinctive" rebellion against tyranny. Nor did they believe in the possibility of creating what they called a "progressive democracy" in Italy under the aegis of the Allies. Consequently, they based their campaign against *attesismo* not only on moral arguments, but also on their conviction that careful organization and planning on all levels of Resistance activity had to take precedence over individual acts of rebellion and on their belief that every people becomes conscious of its power by creating its own history. The Communist Party recognized, in other words, that reliance on the Allies to free Italy would not lead to liberation but simply to another occupation, even if by a friendly and welcome army.

One of the chief concerns of the Action Party was to dissociate the Italian people from the fascist regime, to persuade Italians that unless they took up arms in alliance with the United Nations they would be forever blamed for the aggressions and crimes of which fascism had been guilty. This was no mere opportunistic maneuver, for almost all the Action Party members had resisted fascism long before it became clear that the nazi-fascist armies would be defeated in battle. On October 30, 1943, the Roman edition of *L'Italia Libera* issued one of many similar appeals to the Italian people not to succumb to the blandishments and excuses for inaction offered by the *attesisti*: "In the struggle against nazism lies our only hope for national rebirth. The struggle against nazism, without limit and without fear of the supreme sacrifice, is the only possibility for redemption available to the Italian people. Dishonored by Mussolini and his policy of provocation and aggression, betrayed by Badoglio, who handed over thirty Italian divisions to ten Nazi divisions, fought over by two pseudolegal governments, equally responsible for its ruin, only in this struggle must the Italian people find its future." [33]

The clandestine press of the Liberal Party paid less attention to the question of *attesismo* than did the communists and actionists. Its members were not as experienced in the strategy of ideological and partisan warfare as were those of the other two parties, which could rely on many men who were veterans of conspiratorial activity and of actual military combat in Spain. The Resistance depended on guerrilla and terrorist warfare for its success and required a cohesive organizational apparatus capable of mobilizing vast sectors of the population, neither of which was

[33] "La lotta contro il nazismo unica possibilità di rinascita," *L'Italia Libera,* October 30, 1943, p. 1. (ISRT)

within the possibilities of the Liberal Party. The socialists, on the other hand, waged a persistent campaign against *attesismo* and followed essentially the same line of reasoning as that of the communists and actionists. In November 1943, *Avanti!* struck the same note of opposition to *attesismo* when it declared that "we do not want freedom as a gift presented to us by a King disguised as a liberal, by a repentant general, or by foreign governments. We want the Italian people to regain its freedom with its own sacrifices, with its own war, and we summon all Italians to the struggle against nazism." [34]

The Christian Democratic Party, although impeded by some of the same deficiencies that characterized the Liberal Party, was nonetheless more active than the Liberal Party in its efforts to combat *attesismo* by reason of the support it enjoyed among the Catholic masses, particularly in the rural areas of Italy. It must be noted here that Italian farmers, many of whom identified themselves with the Catholic movement, formed the backbone of numerous partisan units in the regions of Tuscany, Emilia, Liguria, Piedmont, and Veneto. Consequently, it was possible for the Christian democrats to direct their messages of resistance to large numbers of Italians on whose loyalty they could depend.

Yet it was not so much the practical exigencies of organized warfare as it was the moral content of the anti-fascist struggle that was stressed by the Catholic underground press. A typical example of the primarily moral appeal made by the Christian democrats appears in the first issue of *Il Segno*, the clandestine organ of a group of Catholic intellectuals in Rome. On March 1, 1944, *Il Segno* proclaimed that "for us there can be no doubts, no perplexities. This is the hour in which Catholics must awaken once and for all in order to take the place they rightfully deserve in the governing of the affairs of this world. At the point at which we are, after the immense world catastrophe caused by the spiritual disorientation of the rulers of governments, all of which are more or less tied to substantially materialistic theories and pseudodoctrines, we feel the urgent need to take a position, to insert ourselves in politics and to fight our battle. We must do this in order to bring about a return to the fundamental values of life, those of the spirit, to achieve the redemption of man from the enslavement of ideologies that have completely failed, and whose effects are everywhere evident." [35] Although expressed in a somewhat presumptuous and high-sounding manner, this appeal on the part of *Il Segno* was unquestionably motivated by a sincere desire to translate the ideals of Christianity into concrete action. Like *L'Uomo*,

[34] "Punti fermi," *Avanti!*, November 1943, p. 1. (ISRT)
[35] "La nostra ora," *Il Segno*, March 1, 1944, p. 1. (ICP)

Per Il Domani, and other clandestine newspapers published by Catholic intellectuals, *Il Segno* helped awaken the conscience of the lay Catholic population in Italy and performed an important ideological function in the Resistance Movement.

The Catholic press also distinguished itself for its refusal to coddle the disturbed consciences of those persons who liked to pretend that fascism had been entirely imposed on the Italian people, that no significant amount of consent or acquiescence to the dictatorship had ever characterized the attitude of most Italians. *Il Popolo* was often harsh in its judgments of what it called the political immaturity of the majority of Italians, as was *La Punta,* the organ of the Catholic Youth Organization. "It is futile," said *La Punta* in February 1944, "to blame everything on one man and on a regime." The Italian people itself had been at fault, and the first act of redemption was to admit guilt. Only in this way could the nation as a whole rediscover its authentic virtues and enter into battle for the values in which it had learned at great cost to believe.[36]

The question of *attesismo* was also discussed by many partisan newspapers, but from the perspective of men who had already definitively resolved the problem by taking up arms against nazism and fascism. The partisans naturally felt a certain impatience and rancor when they encountered the political arguments used to oppose *attesismo,* since for them one accurately aimed shot at a nazi or fascist soldier was worth more than many eloquent words. The men who joined the volunteer partisan army after September 8 did not require lengthy discourses on the need for resistance to realize that armed action, not *attesismo,* was the only course to follow for those who loved freedom. As expressed by the anonymous author of an article that appeared in the partisan newspaper *Il Partigiano Piemontese* in November 1943, the example set by partisan movements in all nazi-occupied countries was a sufficiently powerful stimulus to action:

Partisan: a name and a banner on which are written the heroic exploits of patriots of all countries devoted to the same cause, the freedom and independence of their lands. We too have the honor of holding the same flag, of meriting the same glorious name! . . .

The "impatient" people, who follow the progress of the Anglo-American Army on the map and find it too slow, who wait for freedom as a gift bestowed by Uncle Sam, and, in the meantime, do not move a finger to fight the German invader or the traitor who threatens at every moment the safety of the patriots, not only do not help the cause of the United Nations but become accomplices

---

[36] "Libertà cosciente," *La Punta,* February 3, 1944, p. 1. (LC)

of the enemy by giving him a free hand: the hand guilty of crime and devastation . . .

To wait while the filthy traitors lend their services to the foul deeds of the police and spies of the Germans, means to extend the stain of dishonor with which the police and spies besmirch the name of Italy.[37]

"The honor of Italy": this was in the final analysis the watchword to which all anti-fascists responded, the ideal that united men and women of all types and all ideologies. The ideal of honor has, to be sure, been misinterpreted and abused by individuals and nations whose actions have been anything but honorable, yet the word in its original sense of merited prestige retains its force, its relevance to the situation in which so many Italians found themselves after September 8, 1943.

But what was the substantial content of this honor? What aspects and phases of Italian history prior to the advent of fascism could Resistance leaders look to as points of reference for the struggle they were waging? What were the political and cultural values to which they referred in substantiating their claim that the Resistance formed an integral part of Italian and European democratic traditions? These are the questions which we shall attempt to answer in the next chapter.

[37] "Partigiano," *Il Partigiano Piemontese,* November 1943, p. 1. (LC)

CHAPTER SIX

THE RISORGIMENTO
AND THE RESISTANCE

One of the purposes of the underground press in Italy was to give its readers the sense that their thought and action belonged to a worthy tradition, that important values of Italy's political and cultural history that had been denigrated, distorted, or ignored by fascism were being reaffirmed by the Resistance. This purpose is reflected principally in the many articles in the underground newspapers that deal with men and ideas of the Risorgimento.

The term Risorgimento, as used here, refers to all of the intellectual and political currents, popular insurrections, and military campaigns which, beginning in the second half of the eighteenth century, were inspired by the ideal of a free and independent Italy and culminated in 1861 in the unification of the country under the aegis of the Savoyard Monarchy. This definition of the Risorgimento corresponds to the interpretation that one finds in the majority of clandestine newspapers and allows the kind of broad perspective that is necessary in considering the problem of historical links and parallels.

The question of the relationship between the Risorgimento and the Resistance has been passionately debated by Italian historians since the end of World War II. In the first place, the fascist regime made a concerted effort to prove that it was the legitimate inheritor of the Risorgimento tradition. Fascist ideologists, from Mussolini himself to Giovanni Gentile, from the historian Gioacchino Volpe to supporters of the neofascist Republic of Salò, believed that the essence of the Risorgimento lay in the struggle of the Italian people to achieve, in the words of Volpe, "unity, power, and greatness." In 1923, Mussolini proclaimed that "between the Garibaldian tradition, the pride and glory of Italy, and the action of the blackshirts, not only is there not an antithesis, but there exists a historical and ideal continuity," and in 1925 Giovanni Gentile defended the exploits of the fascist *squadristi* as having been inspired by "a political and moral need" analogous to that of Mazzini's Young Italy movement.[1] As a consequence of the fascist attempt to incorporate the Risorgimento tradition and claim it as its own, anti-fascist intellectuals have sought to vindicate what they regard as the essentially liberal, democratic, and international character of the Risorgimento. Benedetto Croce was the most prominent defender of this interpretation of the Risorgimento during the fascist epoch itself, and after World War II, his ideas were further developed by Adolfo Omodeo, Arturo Carlo Jemolo, Alessandro Galante Garrone, and other Italian historians who have been influenced in greater or lesser degree by Croce's thought.

The second reason for the intense interest in the relationship between the Risorgimento and the Resistance lies in the fact that, whether objectively valid or not, many Italians who participated in the Resistance felt this relationship as something sacred and often committed themselves to the anti-fascist struggle in the name of ideals and traditions that derived from the Risorgimento.

It would be misleading to suggest that there was unanimity of opinion among Italian Resistance leaders regarding the nature of the link between the Risorgimento and the Resistance. For example, in *Un uomo, un partigiano,* Roberto Battaglia attributed much of the debate on the question to ideological confusion, a lack of firsthand experience with historical problems, and, in some cases, a merely rhetorical exaltation of Italian greatness.[2] The Risorgimento, Battaglia maintained, was the work of a restricted group of intellectuals who believed in the nineteenth-century ideals of liberalism and national independence. The Resistance, on the other hand, was a mass movement involving people from all segments of the population and was essentially revolutionary and international in its aim. Nevertheless, in his *Storia della Resistenza italiana,* published ten years after *Un Uomo, un partigiano,* Battaglia was less inclined to dismiss the question as a product of confusion and rhetoric and devoted many pages of his work to explaining how the Resistance was linked with the Risorgimento.[3]

The postwar controversy between liberal and Marxist historians [4] has centered around Antonio Gramsci's interpretation of the Risorgimento as expressed in the volume *Il Risorgimento.* Most liberal Italian histo-

---

[1] Claudio Pavone, "Le idee della Resistenza," *Passato e Presente,* January-February, 1959, pp. 854–58.

[2] Battaglia, *Un uomo, un partigiano,* p. 181.

[3] See especially Roberto Battaglia, *Storia della Resistenza italiana,* pp. 279, 322, 384.

[4] The main issues in the controversy are analyzed by John Cammett, "Two Recent Polemics on the Character of the Italian Risorgimento," *Science and Society,* Fall 1963, pp. 433–457.

rians—notably Benedetto Croce, Carlo Antoni, Federico Chabod, and Rosareo Romeo—take issue with Gramsci and his communist disciples over their tendency to emphasize the failures rather than the successes of the Risorgimento. Gramsci's interpretation of the Risorgimento as an abortive revolution was based on his assumption that the moderate and radical intellectuals who led Italy's struggle for national independence had deliberately sought to exclude the nation's peasantry—who in the mid-nineteenth century constituted about four-fifths of the Italian population—from participating actively in that struggle. Thus, although the "national" aims of the Risorgimento had been achieved, its "social" and genuinely "revolutionary" potentialities had been blocked. In Gramsci's view, which is still more or less accepted by Italian Marxists, "the famous minority . . . that led our movement for unification was concerned in reality with economic interests more than with idealistic formulas and struggled much more to prevent the people from intervening in the struggle and making it social (in the sense of an agrarian reform) than against the enemies of unification." [5] Liberal historians answer this charge by denying, in the words of Romeo, the possibility of "any alternative to the Risorgimento as it was concretely realized." [6] They charge in turn that Gramsci and his followers "anachronistically reflected the twentieth century interests of the PCI [Italian Communist Party] in stressing the importance of the peasant movement and the Southern Question during the Risorgimento, in underestimating the influence of the European powers on the Risorgimento, and even in using terms like 'national-popular,' supposedly derived from the Russian term *narodnost.*" [7]

The controversy is still alive and has, in fact, important implications for those who are seeking to understand the historical significance of Italian anti-fascism and specifically of the Resistance Movement.

The idea that anti-fascism represented a continuation and amplification of the Risorgimento was not born in September 1943, nor were the life and thought of various Risorgimento patriots first held up as an example to follow during the period of the armed Resistance from September 1943 to April 1945. As early as 1932, the Justice and Freedom Movement in Paris asserted in one of its clandestine booklets that "the liberation of Italy must be the work of the Italians themselves. [The movement] declares that the struggle will be hard and will require the greatest sacrifices. This is the price of the second Italian Risorgimento." [8]

[5] Antonio Gramsci, *Il Risorgimento*, p. 65.
[6] John Cammett, *Antonio Gramsci and the Origins of Italian Communism*, p. 216.
[7] *Ibid.*, p. 215.
[8] This statement appears on the back cover of a booklet entitled *Contro il decennale e per l'azione*, November 1932. (CG)

On November 29, 1935, Michele Giua, who had been imprisoned in Rome on May 15 of that year because of his participation in the Justice and Freedom Movement, sent a letter to his wife that contains a passage praising Vittorio Alfieri's lifelong hatred of tyranny. Censorship of his letters prevented Giua from making a direct parallel between Alfieri's thought and the cause for which he himself had been imprisoned, yet the intent of his letter is unmistakably clear: "If you buy the Sonzogno edition," Giua wrote, "you will find in the appendix to the volume Alfieri's *On Tyranny,* which is a magnificent essay against despotism and in favor of republican government. The proud man from Asti was really awesome in this sense, and who knows how many minds that essay shaped during our Risorgimento." [9] In October 1941, six prominent members of the recently formed Action Committee for the Union of the Italian People—Emilio Sereni and Giuseppe Dozza of the Italian Communist Party, Pietro Nenni and Giuseppe Saragat of the Italian Socialist Party, and Silvio Trentin and Fausto Nitti of the Justice and Freedom Movement—issued an appeal from France that urged Italian intellectuals to "put an end to the Hitlerian-fascist enslavement of thought, to shout the truth as befits your function, to defend Italian culture and the noble traditions of the Risorgimento that are being trampled on by fascism!" [10] And two years later, in May 1943, during a period of confinement in a desolate area of southern Italy, Leone Ginzburg began working on an essay dealing with the values of the Risorgimento. The central idea of Ginzburg's essay was that the Italy in which he and other anti-fascists believed was inconceivable without the preceding achievements of the Risorgimento: "For the Italians of today, the Risorgimento is not simply the name of an historical period . . .; it is, instead, a still vital and jealously guarded tradition to which we refer continuously in order to derive from it standards of judgment and incentives to action." [11]

These are but four of many similar tributes to the Risorgimento that were expressed by precursors of the Resistance during the fascist epoch. But it was not until the actual beginning of an organized partisan movement after September 1943 that the return to the Risorgimento for moral and political inspiration became a widespread phenomenon.

---

[9] *Lettere di antifascisti dal carcere e dal confino,* vol. II, p. 113. Alfieri (1749–1803), although known primarily as a dramatist, has always been credited by Italian political historians with laying the first spiritual cornerstone of the Risorgimento. Mazzini called Alfieri "the first modern Italian."

[10] "Il primo appello per l'unione del popolo," October 1941, reprinted in *L'antifascismo italiano,* edited by Paolo Alatri, vol. II, pp. 404–8. The above-mentioned appeal to the intellectuals is on p. 408.

[11] Leone Ginzburg, "La tradizione del Risorgimento," *Il Ponte,* January 1961, p. 43.

The need for a sense of identification with Italian political and cultural traditions was felt with particular urgency by young people whose formative years had coincided with the rise and triumph of Mussolini's regime. In the underground press of the various anti-fascist youth movements, one finds this need expressed in many articles dealing with the ideals of the Risorgimento.

The largest and most efficiently organized youth movement was Il Fronte della Gioventù, which was founded in November 1943 through the efforts of Eugenio Curiel. Curiel, it will be remembered, also functioned as chief editor of the Italian Communist Party's two principal clandestine organs, *L'Unità* and *La Nostra Lotta,* until he was assassinated by fascist gunmen in Milan on February 24, 1945. Yet Curiel did not want the Fronte to be dominated by communists. He conceived of the Fronte as a movement that would transcend all party interests and that would be genuinely national and democratic in character. He labored incessantly to accomplish this end and achieved notable success, for the Fronte groups were composed, at least initially, of young men and women of diverse political persuasions.

During his student days in Padua in the mid-1930's, Curiel had gradually moved toward a Marxist position and had identified himself closely with the Italian working class movement. At the same time he was not then, nor did he later become, an inflexibly dogmatic communist and in fact drew inspiration from many sources of historical thought and experience. Enzo Modica, Curiel's biographer, stresses that during the period of the Resistance, "Curiel did not know very many of the writings of Gramsci; he was familiar, however, with the best Italian and European traditions, he knew the history of our country, and was profoundly tied to the life of our people. For this reason his Marxism did not reduce itself to an arid enunciation of formulas, but was instead an instrument for the criticism of reality." [12]

Curiel was interested in the parallels and contrasts that existed between the Risorgimento and the Resistance. He studied the writings of Mazzini, Cavour, Settembrini, D'Azeglio, and other Risorgimento patriots for the purpose of determining the extent to which the thought of these men could be assimilated and transmitted by Fronte organizers as part of the ideological war against fascism. His conclusion was that a definite continuity of ideas and ideals existed between the Risorgimento and the Resistance, that both movements were essentially struggles for independence, national unity, and freedom, even though the Risorgi-

[12] Eugenio Curiel, *Classi e generazioni nel secondo Risorgimento,* edited by Enzo Modica, p. xxv.

mento lacked the extensive mass participation that characterized the Resistance.

Curiel's interest in the historical connection between the Risorgimento and the Resistance is reflected in a statement of purpose issued by the central committee of the Fronte in November 1943. In its directive concerned with the problem of reeducating Italian youth, the Fronte committee stated that "patriotic teachers should emphasize the concept of a national struggle and explain the continuity of mass action for freedom and national independence from the Risorgimento to today." [13] Another directive asserted that the Fronte intended to "recall constantly to the youth the struggles for freedom and independence in Italy and to show the continuity of our fight for democracy." [14]

The first underground newspaper to be published by the Fronte organization was a crudely mimeographed *Bollettino del Fronte della Gioventù,* which, although undated, probably appeared in Milan in November or December 1943. The *Bollettino* was the work largely of Curiel himself. From February 1944, to April 1945, Fronte groups were established in almost every important city in central and northern Italy. Each group had its own clandestine organ. In February 1944, the first issue of *La Giovane Italia* appeared in Florence; *Noi Giovani* was published in Turin beginning in May 1944; the first issues of *La Lotta dei Giovani* (Padua), *La Voce dei Giovani* (Genoa), *Per una vita migliore* (Domodossola), and *L'Avvenire d'Italia* (Novara) appeared in May, July, September, and October 1944 respectively. Other Fronte newspapers were founded in Udine, Biella, Cuneo, Savona, Pavia, Modena, Bologna, and Parma from October 1944 to March 1945.

In the fourth issue of the *Bollettino,* Curiel contrasted the fascist and anti-fascist interpretations of the Risorgimento.[15] The fascist schools, he said, had deliberately ignored or distorted those aspects of the Risorgimento that would have induced young students to rebel against tyranny and emphasized only those that could serve the purpose of wars of aggression. They had neglected to tell Italian youth that the Risorgimento was a struggle against oppression and for freedom and independence. It is true,

---

[13] *Direttive per l'organizzazione del Fronte della Gioventù,* p. 14. (ISRT) The first directing committee of the Fronte was composed of the following men: Curiel, Gillo Pontecorvo, and Quinto Bonazzola for the Communist Party; Renato Carli-Ballola and Gianni Baldi for the Socialist Party of Proletarian Unity; Dino Del Bo and Alberto Grandi for the Christian Democratic Party; Giorgio Peyronel and Carlo Sampietro for the Action Party; P. Cattaneo and S. Simonazzi for the Liberal Party; and Baroni and Sebregondi for the Catholic Communist Party.

[14] *Ibid.,* p. 16.

[15] Eugenio Curiel, "Il nostro Risorgimento," *Bollettino del Fronte della Gioventù* (undated), pp. 1–3. (CG)

Curiel continued, that the Risorgimento did not complete the task of building a democratic state and that unification had been achieved amidst the apathy or hostility of large sectors of the proletariat. Yet despite these insufficiencies, "there were episodes, writings, figures" of the Risorgimento that could still stimulate and guide the action of Resistance patriots. Curiel cited in particular Luigi Settembrini's *Le ricordanze,* Giuseppe Cesare Abba's *Noterelle di uno dei mille,* and the historical works of Carlo Cattaneo, Carlo Pisacane, Vincenzo Cuoco, and Pietro Colletta as texts "that ought not to be neglected by any young person who wants to know the country in which he lives and for which he wants to live and struggle." Probably underlying Curiel's emphasis of these men was their combining of scholarly endeavor inspired by the need to give Italians a knowledge of their own political and cultural traditions with concrete political action in support of Italy's struggle for national independence. Also worthy of note is the fact that several of the men cited, most notably Luigi Settembrini, had paid for their convictions with years of imprisonment and exile. The analogy to the lives of many anti-fascists was evident. Indeed, Curiel himself had been imprisoned on the island of Ventotene from 1939 to 1943.

The first issue of the Florentine *La Giovane Italia* of February 10, 1944, made reference to the link of continuity between the ideals of Giuseppe Mazzini and the commitment to freedom that animated the young people associated with the Fronte movement: "By taking the name of 'Young Italy' we do not intend to enter into competition with today's fascist press for the right to inherit the teachings of Giuseppe Mazzini. Instead we affirm our connection with Mazzini above and beyond any specific political programs, and only insofar as we continue, on the basis of his life and thought, a great tradition of clandestine struggle with insurrectional aims against all tyrannies and against all reactionary forms of government." [16]

La Giovane Italia adhered consistently to its initial policy of eschewing a single political orientation, despite the fact that its most active members— Vinicio Ceseri, Aldo Braibanti, Gianfranco Mattei, Gianfranco Sarfatti, Alessandro Susini, Romano Bilenchi—belonged to or identified themselves with the Communist and the Action Parties. Thus it was Mazzini's internationalism, his conception of a family of free nations bound together by a sense of interdependence and solidarity, rather than any of his specific political ideas, which inspired *La Giovane Italia.*

On June 4, 1944, Allied forces liberated Rome. This event was greeted with great enthusiasm by the editors of *La Giovane Italia,* not only be-

[16] "Presentazione," *La Giovane Italia,* February 10, 1944, p. 1. (ISRT)

cause of its military significance but also because of what it symbolized in relation to the communal tradition in Italian civilization. The newspaper indicated that many Risorgimento figures, particularly Carlo Cattaneo, had fought to maintain the tradition of communal and regional autonomy within the larger structure of a unified state. It was precisely this ideal of local autonomy within a framework of national unity that had been one of the characteristic aspects of the Risorgimento and that now, with the fall of "fascist and imperial Rome," was once again a realizable objective. *La Giovane Italia* noted that Italian civilization had begun to assume a unique character with the rise of the medieval communes and stated that "it is because we base our point of view on the most enduring convictions of our Risorgimento, the belief in communal liberty, in democracy, and in a confederation of free Italian cities, that we exult at the fall of fascist and imperial Rome." [17]

Fronte newspapers often discussed the meanings that can be attributed to the words nationalism and patriotism. Two articles in the Turinese *Combattere* of November 1944 were devoted to this problem. The newspaper first sought to clarify the concepts underlying the two terms. Nationalism, the newspaper said, at least in the fascist sense of the word, signified the irrational exaltation of one's own country and a corresponding contempt for the national integrity of other peoples. The fascist brand of nationalism was the expression on a collective level of the unrestrained individualism incarnated in the figure of Gabriele D'Annunzio, who had misunderstood and distorted the teachings of Nietzsche's superman. Italian youth had been led to believe that national glory and territorial expansion were sacred ideals. But behind these so-called ideals "there was nothing but the effort of big capital, the accomplice of fascism, to seize control of new markets." Patriotism, on the other hand, as conceived by the men of the Risorgimento and by Resistance leaders, signified a discriminating attachment and loyalty to the best values embodied in one's own country's national traditions and demanded that men fight for their country only when it was attacked. The only war sanctioned by patriotism, the newspaper concluded, was a defensive war. Fascism had betrayed the Risorgimento, for it had "plunged the Italy of Mazzini and Garibaldi, who were champions of freedom for all nations, into a war of extermination against all the peoples of Europe." [18]

Combattere was typical of Fronte newspapers in its somewhat sim-

17 "Roma liberata," *La Giovane Italia,* June 1944, p. 1. (ISRT)

18 "Nazionalismo-patriotismo," *Combattere,* November 25, 1944, p. 2 (MR); "Professori e studenti a Roma durante l'occupazione," *ibid.,* November 25, 1944, pp. 3, 4 (MR).

plistic use of Marxist formulas to explain all the crimes and abuses of the fascist regime and in its genuine commitment to international democratic solidarity. Also characteristic of the Fronte press was a certain tendency to make appeals to the anti-German rather than anti-nazi sentiments of its readers. This was the motive behind an issue of a Fronte newspaper in Udine, which in October 1944 printed an anti-German poem written by Giovanni Berchet in the early nineteenth century in circumstances only superficially analogous to those of the years 1943 to 1945.[19] Yet this sort of reverse racism, which at any rate only rarely manifested itself, was probably inevitable by reason of traditional Italian resentment against Germany dating back to World War I and still further to the struggle against Austrian domination in the nineteenth century.

The Fronte della Gioventù was not the only nor the first youth movement to find inspiration in the traditions of the Risorgimento. In August 1943, *L'Italia degli Studenti,* published by a group of university students in Rome affiliated with the Action Party, had paid a tribute to Benedetto Croce that was based on the Neapolitan philosopher's defense of a "liberal," enlightened Risorgimento,[20] and in November 1943, the action committee of another youth organization in Rome hailed the beginning of the partisan movement "as not unworthy of the glorious heritage of Curtatone and Montanara." [21]

In *Movimento,* the clandestine organ of a Florentine youth movement affiliated with the Liberal Party but which expressly declared itself to be a nonpolitical "union of young people of every social category who want to be free citizens in a free Italy in a free Europe," [22] one discovers a keen sense of connection with the Risorgimento. The newspaper's references to the patriot poets Giusti and Berchet, to the Garibaldian tradition of guerrilla warfare, to Mazzini's ideal of universal brotherhood, are indicative of the extent to which various aspects of the Risorgimento inspired many young people to join the Resistance. In fact, *Movimento's* program was built on "the same supreme principle of freedom that once inflamed the hearts of our heroes of the Risorgimento." [23] A quote

[19] *Periodico del Fronte della Gioventù,* October 15, 1944, p. 2. (MR)
[20] "Lettera aperta degli studenti italiani a Benedetto Croce," *L'Italia degli Studenti,* August 16, 1943, p. 3. (ISRT)
[21] "Universitari dell'Italia invasa!", *Studenti, Intellettuali, Insegnanti del C.L.N.,* November 17, 1943, p. 1. (INS) On May 29, 1848, a battle was fought in the region of Curtatone and Montanara between thirty-five thousand Austrian troops under the command of General Johann Radetzky and a force of five thousand Tuscan volunteers, many of whom were inexperienced students, who struggled heroically until overwhelmed by the Austrians.
[22] "Programma," *Movimento* (undated, but probably late June 1944), p. 1. (ISRT)
[23] *Ibid.*

from Mazzini's essay *Dei doveri dell'uomo,* "without freedom there can be no morality," became the newspaper's watchword. *Movimento* reminded any of its readers who might be skeptical about the military strategy being employed by the Resistance that the partisans fighting in the mountains against superior enemy forces were practicing a method of warfare that Garibaldi had used with success against the Austrians. In truth, *Movimento* said, the partisan bands were fighting with a "tenacity of purpose which even our fathers of the Risorgimento were never able to demonstrate." [24]

The "tenacity of purpose" that characterized the action of many partisan units can be legitimately attributed in some measure to the Risorgimento tradition. The conviction that military and political problems are inseparable formed an integral part of the struggle waged by the Italian partisan movement and often derived from the teachings of Risorgimento patriots, in particular Garibaldi and Mazzini. The principal reason why the Communist Party named their partisan units the "Garibaldi Assault Brigades" was because Garibaldi had led a volunteer "people's" army whose aim was to defeat the Austrians in order to give Italy freedom and independence. The partisan newspaper *Il Combattente* spoke of "the heroic Garibaldian tradition of the Risorgimento" as inspiring the Garibaldi brigade in Spain and later the formation of Garibaldi partisan units after September 1943,[25] and *Il Garibaldino Piemontese* explained that Italian partisans felt a close tie to Garibaldi because "he had fought not only for the freedom and independence of Italy but also for a more just social order." [26] In reality, Garibaldi was not as democratic and equalitarian as the partisans liked to imagine, and there can be no doubt that in 1943 his name was too enfolded in legend to permit a realistic evaluation of his aims and achievements. Yet the fact remains that Garibaldi was not a mere military adventurer, that he did fight in the name of transcendent political ideals.

Mazzini, too, had devoted his life to the cause of Italian unity and independence and had always subordinated the military aspects of the Risorgimento to the larger political and moral values that he believed Italy should embody in the family of nations. Mazzini's teachings formed the ideological basis of numerous partisan newspapers, particularly those written by men associated with the Action Party. The name *Partito d'Azione* was in fact chosen in order to indicate that its members were in

---

[24] "Il dovere dei giovani," *Movimento,* July, 1944, p. 2. (ISRT)
[25] *Il Combattente,* November 25, 1943, p. 1. (MR)
[26] "Nel nome glorioso di Garibaldi," *Il Garibaldino Piemontese,* December 1943, p. 1. (CG)

name and spirit directly linked with the Action Party which, under the guidance of Mazzini, had brought together during the Risorgimento the most militant and progressive forces of the new Italian democracy.

One of the most outstanding partisan leaders produced by the Italian Resistance Movement, namely, Tancredi "Duccio" Galimberti, was imbued with Mazzinian ideals.[27] Galimberti organized the actionist partisan units in the province of Cuneo in Piedmont, and his influence is reflected in *Il Partigiano, Il Partigiano Alpino, Il Pioniere, Giustizia e Libertà,* and other partisan newspapers. An issue of *Il Partigiano* in August 1944 asserted that the Risorgimento had been achieved in concord with and respect for the national aspirations of other peoples struggling for independence. Garibaldi, the newspaper said, had fought for the freedom of Uruguay, and Santore Santarosa had died fighting for Greek independence against the Turks. These men symbolized the universal idealism of the Risorgimento. But Mazzini was among all Risorgimento patriots the man most dedicated to universal as well as national freedom. "No one better than Mazzini expressed this national sentiment elevated to a universal vision of all countries with which the heroes of Italian independence were imbued." Although fascism had interrupted the Mazzinian tradition, the newspaper concluded, it was being reaffirmed by Italians who were fighting not only in Italy but in partisan units in France and Yugoslavia.[28]

In June 1944, the partisan newspaper *Il Pioniere* published an article honoring Paolo Braccini, one of eight members of the military command of the Liberation Committee in Turin who had been executed by a fascist firing squad on April 5 of that year. Braccini had conducted himself with exemplary courage and dignity both during his trial and in the last minutes before execution, a fact that prompted *Il Pioniere* to say that "in this man the Mazzinian concept of the unity of thought and action had been fully realized." [29] Passages, epigrams, and slogans written by Mazzini were constantly used by *Il Pioniere* to spur on the partisans. An issue dated July 7, 1944, was headed with a quotation from Mazzini's *Dei doveri dell'uomo*: "Without freedom no true society can exist, because there can be no association between free men and slaves, but only domination of some men by the others." The Mazzinian motto "We love

[27] The Mazzinian ideals of Galimberti are discussed by Mario Giovana, *Tempo d'Europa*, passim.

[28] "Il secondo Risorgimento," *Il Partigiano*, August 1, 1944, p. 1. (CDE)

[29] "Paolo Braccini," *Il Pioniere*, June 30, 1944, p. 4. (CG) For a full, well-documented account of Braccini's trial and execution, see Giampaolo Pansa, *Storia e documenti del primo Comitato Militare del C.L.N. regionale piemontese;* see also Braccini's letters in *Lettere di condannati a morte della Resistenza italiana*, pp. 88–91.

our fatherland because we love all fatherlands" was prominently featured on the first page of *Il Pioniere* and of many other partisan newspapers; and in April 1944, *Giustizia e Libertà* announced its intention to publish periodically passages from the works of Mazzini because "we are certain that the pure faith of the founder of Young Italy, which once inspired our struggle for freedom, will again be able to show us the path to take for our honor and national rebirth." [30]

Among the episodes of the Risorgimento most often cited by the communist press as an incentive to action was "the five days of Milan," a popular insurrection against the occupying Austrian Army that took place from March 18 to 22, 1848. This insurrection, which cost the lives of several hundred Italian revolutionaries, had resulted in the withdrawal of fifty thousand Austrian troops under the command of General Johann Radetzky. But only several months later Radetzky was able to make a triumphant return to Milan because of the inability of the various Italian states to resolve their internal differences and present a solid front to the invader. In March 1944, *La Nostra Lotta* recalled this episode as both an example to follow and as a warning to Resistance patriots against the "conspiracies" of the ruling class in Italy: "The five days of Milan are one of the most memorable examples of a victorious popular insurrection, and not only because its fighters were almost all men of the popular classes—its dead and wounded were in great part workers and artisans, professional men and students—but above all because the struggle was desired and undertaken by the people against the will of the privileged classes, it was tenaciously completed against all the tricks and deceits of the city's patrician rulers who, by compromising with the enemy, wanted to force the people to put down its arms. The lesson of 1848," concluded *La Nostra Lotta*, "must not be forgotten." [31] This appeal was echoed by many other communist newspapers. For example, *Insorgiamo!*, the clandestine organ of a group of Milanese industrial workers, published an article in November 1944 entitled "Radetzky Yesterday, Kesselring Today," in which "the five days of Milan" were referred to as "a tradition passed down from generation to generation, an indestructible memory. . . . Just as then, the liberation of our city and the future of our country depend on the unified action of all citizens, of all the people." [32] Exactly who "the people" was remained unexplained by *Insorgiamo!* This kind of generic appeal to "all the citizens, all the people" was frequently

[30] "Parole di un italiano," *Giustizia e Libertà*, April 1944, p. 4. (CG)

[31] "Le cinque giornate di Milano e la situazione odierna," *La Nostra Lotta*, March, 1944, pp. 1–5. (LC)

[32] "Ieri Radetzky, oggi Kesselring," *Insorgiamo!*, November 1, 1944, p. 1. (IG)

characteristic of communist clandestine newspapers and was motivated by the desire of the Italian Communist Party to place itself at the vanguard of a national resistance movement embracing people from all classes and segments of Italian society.

The communist political press often based its attacks against prominent Italian intellectual and cultural figures who had supported fascism by evoking the moral purity of Risorgimento patriots. On April 20, 1944, the Roman edition of *L'Unità* declared that "in the past twenty years Italian culture has frequently betrayed the duty and dignity embodied in the glorious tradition of the leaders of the Risorgimento." [33] But of more importance to the Italian communists was the necessity of convincing the Italian people that it could fight bravely for a cause in which it believed. Here again the Risorgimento provided the key to militant action. A Florentine edition of *L'Unità* dated December 15, 1943, contained a summary and brief excerpts of an article written by Palmiro Togliatti that exemplifies the practical use made of the Risorgimento tradition by the Italian communists. The article had appeared originally in the Moscow *Pravda* of November 12, 1943, when Togliatti was still living in the Soviet Union. Togliatti had attempted to explain the reasons for the sudden collapse of the Italian Army and the equally sudden resurgence of partisan brigades in Italy: "Why was the Italian Army beaten in the fascist war?" Togliatti asked. "Because the Italian people did not want to fight for an unjust cause and suffered from its subservience to nazism. Now that it is a question of struggling against nazi-fascism, the Italian nation is returning to its best traditions, those which in the Risorgimento call to mind the name of Garibaldi; already two Italian divisions fighting in Yugoslavia have passed over to the partisans, one of them taking the name of Garibaldi." [34] The military exploits of Garibaldi, who as leader of a volunteer citizen army had made such a decisive contribution to the cause of Italian independence, were constantly cited by *L'Unità* as examples to follow in the partisan war against fascism.

The Christian democrats' *Il Popolo*, on the other hand, emphasized the patrimony of spiritual values, the tradition of self-abnegation and sacrifice, bequeathed by the Risorgimento to the Resistance. *Il Popolo* also stressed in particular its conviction that the Catholic masses of workers and farmers had first become a part of the main stream of Italian national life as a result of the Risorgimento and that it was now up to the Resistance to widen still further the popular base of Italian democracy.

[33] "L'esecuzione del traditore Giovanni Gentile," *L'Unità*, April 20, 1944, p. 1. (IG)

[34] "Un importante articolo di Ercoli," *L'Unità*, December 15, 1943, p. 1. (ISRT)

An important aspect of the Christian Democratic Party's indebtedness to the Risorgimento is illustrated in an undated issue of the newspaper *L'Uomo,* published by a group of Catholic intellectuals in Rome. The editors of *L'Uomo* accused the "imperialists" in fascist Italy and nazi Germany of failing to understand "the vaster realm of ideals, of collaboration and purposes that is embodied in the European consciousness of all peoples." This consciousness of belonging to a family of interdependent European nations, which "the Napoleonic meteor had dangerously compromised and betrayed," had been reaffirmed in the period that began with the revolutionary movements of 1848. Its greatest champion had been Giuseppe Mazzini: "Did not Giuseppe Mazzini," the newspaper asked rhetorically, "realize that the Young Italy movement would immediately lose its appeal and substance unless it became a voice, a means of expression, an integral part of that Young Europe that the Italians themselves were invited to join?" [35] *Il Popolo,* too, made frequent references to the necessity of countering imperialist propaganda with the teachings of Mazzini, as did *La Punta* and other Catholic newspapers.

One of the striking features of the socialist newspaper *Avanti!* is its many references to the Resistance as Italy's "second Risorgimento" and to the partisans as "patriots of the second Risorgimento." An editorial published in *Avanti!* on July 1, 1944, for example, blamed the Italian people for having allowed fascism to wrench from its grasp the freedoms of speech, press, and assembly that had been won by the Risorgimento and predicted that the Resistance, "this second, this true Risorgimento," would eventually create a new socialist democracy in Italy.[36]

Unlike the Socialist Party, the Liberal Party could not re-establish ties with an organized, cohesive political movement that antedated the fascist era. The liberals could, however, make claim to a broadly liberal tradition in Italian political history that began in the latter part of the eighteenth century in the form of various individual initiatives such as that of Pietro Verri's *Il Caffè* in Milan, was continued in the mid-nineteenth century by such eminent statesmen as Camillo Cavour and Bettino Ricasoli, and was further developed after World War I by Luigi Einaudi, Benedetto Croce, Luigi Albertini, and others.

In 1764, Pietro Verri, a Milanese political economist who had been profoundly influenced by eighteenth-century French rationalism and English empiricism, founded the newspaper *Il Caffè,* with which he waged courageous campaigns for free trade, democratically oriented tax reforms, and the abolition of torture from the penal code and sought to

[35] "Europei nella coscienza," *L'Uomo* (undated), p. 3. (LC)
[36] "Nuovo Risorgimento," *Avanti!,* July 1, 1944, p. 2. (ISRT)

convince Italians that the first step toward national unity was to acquire a civic and moral education. The newspaper appeared for only two years but left a permanent mark on the political consciousness of the intellectual and liberal élite in northern Italy.

In November 1944, Giulio Grasselli, Paolo Serini, and several other liberal intellectuals in Cremona founded a clandestine newspaper that they named *Il Caffè* in tribute to their illustrious predecessor. The first editorial explained that the editors of *Il Caffè* were weary of the abstractions and rhetoric that had characterized both fascism and certain segments of anti-fascism and stated their intention to continue the work of Verri, who had led the revolt against rhetoric and promoted the concrete, scientific study of Italian economic and political problems: "The re-evocation of the title of the newspaper published in Milan from 1764 to 1766," said the editors of *Il Caffè*, "is not a complacent act on the part of initiates or erudite scholars, but rather the deliberate vindication of the liberal tradition of northern Italy. *Il Risorgimento* recalls the title of Cavour's newspaper; *Il Caffè* is linked with the newspaper published by Verri. But there is another reason that has induced us to choose the title *Il Caffè*: the ideally Lombard spirit of practical initiative that animates us. The lesson of the liberals to which we look for inspiration is that study of political and social problems must always be rooted in concrete historical experience." [37] In this same issue of November 1944, Filippo Jacini praised Cavour, Ricasoli, Spaventa, and other nineteenth-century conservative Italian liberals for their ability to accomplish practical and constructive tasks and for their refusal "to confuse liberty with license, legality with inertia, impartiality with agnosticism, a vigilant national consciousness with expansionistic megalomania." [38]

The defense of a liberal, enlightened, constructive Risorgimento was also characteristic of the Liberal Party's principal organ *Risorgimento Liberale*. In fact, the first issue of the newspaper published during the interim forty-five days between July 25 and September 8, 1943, made a special point of distinguishing the main current of nineteenth-century Italian political experience from that of Germany. "The Risorgimento in Italy," the newspaper claimed, "signified a return to the center of European life, a reestablishment of close ties with the ideals and dominant principles in accordance with which the free states of the West had been formed. A Cavour, not a Bismarck, was the political and diplomatic genius of the Italy of that era. And Mazzini spoke of Young Italy as presupposing

---

[37] "Le nostre ragioni," *Il Caffè*, November 1944, p. 1. (INS)

[38] Filippo Jacini, "Appunti circa l'indirizzo del nuovo Partito Liberale," *Il Caffè*, November 1944. The article is reprinted in Filippo Jacini, *Carattere*, p. 76.

and as looking forward to a Young Europe." The present war between liberalism and totalitarianism, the newspaper concluded, was in reality a war between the values of Cavour and those of Bismarck.[39]

The Action Party, despite its revolutionary stance and intransigent opposition to almost all elements of the pre-fascist state, was nonetheless more imbued with Risorgimento idealism than any of the other parties. For the actionists, the Risorgimento had produced Italians of great moral stature, and this achievement alone deserved to be honored by anti-fascists. In the first clandestine issue of *L'Italia Libera* of January 1943, the party had made the following declaration: "Italians! In all the centers of Italy the Action Party has been established; in repudiating every form of factionalism and sectarianism our party once again takes hold of the flag of the Risorgimento, which the Fascist autocracy has torn and defiled." [40]

Although the Action Party attracted people from many diverse political backgrounds, it was composed largely of men and women who identified themselves with a series of liberal and socialdemocratic movements of the 1920's and 1930's led by such renowned anti-fascists as Piero Gobetti, Ernesto Rossi, Gaetano Salvemini, Carlo Rosselli, and Piero Cala-mandrei. All of these men had meditated deeply on the contribution made by the Risorgimento to the ideals of freedom and justice.

The strong sense of indebtedness to the Risorgimento that animated the actionists—many of whom had personal ties of affection and esteem with the generation of anti-fascist intellectuals mentioned above—emerges in an article published in one of the last clandestine issues of the Florentine *La Libertà*. The issue is not dated, but doubtless it was published on August 11 or 12, 1944, since it bears the subheading "special issue for the insurrection" and is dedicated to "our comrades in northern Italy" who were about to enter the decisive phase of the Resistance struggle. On August 11, Allied troops entered Florence:

At the same time that our contacts with our comrades of southern and central Italy are reopened, those with our comrades of the North are closed: a fatal, dramatic turning point of the war, which cuts the nation into two parts, physically isolated from each other, but spiritually united by a single faith. Nobody can say how long this separation will last: but we feel its bitterness burn within us, because in the North of Italy we see that same industriousness, that spirit of initiative, that calm and serene faith, that organic connection between thought and action that made our Risorgimento a great

[39] *Risorgimento Liberale,* August 18, 1943, p. 1. (CG)
[40] *L'Italia Libera,* January 1943, p. 1. (ISRT)

event and that today still constitute the most enduring bases for the continuity and profundity of every political movement.[41]

Another example of the Action Party's indebtedness to the Risorgimento appears in a clandestine manifesto circulated in Trieste in June 1944. This manifesto, written by Giani Stuparich and Ercole Miani, deals with the nationalistic rivalry between Slavs and Italians in Venezia Giulia and is entitled "Garibaldi." "The life of Garibaldi," wrote Stuparich and Miani, "as opposed to that of all corrupt militarists, demonstrates that the salvation of the Italian people lies in the tradition of freedom, in a repudiation of all forms of nationalistic egotism and imperialistic hystericism. A people who could produce a Garibaldi cannot base its life on bayonets and the abuses of a police state." [42] Here again the figure of Garibaldi, though barely visible behind the legendary aura that surrounded him, was looked to by Resistance leaders as the very incarnation of Italy's democratic aspirations.

Among the politically independent anti-fascist movements that conceived of the Resistance as a continuation of the Risorgimento tradition, the most important was the Italian segment of the European Federalist Movement.

Immediately after the outbreak of World War II, a small group of anti-fascist intellectuals imprisoned on the island of Ventotene succeeded in reaching agreement about the need for a federation of European states that would replace the existing structure of sovereign and mutually hostile nations. Altiero Spinelli and Ernesto Rossi were the principal promoters of federalism at Ventotene and were responsible for two federalist manifestoes that were illegally circulated in Italy in June and August 1941. In August 1943, a few weeks after the fall of Mussolini, Spinelli, Rossi, and several of their colleagues who had been amnestied by the Badoglio government went to Berne, Switzerland, to resume their work for the Federalist Movement. On August 29, 1943, Spinelli and Rossi, in conjunction with Luigi Einaudi, reissued the second manifesto of August 1941, in the hope of enlisting the support of the newly resurrected anti-fascist parties in Italy. In little more than a year the Federalist Movement did in fact succeed in receiving the official endorsement of the five major parties, as well as of numerous minor parties and organizations that functioned outside the Committees of National Liberation.

---

[41] "Ai compagni dell'Italia Settentrionale," *La Libertà,* August 1944, p. 1. (ISRT)

[42] The manifesto written by Stuparich and Miani is cited textually by Franco Ventura, "La stampa clandestina a Trieste dal 1943 al 1945," *Il Movimento di Liberazione in Italia,* January-March 1957, p. 15.

Federalism, as a solution for the evils of the centralized, totalitarian state created by fascism, formed an integral part of the Action Party's platform and was also accepted with more or less enthusiasm by the other parties in the anti-fascist coalition. Hence it was not too difficult for them to extend the federalist principle to all of Europe and, indeed, to the entire world, although in the minds of many anti-fascist leaders the idea remained more of a utopian dream than an immediately realizable objective.

An unbroken tradition of federalist thought existed in Italy from Mazzini, Cattaneo, and Ferrari in the nineteenth century to the Italian members of the European Federalist Movement during World War II. This continuity of federalist thought was referred to in a report issued in March 1945 by the newspaper *L'Idea Federalista,* the clandestine organ in northern Italy of the European Federalist Association, which had held its first meeting in Florence on January 27, 1945. In a message directed to the Committees of National Liberation and to the partisans of northern Italy, the newspaper made the following declaration:

Just as in France seven Resistance Movements have endorsed the program of supranational unity, so in the same way—and for greater reason—we have the duty of supporting European federation in Italy. Therefore we have established the European Federalist Association, which has assumed the task of unifying all of the progressive forces of the nation, whose strength has been tested in the struggle against the oppressor, in order to reaffirm that character of universal humanity and brotherhood that distinguishes this war from all others. The unanimity of consensus obtained by the E.F.A. is proven by the support given to it by all the Italian political parties, and by a great number of independent groups, each of which is officially represented on the Association's directing committee. We think that this consensus demonstrates that now more than ever before the time is ripe for the effective application of the federalist program, which from Mazzini and Cattaneo to Eugenio Colorni has always had its strongest defenders in Italy.[43]

Colorni, in addition to editing the Socialist *Avanti!* in Rome, had before his death in May 1944 worked assiduously for the federalist cause and had exerted a powerful influence on the thinking of those Italian socialist leaders whose conception of socialism was still closely tied to the original internationalism of the party's founders in the 1890's.

Almost all of the anti-fascist parties repudiated the Monarchy and were committed in principle to a republican form of government. (Because of their uncertainty as to the actual sentiments of the masses of

[43] "Ai C.L.N. e ai Partigiani dell'Italia del Nord," *L'Idea Federalista,* March 1945, p. 1. (LC)

Italians with regard to King Victor Emmanuel III, many of the parties feared a plebiscite on the issue of the monarchy and would have preferred to have a constituent assembly proclaim the republic. Nevertheless, despite their intense commitment to republicanism, the parties comprising the Committees of National Liberation finally agreed reluctantly to settle the institutional question by means of a national plebiscite after the war.) But whereas republicanism was only one aspect of the programs advanced by other parties, it represented the raison d'être of the Italian Republican Party and provided the ideological rationale behind the party's support of the Federalist Movement. The idea that republicanism and federalism were inseparable was at the basis of the party's letter of endorsement, which was printed in the federalist newspaper *L'Unità Europea* in January 1945. After making reference to Carlo Cattaneo, Giuseppe Ferrari, Giovanni Bovio, and "other leaders of the Italian Republican school who—like Mazzini—gave concrete expression to their aspirations in the formula: The United States of Europe" and after honoring Garibaldi, "in whose name for many generations the concept of European solidarity was a tangible reality," the Republican Party affirmed its support of the Federalist Movement in taking note "of the urgent need for a solution of the European problem in a federative sense, in order to avoid the periodic outbreak of wars that destroy human lives and wealth, and corrupt the consciences of men." [44] This statement, which was written in October 1944, represents one of the most significant examples of the link connecting the Risorgimento with the Resistance and is illustrative of the ideological contribution made to the Resistance by minor political parties not officially associated with the Committees of National Liberation.

The Risorgimento was not, of course, the only historical point of reference to which Resistance leaders looked for moral and political inspiration. *Fratelli d'Italia, Risorgimento Liberale, Movimento,* and many other clandestine newspapers often cited passages from Dante's *Divine Comedy* to remind their readers of the necessity to maintain dignity and courage in misfortune. Virgil's explanation to Cato concerning the purpose of Dante's voyage—"he goes to win his freedom;/ and how dear that is the man who gives his life for it best knows"—and Ulysses' exhortation to his men, beginning "You were not born to live like brutes,/ but to press on toward manhood and recognition!" were the passages most often quoted as guides to action. The Florentine socialists hailed the liberation of Florence and called for the intensification of

---

[44] "Adesioni repubblicane e mazziniane," *L'Unità Europea,* January-February 1945, p. 2. (LC)

partisan action by evoking the memory of "the last heroic defense of the Florentine Republic" in 1530.[45] Episodes in French history from the Bastille to the revolutionary Paris Commune of 1871 were recalled by the partisan newspaper *Scarpe Rotte* and by *L'Azione Comunista* as precedents for popular uprisings against the bastions of autocracy.[46] A Milanese edition of *Avanti!* in September 1944 refuted the charge that the doctrine of socialism had no native roots in Italy by claiming that there were prefigurations of Italian socialism in the thought of Saint Francis of Assisi, Tommaso Campanella, and Vincenzo Russo and by referring to the original contribution made by Italian Marxist and democratic socialists of the post-Risorgimento period, such as Antonio Labriola and Filippo Turati.[47] *La Voce d'Italia,* the organ of the Genoese Liberation Committee, and *Risorgimento Liberale* spoke of the commitment to democracy and national independence that animated the Italian Army in the battles of the Piave and Vittorio Veneto during World War I.[48] *La Compagna,* published by a group of Turinese women socialists, quoted epigrams of Thomas Paine—"My country is the world, and my religion is to do good"—and of Voltaire—"I disapprove of what you say, but I will defend to the death your right to say it"—[49] and *L'Opinione* cited a passage from Montesquieu's *Reflections and Thoughts,* in which the French philosopher spoke of the indestructible bond linking the actions of each individual with the destiny and welfare of all humanity.[50]

None of the historical figures and episodes mentioned above, however, was felt with the same intensity as was the Risorgimento, simply because Italians are no different from other peoples in their tendency to find the deepest sources of political inspiration in their own collective struggles for national freedom and independence. The fascist regime had made a concerted attempt to present itself as the legitimate heir to the Risorgimento tradition. In response to this challenge, the clandestine press assumed the responsibility of reevaluating the Italian people's struggle for freedom in the nineteenth century within a new framework of democratic values.

This return to the Risorgimento, this commitment to the traditions and

45 "Liberazione," *Avanti!*, August 11, 1944, p. 1. (ISRT)

46 "Alons [*sic*] Enfants de la Patrie," *Scarpe Rotte,* July 15, 1944, p. 2 (CG); "Il comune di Parigi," *L'Azione Comunista,* April 4, 1944, pp. 1, 2 (ISRT).

47 "Tradizione nostra," *Avanti!*, September 4, 1944, p. 3. (INS)

48 "Serriamo le fila," *La Voce d'Italia,* November 21, 1943, p. 1 (LC); "Orientamenti programmatici del P.L.I." *Risorgimento Liberale,* April 1944, p. 1 (INS).

49 *La Compagna,* September 1, 1944, p. 1. (INS)

50 *L'Opinione,* September 13, 1944, p. 1. (INS)

values of a bygone era has been severely condemned in recent years by extreme left-wing groups, who accuse the Resistance of *passatismo,* of a slavish adoration of the past that prevented the anti-fascist struggle from culminating in a proletarian revolution in Italy. These extreme left-wing groups, whose principal organ is the magazine *Classe Operaia,* are correct as far as they go, since there can be no doubt that all parties in the anti-fascist coalition, including the Communist Party, did not conceive of the Resistance as an instrument with which to create a state entirely dominated by the working class. They are right also in claiming that *the restoration* of liberal institutions and constitutional government, which were first established in a united Italy as a result of the Risorgimento, was of primary concern to the Italian Resistance as a whole. What *Classe Operaia* fails to realize is that historical factors exert a powerful influence on even the most revolutionary movements. Before the advent of fascism, Italy had been a nation whose political life, with all its admitted insufficiencies, was based on some of the best and most viable aspects of bourgeois civilization. Italy is also an overwhelmingly Catholic country in which millions of people are emotionally, if not always intellectually, committed to the teachings, traditions, and rituals of the Church. The historical reality of Italian liberalism and Catholicism made it imperative for Resistance leaders *who wanted to enlist mass support* to link the present struggle with the past, to find a point of ideological equilibrium between traditional values and revolutionary aspirations. Viewed from this perspective, it becomes clear that the return to the Risorgimento fulfilled a mediating function between the forces of conservatism and progress which, in my opinion, was indispensable to the at least partial success of the Italian Resistance Movement.

It cannot be denied that there were many superfluous, merely rhetorical elements in the effort of Resistance leaders to generate enthusiasm for their cause by linking the anti-fascist struggle with the Risorgimento and other episodes in Italy's past. Yet had it not been for this effort, it is unlikely that the necessary and fruitful debate carried on by the anti-fascist parties concerning the origins of fascism and the significance of the Resistance in Italian history would have taken place. The return to the Risorgimento compelled anti-fascist intellectuals to extend their discussion beyond the period of unification and to reexamine the strengths and especially the weaknesses of the unified Italian State that existed prior to the advent of fascism. It also helped them to see the Resistance as part of a continuous historical process with links in the past and meaning for the future, rather than as a sudden and self-contained phenomenon.

The followers of *Classe Operaia* attribute what they regard as the total failure of the Resistance to the fact that, in accordance with a characteristically Italian tradition, it set brother against brother rather than son against father. It was a fratricidal war, they assert, whereas the true purpose of the Resistance should have been patricide. The weak point in this admittedly seductive argument is that patricide is often committed by persons who project onto the father all of the faults, guilt, and deficiencies from which they themselves suffer. Expressed in more general terms, the radical denial of all traditional values, the projection of revolutionary programs completely divorced from the past, provides a convenient way of avoiding the painful task of self-analysis. To the lasting credit of many Italians engaged in the anti-fascist struggle, this task was not only not avoided but was also willingly accepted as part of the price for freedom.

CHAPTER SEVEN

THE ANATOMY OF FASCISM

The fascist seizure of power in Italy has been variously explained by historians, political scientists, economists, sociologists, and psychologists. Some have regarded it as one of several forms of modern totalitarianism whose mass appeal must be attributed to the crisis of liberal ideology following World War I; some as the product of certain deficiencies in the Italian character; some as a conspiratorial reaction on the part of Italy's ruling class to the rise of militant, messianic socialism in the Italian working class; some as a collective neurosis characterized by a need to escape from the burdens of individual freedom through reliance on the commands of an all-powerful father figure; and some as the natural outcome of preceding patterns of Italy's historical development, which led inevitably to the formation of a centralized, dictatorial state. (In footnotes to this chapter certain of the findings and conclusions of representative scholars belonging to one or the other schools of thought mentioned above are cited.) Considering their direct personal involvement in the phenomenon with which they were dealing and the inaccessibility of basic sources of historical information, the ideologists of the Resistance made some remarkably accurate analyses of the roots of Italian fascism, analyses that have been borne out by scholarly studies of fascism undertaken during the past thirty years. These have refined and modified but not substantially invalidated many of the opinions expressed in the clandestine press.

The most conspicuous lacunae in the analyses provided by the clandestine press lie, as one might expect, in the areas of psychology and sociology, since neither of these two disciplines were developed in Italy in an organized fashion during the fascist period and since both require a type of research methodology and documentation that for obvious practical reasons propaganda warfare does not admit. Yet even the psychological aspects of the fascist phenomenon discussed in such books as Erich Fromm's *Escape from Freedom* (1941) and Eric Hoffer's *The True Believer* (1951) are occasionally explored in the underground press, while the findings of modern sociology with regard to the type of political attitudes and social conditions that may easily give rise to totalitarian movements often confirm the judgments of Resistance leaders during the years 1943 to 1945.

I
The Communist Views: Theory and Realpolitik

The position taken during the Resistance by the Italian Communist Party with respect to the problem of the roots of fascism in Italy did not suddenly crystallize in 1943. In fact, most of its essential elements had been stated as early as January 1926, when the third party congress of the Italian communists took place in Lyons, France. In addition, as indicated in chapters II and III, Antonio Gramsci in *L'Ordine Nuovo* and Palmiro Togliatti in *Lo Stato Operaio* had attempted during the mid-1920's to formulate an interpretation of the fascist phenomenon based on the doctrines of Marx and Lenin.

The principal result of the party's deliberations in 1926 was a document known as the *Lyons Theses*, the central portion of which dealt with "the class struggle and fascism." This document stated that the aim of the Italian ruling class after unification was to hold the masses of workers and farmers in subjection in order to prevent the formation of a proletarian state. But the complete realization of this aim had been frustrated by dissension between two factions of the ruling class. One faction, headed by the magnates of heavy industry, large agrarian landowners, and banking interests, was essentially authoritarian and anti-democratic; the other, composed of smaller industrial and commercial organizations with closer ties to the people, had tentatively supported the liberal, constitutional regime established in Italy in the 1860's. After World War I, the contradictions inherent in the bourgeois liberal state became apparent. Threatened by a militant working class and the specter of bolshevism, the formerly opposed factions of the ruling class closed ranks and saw that their only hope for salvation lay in the creation of a centralized, authoritarian regime. The fascist movement, founded in 1919, provided the ruling class with the necessary men and methods with which to carry through its counterrevolutionary schemes. "Fascism," the communist document concluded, "as a movement of armed reaction whose purpose is to disunite and disorganize the working class in order to immobilize it, forms part of the traditional policy of the Italian ruling classes, and of the struggle of capitalism against the working class." [1]

Theses four, five, and six dealt with the economic structure of Italian

---

[1] *Il fascismo,* edited by Costanzo Casucci, pp. 269, 270.

society. Capitalism, the communist document asserted, was the predominant element of Italian society. But industrialism, the essential feature of capitalism, was weak in Italy. Furthermore, its possibilities for development were limited, and it could not absorb the activities of the majority of the Italian population. Opposed to industrialism was an agriculture that continued to present itself as the basis of the nation's economy. Between the industrial and agrarian sectors there was a persistently restless and disoriented petty bourgeoisie that at times tended to veer to the left, at other times to cling desperately to rightist political doctrines. The intrinsic weakness of Italian capitalism forced the industrial class to adopt certain expedients to guarantee its control over the entire economy. These expedients rested chiefly on a system of economic compromises and agreements between the industrialists and the most powerful agrarian class—the large landowners. The social, political, and economic crises of the years following World War I had, however, indicated to the industrial class that these expedients were no longer adequate. Consequently, "For the tactic of agreements and compromises fascism substitutes the proposal to achieve an organic unity of all the forces of the bourgeoisie in a single political organism under the control of a single central apparatus that would direct together the party, the government, and the state. This proposal corresponds to the will to resist to the utmost every revolutionary assault, which allows fascism to gather the support of the most resolutely reactionary parts of the industrial and agrarian bourgeoisie." [2]

During the early phases of the Resistance, the Italian Communist Party reasserted the position it had taken in the *Lyons Theses* of 1926, insisting that, far from representing a radical break with the pre-fascist liberal state in Italy, fascism was nothing but the logical outgrowth of a policy that had traditionally characterized the role of the Italian ruling class. In accordance with Marxist theory, the Italian communists conceived of class struggle as the primary motive force in human history. Fascism had been merely an instrument, a means of seizing and maintaining political power for the purpose of protecting specific class interests. Whereas the class struggle had not as yet reached the stage of direct armed conflict in some capitalist countries, thereby permitting the continued functioning of democratic institutions in the United States, Great Britain, France, and elsewhere; in Italy this struggle manifested itself

[2] The *Lyons Theses* have been reprinted almost in their entirety in *L'antifascismo italiano,* edited by Paolo Alatri, vol. I, pp. 415–46. The quote cited above appears on p. 416. For a discussion of the *Lyons Theses,* see John Cammett, *Antonio Gramsci and the Origins of Italian Communism,* pp. 170–76. It should be noted that certain features of the analysis of fascism in the *Lyons Theses* are confirmed by Barrington Moore, Jr. in his brilliant study *Social Origins of Dictatorship and Democracy.*

in its most violent form after World War I and culminated in the temporary victory of reaction.

According to the Italian Communist Party in 1943, a proof of the merely instrumental character of fascism lay in the general tendency of Italian capitalists to dissociate themselves from Mussolini's regime as soon as it became clear that fascism would be defeated in the war against the Western democracies and the Soviet Union. In November 1943, the Communist Party's theoretical organ *La Nostra Lotta* declared that, until the spring of 1942, the forces of Italian capitalism and imperialism had remained closely tied to fascism and Hitlerism. But when the German Army began to suffer its first defeats and when the Allies threatened invasion of the Italian mainland, these reactionary elements had chosen to save capitalism by abandoning fascism and by seeking to gain the good will of the British and American governments. This decision had led to the downfall of Mussolini and to the formation in July 1943 of the Badoglio regime, which was "the regime of Italian finance capital and of all the corrupt forces of the country, of the army officers and the Monarchy, of the large agrarian landowners and the high bureaucracy, in a word of the same conservative and reactionary Italy that had given life and substance to fascism." [3]

Until early April 1944, when Palmiro Togliatti returned to Italy from the Soviet Union and persuaded the central committee of the Italian Communist Party to modify its intransigent anticapitalism, the point of view expressed in *La Nostra Lotta* formed the basis of the position taken by all the major organs of the communist press. For example, in October 1943, *L'Unità* spoke out vehemently against the irremediable corruption and failure of the capitalist ruling class in Italy, which had created and supported fascism: "We are witnessing in Italy," said *L'Unità,* "the multiform phenomenon of an organism in the process of decomposition. And what is decomposing is the ruling class, whose putrefaction gives off pestilential miasmas that poison the air we breathe." [4] And two months later the communist newspaper appealed to the workers "to fight for their class interests against the Germans, against the fascists, against the profiteering bosses." [5]

After April 1944, as a consequence of Togliatti's initiative and of the Soviet Union's recognition of the Badoglio regime, the Italian communists ceased their attacks on the ruling capitalist class as a whole and instead began to distinguish between enlightened and reactionary capital-

[3] "La natura classista del fascismo," *La Nostra Lotta,* November 1943, p. 4. (LC)
[4] "Il maresciallo traditore," *L'Unità,* October 14, 1943, p. 1. (ISRT)
[5] "Il PCI chiama i lavoratori alla lotta," *L'Unità,* December 15, 1943, p. 1. (ISRT)

ists in a fashion reminiscent of their attitude during the period of the Popular Front from 1935 to 1939. In addition they began to examine some of the non-economic roots of fascism. The communist press gave some prefunctory attention to certain peculiarly Italian sociological phenomena in explaining the rise of fascism, such as the traditional dissension within the working class movement between Catholics and communists that had allowed the fascists to exploit the fears of both for their own ends. It also made occasional reference to the grave deficiencies of many Italian intellectual leaders, who had not only failed to uphold the values of a free culture but had actively contributed to the creating of a fascist ideology and to the consequent seduction of large segments of Italy's semi-educated lower and middle classes. But notwithstanding their somewhat more moderate and sophisticated analyses during the latter phases of the Resistance, the Italian Communists never abandoned their interpretation of fascism based on the assumption that fascism could be adequately explained only in terms of the material conditions and class relationships which existed in Italy after World War I.[6]

[6] Three comprehensive works that exemplify Marxist-oriented interpretations of fascism are Angelo Tasca's *Nascita e avvento del fascismo* (1937), Daniel Guérin's *Fascism and Big Business* (1939), and Paolo Alatri's *Le origini del fascismo* (1963). These historians are however far more subtle and sophisticated in their application of Marxist ideas to the fascist phenomenon than were the writers of the communist press during the Resistance. They share a common assumption, namely, that the seeds of fascism are latent in every capitalist society, but also recognize that "objective material factors" are not the only determinants of human action, that it is necessary to explain, in the words of Guérin, "how these factors are reflected in the consciousness of men."

Tasca attributes the success of the fascist movement in large measure to the fact that many of Italy's liberal leaders rallied behind Mussolini's campaign against "the betrayal of Versailles." He maintains that "if the Italian ruling class had not yielded to the blackmail of Mussolini and the Nationalists," it might have succeeded in thwarting the fascists' march to power (p. 49). Tasca also places emphasis on the conspiratorial activity of Italy's large agrarian landowners, who in August 1920 banded together to form the General Confederation of Agriculture for the purpose of destroying the entire network of socialist cooperatives that Italian agricultural workers had created after World War I. But he does not attribute fascism's success only to a capitalist conspiracy. For example, he insists in very un-Marxist fashion that Mussolini's initial campaign "against the state" appealed to the "latent anarchy" of the Italian people. He also dwells at length on Italy's national inferiority complex, which was so cleverly exploited by Mussolini in his championing of the Italian people's right to create an empire equal to that of Britain and France. Tasca's work is remarkably thorough and perceptive, and helps us to see in clearer perspective the limitations of any single-cause analysis of the fascist phenomenon such as that advanced by the Italian communists during the period of the Resistance.

Guérin's study is useful in terms of the documented evidence it supplies to prove the indispensable financial support fascism received from the principal Italian banks, from the magnates of heavy industry and from their counterparts in agriculture. The assumption on which Guérin operates is simply that "the state has always been the

II
The Actionist View: Fascism as Political and Social Corruption

Unlike the communists, the ideologists of the Action Party avoided attributing the rise and triumph of fascism only to large, impersonal forces such as the capitalist system, the class struggle, and "material conditions." Without ignoring the role played by the magnates of heavy industry in financing the fascist movement and although fully aware of the economic motives underlying the fascists' use of terrorist anti-labor squads, they recognized that fascism—in its Mussolinian form, that is—was after all rooted in the concrete historical experiences and prevalent psychological characteristics of the Italian people. They were, in short, unwilling to content themselves with ready-made formulas. The actionists' greater sophistication and sensitivity to the complexity of historical problems were the products in large measure of the intellectual inheritance bequeathed to the party by Piero Gobetti, Gaetano Salvemini, Carlo Rosselli, and Silvio Trentin, all of whom had considered the fascist phenomenon on many levels of interpretation.

In *The Action Party and Socialism*,[7] one of many similar clandestine booklets issued by the Action Party during the period of the Resistance, Carlo Bandi raised an important question that the communists were either unable or unwilling to consider. Bandi noted that if fascism was a dogmatic religion of power that rested on dictatorial control of the nation's

---

instrument by which one social class rules over other social classes" (p. 3). He shows that despite the change in Italy's political system that took place as a result of the fascist seizure of power, no corresponding change occurred in the nation's social and economic order. Therefore, Guérin concludes, the political transformation obviously served the interests of the pre-fascist ruling class. He devotes considerable attention to showing how fascism used mysticism and social demagogy to forge unity among the Italian people, but he treats these psychological aspects of the fascist phenomenon as merely outgrowths of a more primary economic reality.

Alatri's work is helpful for the light it sheds on various Italian political and cultural movements in the early twentieth century that foreshadowed aspects of fascism. He points out that the fascists' exaltation of imperial Rome had been anticipated by the nationalist Enrico Corradini in the newspaper *L'Idea Nazionale* in 1911; that Corradini's "vacuous and rhetorical" brand of nationalism, Filippo Marinetti's futurist movement, and the political writings of Giovanni Papini on the eve of World War I had all been based on a glorification of war and violence, which became typical features of fascist ideology. But Alatri also touches on another phase of the fascist phenomenon with which the underground press of all parties except the communist was concerned, namely, "the conformist, vulgarly Machiavellian education of many Italians, which had the chance to develop fully under fascism" (p. 31). Thus Alatri concedes that fascism owed its success to many factors, including certain character deficiencies prevalent among Italians.

[7] Carlo Bandi, *Partito d'Azione e socialismo*, December 1943. (LC)

political life, the question remained as to why this religion and this particular form of dictatorship had had such extensive mass support in Italy for close to twenty years. In answer, Bandi first made an unflattering appraisal of the Italian people's level of political consciousness. Fascism had appealed to large segments of the Italian population because it played on their susceptibility to a type of demagogic, high-sounding rhetoric that a more politically mature people would have immediately rejected. This susceptibility to demagoguery derived in turn from the feeling of insignificance and powerlessness that characterized the state of mind of many Italians, who responded eagerly to the ideal of an all-powerful state that promised to resolve all their problems. In the second place, fascism reflected in Italy the same desire for social and economic justice felt by peoples throughout the world after World War I, when political freedom was no longer regarded as the only criterion for a democratic society. This was a legitimate desire, which the fascist movement exploited for opportunistic motives. The crucial problem lay in the fact that the legitimate social and economic aspirations of the Italian people had not been satisfied by the various liberal regimes that had held power in Italy since unification, and a vacuum was thereby created that was easily filled by fascism. Thus Bandi concluded that fascism had gained power because of the political immaturity of the Italian masses and the ineptitude of the liberals who had guided the Italian nation from 1870 through the end of World War I.

Certain aspects of Bandi's analysis were reconsidered in the first issue of *Lo Stato Moderno*,[8] a "magazine of political, economic, and social criticism" founded by Mario Paggi, a Milanese lawyer and a veteran anti-fascist conspirator, in July 1944. In attempting to fulfill one of the main purposes of the magazine, which was "to seek the causes of the appalling decadence" that had led Italy to fascism, Paggi observed that soon after unification, when the heroic enthusiasms of the Risorgimento gave way to the practical tasks of national development, the Italian middle class fell back into apathy and passivity. Instead of becoming actively engaged in shaping the destiny of their country, this class—professional men, small businessmen, certain segments of the government bureaucracy and of white-collar workers, small farmers—acquired an attitude, cleverly exploited by fascism, of reliance on the favors of a paternalistic state. Although sympathetic to the idea of an extension of democratic rights to the masses of Italians, the middle class had failed to act on its beliefs and had therefore not provided the leadership given by its

[8] Mario Paggi, "Il problema dei ceti medi," *Lo Stato Moderno*, July 1944, pp. 8–10. (MR)

counterparts in other Western nations. At the same time, Italian capitalism had immediately assumed a monopolistic character in the period following unification, which also witnessed an increasing amount of subsidization by the state of large industrial complexes in northern Italy. The psychological and moral effects of this situation had been disastrous, said Paggi, for Italy emerged from the crisis of World War I without a solid tradition of democratic achievements to which people of all classes could look with a sense of national pride. On the one hand, the various strata of the Italian bourgeoisie, which Paggi branded as "cowardly, intellectually mediocre, and parasitic," clung to their conception of the state as an instrument with which to safeguard their own interests. On the other hand, the Italian working class lacked the experience required to assume a role of political leadership and remained tied to a kind of narrow parochialism that alienated it from other potentially democratic sectors of the population. Mussolini had profited by this polarization of economic and political forces in postwar Italy, since the bourgeoisie and the working class were so hostile to each other that they could not agree on a common program of action for the national welfare with which to counter the propaganda of the fascist movement.[9]

[9] Many of the opinions expressed by Bandi and Paggi, as well as those of *L'Italia Libera, Chiarezza,* and other clandestine organs of the Action Party, have been confirmed by scholars working in a variety of disciplines since the early years of World War II.

In *The Civic Culture,* the political sociologists Gabriel Almond and Sidney Verba tend to corroborate the views of Bandi and Paggi regarding the low level of political maturity of most Italians. This inquiry into the political attitudes of representative Italians, Mexicans, Americans, Englishmen, and Germans was made mainly in 1959 and therefore provides us with important yet only inferential evidence concerning the problem with which we are dealing. But if in the early 1920's Italians had approximately the same attitude toward civic affairs as they had in 1959, when according to Almond and Verba "only one in ten Italians believed that the ordinary man has an obligation to take an active role in his community" (p. 170), it is likely that most Italians remained aloof from the political scene while the fascists were proceeding to the conquest of power. A fanatical minority was thus able to impose its will on a passive, indifferent majority. In the light of Almond and Verba's findings, it might be said with some justification that the Resistance from 1943 to 1945 was an exceptional event in Italian history in that it temporarily forged a high sense of democratic and collective responsibility in the masses of people.

With regard to Bandi's assertion that the Italian susceptibility to demagoguery derived from a widespread feeling of powerlessness and insignificance, one finds some illuminating insights in Erich Fromm's *Escape from Freedom* and Eric Hoffer's *The True Believer.* Fromm's analysis rests fundamentally on the assumption that modern man lives in an impersonal, mechanized world so complex in its nature and so filled with baffling and hostile elements as to render even the strongest individual susceptible to the appeals of chiliastic political movements. In times of trouble and upheaval such as our own, Fromm maintains, the yearning for submission to authority that is always latent in many human beings becomes an active, propulsive

The main Action Party organ, *L'Italia Libera,* attributed the success of fascism in Italy in large measure to the irresolute character of King Victor Emmanuel III, whose failure to take a principled stand against Mussolini had severely damaged the forces of anti-fascism in the early and mid-1920's. The King was the living symbol of authority and of the continuity of the unified Italian state for millions of Italians. Therefore his refusal to enlist the support of the army and of the police against the fascists at the time of the march on Rome in October 1922, and subsequent rubber-stamping of Mussolini's anti-democratic decrees and laws in 1923 and 1924, gave the fascists a prestige that they could not have acquired in any other way. Unworthy of his forebears, who had laid the

---

force. The responsibility of individual freedom becomes excessively burdensome. Men with an inordinate lust for power, which is itself rooted in weakness, in an inability to experience life creatively, offer their followers a way out of their personal dilemmas. In order for fascism to succeed, Fromm concludes, it is necessary that a vast number of people feel personally inadequate. The societies of Italy and Germany were fertile soil for the rise of fascism, for in both there was a widespread sense of "the insignificance and powerlessness of the individual" (p. 240).

Hoffer is not concerned specifically with fascism but rather with the psychology behind mass movements in general. Nevertheless, many of his generalizations are pertinent to the character of the fascist movement at its inception, as well as to the types of individuals who tended to submit passively to Mussolini's demagoguery. Indeed, the book begins with "the truism that many who join a rising revolutionary movement are attracted by the prospect of sudden and spectacular change in their conception of life." This attitude was certainly characteristic of many of Mussolini's early followers, as were the "unifying agents" of hatred and the cult of action, which Hoffer claims to be peculiar to almost all mass movements, be they religious, social, or nationalist in purpose.

Implicit in Paggi's assertion that the pre-fascist liberal state lent vast amounts of aid to Italian industrialists is the conviction that the fascist state continued and developed liberal practice to the detriment of Italian democracy. The American historian Richard Webster, in a paper read at the American Historical Society conference in Washington (December 1964), produced much evidence to substantiate Paggi's implication that, with the exception of the internal political sphere, there was a definite continuity between the policies of the liberal Italian state and those of the fascist government. Webster made the following points: (1) the idea that heavy industry was a national interest antedates and anticipates fascism, as evidenced by the fact that, beginning in the late nineteenth century, the Italian state began subsidizing large military and industrial complexes and continued to do so under fascism; (2) government, heavy industry, and banking were closely interrelated both before and after fascism; (3) autarchic and imperialistic tendencies show themselves even during the Giolitti period and in fact expansionism (the Libyan campaign of 1912 and 1913) was as characteristic of the liberal state as it was of fascism.

As for the importance attributed by Paggi to the polarization of political and social forces in Italy after World War I, almost all students of fascism agree that Mussolini profited by the faction-ridden character of Italian life during the early 1920's. For example, the historian Leo Valiani maintains that the fact that capitalism did not erect a dictatorship to protect its interests in many countries of western Europe and in the United States belies the Marxist thesis and forces us to examine the specifically Italian situation after World War I. This situation, he says,

foundation for Italy's constitutional and parliamentary government, King Victor Emmanuel III had been guilty of helping the fascists to dismantle the entire structure of the political state created by the Risorgimento.[10]

But *L'Italia Libera,* like other Actionist publications, did not place the entire burden of guilt on the King. Indeed, it saw the roots of fascism as extending into nearly every area of Italian national life. Even if Italian universities merited their reputation as guardians of the humanistic tradition passed on to the country by the scholars and poets of the Renaissance, the newspaper said, it could not be denied that these same universities had become monopolized by the privileged classes, that they did

---

was characterized by a dramatic polarization of political and social forces. The regular Italian Army and many of the discharged war veterans looked upon Catholic and socialist opponents of Italian intervention with the utmost contempt. The large industrialists who had profited from the war and who continued to prosper after the war in an inflationary economy directed their hostility against the entire organized working class, whose aspiration for social and economic justice had been catalyzed by the Russian Revolution. From 1919 to 1922, Valiani states, Italy was a fragmented, divided country, and it was precisely this disunity that allowed the rising fascist movement to gain a solid foothold.

On a more general and theoretical level of interpretation, the political sociologist Seymour Lipset asserts in *Political Man* that "a system in which the support of different parties corresponds too closely to basic social divisions cannot continue on a democratic basis, for it reflects a state of conflict so intense and clear-cut as to rule out compromise" (p. 31). This particular point was made repeatedly by the Action Party ideologists, and in fact the mutual hostility dividing the principal Italian anti-fascist parties after World War I did facilitate the rise of the fascist movement because it rendered interparty solidarity against fascism nearly impossible. Also pertinent is Lipset's observation with respect to the relationship between the way political power is wielded and the stability of a democratic state: "If the outcome of the political game is not the periodic awarding of effective authority to one group, unstable and irresponsible government rather than democracy will result: This state of affairs existed in pre-Fascist Italy, and through much, though not all, of the history of the third and fourth French Republics, which were characterized by weak coalition governments, often formed among political parties having major interest and value conflicts with each other" (pp. 45, 46). That Italy was in fact ruled immediately after World War I by a weak coalition government incapable of meeting the fascist challenge decisively has been confirmed by most historians and political scientists, including such staunch defenders of political liberalism as Luigi Salvatorelli and Federico Chabod.

[10] Like many other political scientists of liberal-democratic persuasion Dante L. Germino in *The Italian Fascist Party in Power* places an especially heavy burden of responsibility for failure to meet the challenge of fascism decisively on Prime Minister Luigi Facta, who preceded Mussolini in power, and on King Victor Emmanuel III: "Although he pledged himself to restore the dignity and authority of the state, Facta actually did little or nothing to halt the building up of Fascist armed gangs. Nor was the Italian monarchy a rallying point for supporters of a constitutional regime: concerned above all with the preservation of his crown, the weak-willed Victor Emmanuel III, who later became the complete captive of Fascism, was a political force of negligible significance" (p. 7).

nothing to make the possibilities for self-development more easily accessible to the masses of people, that too often they employed professors whose method of teaching was "dogmatic and rhetorical," that they rewarded rote learning far more frequently than original, creative thinking. Instead of encouraging critical thought, Italian universities had produced a whole class of educated conformists incapable of resisting the irrational appeals for "action at all costs" that emanated from the fascist movement.[11] If fascism was "the creation of the reactionary upper bourgeoisie," *L'Italia Libera* noted in September 1943, it spread rapidly and found fertile soil in a country filled with "adventurers and opportunists, with many persons of the middle class who felt disappointed and frustrated with their lot in life," and with millions of individuals who could not distinguish between genuine patriotism and chauvinistic rhetoric.[12] These same harsh, unflattering judgments were expressed repeatedly by *L'Italia Libera,* which perhaps explains in some measure why the Action Party gained the support of only a small minority of Italians.

Among publications edited by youth movements associated with the Action Party, the one that offered the most penetrating analysis of the fascist phenomenon was the magazine *Chiarezza,* the organ of the Italian University Students Association. The leading article in the first issue of *Chiarezza* (May 1944), entitled "The Will to Renewal," [13] began with a description of the psychological atmosphere that prevailed in Italy following the end of World War I. Amidst the chaos that afflicted the Italian economy after the war, the magazine said, millions of Italians felt socially displaced and politically disoriented. The returning war veterans, many of whom were unable to find employment, felt doubly cheated of their just rewards when they read of the shoddy treatment given to the Italian representatives at the Versailles Conference. But then their faltering hopes for a new era of Italian prestige and greatness were suddenly revived by "the rhetorical, decadent brand of nationalism" of Gabriele d'Annunzio, whose occupation of Fiume in September 1919 triggered a whole series of chauvinistic street demonstrations in cities and towns throughout Italy. *Chiarezza* ascribed this wave of extremist nationalism principally to a characteristically Italian inferiority complex, which found its expression in an exaggerated compensatory assertion of power. Just as d'Annunzio's exploits, although formally repudiated by the Italian government, were greeted with a burst of enthusiasm throughout Italy, so in the

---

[11] "La riforma della scuola e del costume," *L'Italia Libera,* February 20, 1944, p. 1. (ISRT)

[12] "Il ritorno," *L'Italia Libera,* September 1, 1943, p. 2. (CG)

[13] "Volontà di rinnovamento," *Chiarezza,* May-June 1944, pp. 2–8. (CG)

same way the nationalistic rhetoric of the fascist movement began to attract many thousands of displaced, semi-educated persons who lacked an alternative ideal that would have protected them from Mussolini's demagoguery.

It was precisely "the superficial political education of so many Italians," observed *Chiarezza,* that allowed fascist propagandists to gain a solid foothold in Italian political life. But the profoundest reason for the steady advances made by the fascist movement in the early 1920's lay in "the skepticism and political weariness of the Italians." The real threat to Italian democracy was the widely prevalent attitude among Italians "of passive indifference to public affairs, of expecting external events to resolve their problems." Most Italians, *Chiarezza* claimed, had been neither strongly anti-fascist nor pro-fascist but merely indifferent to what they regarded as another manifestation of the eternal struggle for power waged by ambitious, cynical men in all countries and in all ages. Thus a fanatical minority was given the opportunity to impose its will on a passive, neutral majority. At the same time other social and political factors enhanced the prestige of the fascist movement. The fear of socialism prevalent among the Italian middle and upper classes was intensified by the Bolshevik Revolution and by various attempts on the part of the Italian labor movement to initiate a revolutionary transformation of Italian society modeled on the Soviet pattern. In reaction to this, Italian industrialists, landowners, and bankers immediately took countermeasures, among which was the financing of the newly created fascist "squads" composed of young men who viewed the workers' councils, farmers' cooperatives, and other such working-class initiatives as treasonous assaults against the dignity of the Italian national state. The violent methods of the squads could have been counteracted had the liberals who were steering the Italian ship of state at this juncture taken appropriate measures. The inability of the liberals to take decisive action was conditioned by their confusion about the totalitarian character of fascism. Even liberals of Croce's ilk, said *Chiarezza,* had in the early 1920's looked with favor on the fascist movement, so great was their fear of working-class militancy. All of these factors culminated in the fascist advent to power in Italy, the gradual undermining of democratic institutions and electoral procedures, and the establishment of a dictatorial government.

Chiarezza also saw the roots of fascism in certain features of Italy's historical development. The basic historical problem, the magazine observed, was that political liberalism and nationalism were contemporaneous phenomena in Italy. Whereas in England and France liberalism had developed only after many centuries of political unity during which these two countries had acquired a secure sense of their national dignity and power, the only unifying force in Italy up to the nineteenth century had been the feeling of pride in a cultural tradition dating back to the era of Roman civilization. Thus when liberal political ideals began circulating in Italy after the French Revolution, they immediately became associated in the minds of Italians with the struggle for national unity and independence. One of the results of this simultaneous emergence of liberalism and nationalism was "the idea of Italy's mission and *primato di civiltà,*" as reflected in the thought of Giuseppe Mazzini, Vincenzo Gioberti, and many other nineteenth-century Italian political thinkers. Mazzini and Gioberti had, to be sure, emphasized the cultural and spiritual values embodied in Italian traditions, but it was not long before the idea of a cultural mission began to be translated into political and "imperialistic" terms. *Chiarezza* noted in this regard that, after unification, the literature of political thought produced in Italy contained countless "polemics against the parliamentary regime and imprecations against the cowardice of Cavour's successors, who were attending to the job of balancing the state budget and did not want to hear anything about foreign adventures." The various nationalistic movements that took root in Italy during the first two decades of the twentieth century, *Chiarezza* concluded, found it relatively easy to exalt the principle of national greatness at the expense of a still insufficiently developed tradition of political liberalism, as proved by the alliance between the followers of Mussolini and those of the nationalist Enrico Corradini at the outset of the fascist epoch.

III
Socialist Interpretations of Fascism

Like the Action Party, the Italian Socialist Party also ascribed the growth of fascism to a multiplicity of interdependent factors. In June 1944, in an article commemorating the twentieth anniversary of the death of Giacomo Matteotti, *Avanti!* gave the following answer to the question: Who is responsible for fascism?:

[At the time of the assassination of Matteotti, in June 1924], fascism had been in power for twenty months, a power made possible by the presumptuous and unrestrained ambition of Mussolini, by the violence of a minority of war-crazed psychopaths, by the cowardice of a bourgeoisie that feared the progress of the proletariat, by the illusions of many young people attracted by patriotic rhetoric, by the complicity of the police and of many of the courts, and by the complicity of a contemptible king and his family.[14]

[14] "Nel ventennale del martirio di Giacomo Matteotti," *Avanti!,* June 1944, p. 1. (ISRT)

The socialists maintained that, after centuries of a servile, corrupt existence, the Italian people had at long last won its political independence in the nineteenth century, but only through the sacrifices of an exiguous number of heroic men. The Risorgimento had been "a brief period of moral resurrection" followed by seventy years of pseudodemocracy that culminated in the triumph of fascism.[15] According to the socialists, Italy's intervention in World War I, which was never considered an authentic struggle for democracy either by the Socialist Party itself or by the overwhelming number of Italian workers and farmers, had set the stage for a fascist-type reaction. The reason for this was that Italy's entrance into the war, despite widespread popular opposition, had undermined the Italian people's confidence in its ability to shape its own destiny and had broadened the gap that traditionally separated the masses from the ruling bourgeois élite. The result was an attitude of cynical indifference to politics that was easily exploited by fascism.

The Socialist Party's organ *L'Edificazione Socialista* placed the blame for fascism squarely on the shoulders of the Italian bourgeoisie, which the newspaper characterized as being composed predominantly of "culturally ignorant parvenus" who involved themselves in politics and the state only when they were necessary to suppress strikes and to protect the interests of the capitalist class.[16] In comparison with its counterparts in other capitalist countries, the Italian bourgeoisie was irremediably backward, incapable of providing an example of moral rectitude to other segments of the population. Thus, in the socialist analysis, the economic motives that induced some members of the Italian ruling class to support and others to tolerate fascism were inseparably linked with this class' lack of moral fiber.

IV
The Catholic View: Fascism as Moral Corruption

It was precisely the moral component of the problem of fascism that was most frequently stressed by the various clandestine organs of the Christian Democratic Party, whose leading ideologists, and in particular Alcide De Gasperi, drew inspiration chiefly from the writings of Giuseppe Toniolo. Toniolo (1845–1918), whose career as a professor of economics at the University of Pisa coincided exactly with the period between the end of the Risorgimento and the outset of the fascist era, devoted his life to the problem of reconciling Christian teachings with the development of modern industrial capitalism in Italy. Although opposed

---

[15] "I problemi della ricostruzione," *Avanti!* (undated), p. 1. (ISRT)
[16] "Una questione di costume," *L'Edificazione Socialista,* July 5, 1944, p. 1. (CG)

to the utilitarian and individualistic doctrines of Adam Smith, Toniolo was convinced that a liberal, enlightened capitalism that offered the possibility of self-advancement to all members of society formed the basis of a way of life that Catholics could accept without doing violence to their spiritual beliefs. He did not subscribe to the notion prevalent in his time that men were pawns in the hands of the "objective laws" of social and economic history, for in his opinion these so-called laws were nothing but rationalizations for the rampant materialism that had afflicted both the bourgeoisie and the working class after the French Revolution. Bourgeois acquisitiveness and Marxian socialism were both products of the same materialistic culture that Toniolo rejected in his effort to create the ideological groundwork for an authentic Christian democracy. He insisted in all his writings that within limits men could and must shape economic institutions and systems of government in accordance with moral principles deriving from Christianity in its purest evangelical sense.[17]

By reason of Toniolo's influence, during the Resistance the Christian Democrats found themselves in a somewhat ambivalent ideological position with respect to the problem of fascism. On the one hand, they shared the left-wing parties' negative appraisal of the pre-fascist liberal state, since it was this state that had allowed the enlightened, democratic capitalism championed by Toniolo to be transformed into a system of monopolistic oppression. Christian ideals had not been the motivating force in the lives of Italy's lay intelligentsia during the period preceding fascism. Indeed, fascism had been able to gain power because of the religious agnosticism and opportunistic indifference to the plight of the masses that had characterized the secular leaders of Italian political and economic life since unification.[18] But on the other hand, because of the emphasis they placed on the need for a revival of moral energy in the Italian people and because of their belief in the reconcilability of enlightened capitalism with the welfare of the nation as a whole, the Christian Democratic Party could not accept the idea so frequently advanced by the Communist and Socialist Parties that fascism owed its existence primarily to the contradictions inherent in the capitalist system itself, whether enlightened or reactionary in form. As a consequence, certain of their judgments concerning the roots of fascism were strikingly similar to those offered by the left-wing parties, while others reflected their belief in the primacy of the moral factor in human history.

In an undated issue of the newspaper *Democrazia,* Alcide De Gasperi

---

[17] For the essential elements of Toniolo's life and thought, see Giuseppe Toniolo, *Scritti scelti,* edited by Antonio Boggiano Pico.

[18] This point of view is expressed most forcefully in an article entitled "I C.L.N. e lo stato democratico italiano," *Il Popolo,* February 28, 1945, p. 1. (LC)

gave expression to his party's ambivalent attitude toward the problem of fascism in an article devoted to the teachings of Toniolo.[19] De Gasperi indicated his agreement with the left-wing parties regarding the necessity of effecting a radical restructuring of Italian political and economic institutions, since the inequality of opportunity and system of inherited privileges that had always characterized Italian society rendered the masses of people dangerously susceptible to fascistic demagoguery. A revival of political freedom and of local self-government, De Gasperi said, would have to be accompanied by democratically inspired legislation in the economic and social spheres. But, he continued, the Italian people must not be led to believe that fascism could be defeated by political and legislative actions alone. Nothing could be more false, for the essential problem lay in the need for moral education. Fascism was the product of the low level of private and public morality in Italy, so that the only lasting remedy for it was a fundamental reformation of moral standards and conduct. Toniolo had been correct, De Gasperi concluded, when he wrote that "we must not base all our hopes on a change of juridical institutions or of political systems," while at the same time neglecting *la riforma del costume,* the upgrading of moral and civic norms of conduct.

Yet on page two of this same issue of *Democrazia* an article entitled "In What Way We Are Anticapitalists" spoke of the capitalist system and of the bourgeois class in terms reminiscent in some respects of the communist and socialist press:

> The capitalist regime, now at the end of its existence, is not that abyss of horror depicted by the facile pens of demagogues, but it does have a great responsibility for the bloody conflicts that are tormenting us. In a society that really feels human solidarity there ought not to be any place for capitalism. . . . The bourgeoisie, by reason of its fear of losing its wealth and by becoming the pawn of capitalism, threw itself into the arms of Mussolini . . .
>
> We are not revolutionaries and we want political changes to take place without destroying social classes; therefore in a world that will be based on the freedom of all citizens and on social justice there is a need for capital. But it will be a place reserved for that which serves the common welfare and will be secondary to that occupied by labor, which will have a leading role in reconstruction and, consequently, the right to a large voice in public affairs.[20]

In February 1945, the Christian democratic newspapers *Il Popolo* and *Per il Domani* both attributed the relative ease with which the fascist regime gained power in Italy to the insufficiencies and inequities of the

---

[19] Alcide De Gasperi, "La nostra democrazia cristiana e le sue tradizioni," *Democrazia* (undated), p. 1. (INS)

[20] "Come siamo anticapitalisti," *Democrazia,* p. 2. (INS)

pre-fascist liberal state. *Il Popolo* spoke of the liberal regime's "abdication of the noble civic mission of the state, its non-intervention in the economic and social world," and *Per il Domani* stated that the development of capitalism, which was originally based on the principles of individualism and liberalism, had ended by crushing liberalism through the growth of immense aggregates of power concentrated in the hands of the few.[21] On the basis of this premise, the newspaper said, the Christian democrats agreed with the parties of the left on the impossibility of returning to the system that prevailed before fascism. The danger of a resurgence of fascism could only be avoided by attacking the abusive forms of capitalist power at their roots, through a decentralization of the economy. *La Fiaccola,* another Christian democratic publication, also blamed the bourgeois class for its selfishness and narrow class interests, as did the Florentine representatives of the party in a clandestine pamphlet entitled "The Social and Political Mission of Christian Democracy" published in June 1944.[22]

But the predominant moralism of the Christian democrats is evident in an earlier issue of *Per il Domani,* which made no mention whatever of the bourgeois role in supporting fascism and instead asserted that "opportunism and conformism were almost everywhere in the ascendancy in the early 1920's, that very few Italians had had the courage to oppose fascism," to take a principled stand even at the cost of remaining isolated. Fascism could be crushed, the newspaper said, if the Italian people realized that "strength of character, moral rectitude, coherence between thought and action were as necessary in public as in private life." [23] The lack of these qualities, according to *Il Popolo* and *Per il Domani,* had accounted for the Italian people's inability to recognize the true nature of fascism's "sham élite," its "counterfeit doctrines," its "aberrational" exaltation of power and violence.[24] Thus, in the final analysis, although willing to admit that economic and political factors had to be considered in explaining why fascism gained power, the Christian democrats insisted on the more essential importance of the Italian people's moral failure to resist the onslaught of fascism.[25]

[21] "I C.L.N. e lo stato democratico italiano," *Il Popolo,* February 28, 1945, p. 1. "Libertà, capitalismo e forme collettive," *Per il Domani,* February 1945, p. 1. (LC)

[22] *La missione sociale e politica della Democrazia Cristiana.* (ISRT)

[23] "Per una nuova coscienza della libertà," *Per il Domani,* September 1944, p. 1. (CG)

[24] "La repubblica sociale," *Il Popolo,* December 1943, p. 2. (ISRT)

[25] The leftist, anti-bourgeois cast of the political thought of Italian Christian democrats during the period of the Resistance derived in large measure from their awareness that the social inequities left unremedied by the liberal-bourgeois constitutional monarchy of the years 1870 to 1918 had greatly facilitated the fascist

V
The Liberal View: Fascism as the Loss of the Will to Freedom

Among the five principal parties in the anti-fascist coalition, the liberals were for obvious reasons the most anxious to defend the democratic character of the governments that had ruled Italy up to the advent of fascism. In April 1944, the main party organ *Risorgimento Liberale* made a spirited defense of Italian liberalism, which, the newspaper said, "had created and guided the Risorgimento," laid the groundwork for the considerable economic development and prosperity that Italy had enjoyed in the early part of the twentieth century, and made

---

conquest of power. Illuminating in this regard are the sociopolitical facts revealed in 1929 by Herbert W. Schneider and Shepard B. Clough, who in that year published a pioneering study in the field of political sociology entitled *Making Fascists*. In attempting to explain the multifaceted character of the fascist state, Schneider and Clough devoted themselves to "an examination of the social bases of cohesion" in fascist Italy, and sought through interviews with representative supporters of fascism to establish the attitudes of social and economic groups, sources of loyalty and belief, and other similar problems of permanent interest to political sociologists. Schneider and Clough discovered in the first place that "Fascism was in its origin a northern product," that its appeal to the ignorant, mainly illiterate and semi-literate masses of southern Italy was at first negligible. It was only after fascism became a powerful force in Italian political life, in 1921 and 1922, that significantly large, cohesive nuclei of fascist power were established in the South. The crucial inference that can be drawn from this finding, which has been corroborated by many historians of fascism, is that an inert mass of uneducated people without hope or alternative ideals is easy prey for a fanatical minority of "true believers": in 1921, according to statistics furnished by the Italian government and cited in *Making Fascists,* twenty-seven percent of Italians were illiterate, most of whom lived in the southern half of the country. The grim reality behind this statistic, coupled with the widespread unemployment and poverty that plagued millions of Italians throughout the period 1870 to 1922, gave fascism the kind of appeal that would have been inconceivable in a more prosperous, equalitarian, progressive society. Hence the Christian democratic resisters, anxious to translate Christian ideals into tangible reality, could not but assume a critical attitude toward the type of conservative liberalism that had allowed such conditions to prevail for so long.

With regard to the Catholic anti-fascists' contempt for the "sham élite" and "counterfeit doctrines" of fascism, it will be remembered that it was precisely this aspect of the fascist mentality that aroused the wrath of such eminent Catholic precursors of the armed Resistance as Giuseppe Donati and Don Luigi Sturzo, for whom most components of fascist ideology were incompatible with the teachings of the Catholic Church and with Catholic doctrine.

The severity with which the Christian democratic ideologists such as Alcide De Gasperi judged the behavior of Italy's middle bourgeois class at the time of the fascist conquest of power was also, according to many historians, based on a sound evaluation of the facts in the case. For example, in *Italy from Napoleon to Mussolini*, René Albrecht-Carrié offers the following characterization of the Italian middle class mentality in regard to fascism: "This actual behavior of the Fascists, their willingness to use violence against the elements of the left, whatever the socialistic tinge of their language when speaking of social and economic problems, is what

possible Italian victory in World War I.[26] In November 1944, *Il Secolo Liberale,* published in Genoa, categorically affirmed that only the liberal conception of the state and society was incompatible with fascism on all levels, whereas communism, socialism, and Catholicism had each contributed an essential ingredient of its ideology to Mussolini's regime: "From communism in fact the fascist regime borrowed the formula of 'permanent revolution' and the practice of a single-party dictatorship; from socialism, the idea and the program of so-called social legislation. . . . From Catholicism, it borrowed the principle and practice of hierarchy. To the liberals, mistakenly made by fascism to appear as backward conservatives, to men linked with the ideal continuity of a still brief national life based on constitutional guarantees and on the belief in certain fundamental civic values, which our fathers wanted, obtained and respected, to us, fascism denied everything." [27] In truth, it should be noted that there was one important feature of the political philosophy of Italian liberals that fascism did *not* deny—their violent anti-communism, which *Il Secolo Liberale* and other Liberal Party organs usually neglected to mention.

Sustained chiefly by the thought of Benedetto Croce, who in his *History of Italy from 1871 to 1915* had persuasively described the accomplishments of Italian liberalism, the Liberal Party refused in theory to see a cause-effect relationship between the insufficiencies of the pre-fascist state and the rise of fascism. In practice, however, the Liberal Party recognized the need, as expressed by *Risorgimento Liberale* in November 1943, for "a profound transformation" of Italian society. It could not be denied, the newspaper said again in June 1944, "that fascism, which arose as a movement supported by petit bourgeois elements who found the return to normal life after the great war intolerable, was subsidized and strengthened by industrialists and agrarian landowners who saw in it

---

rallied to them a substantial support from the middle class. The phenomenon need not surprise us and we have seen it repeated in Germany where the same group provided some of the staunchest support of the Nazis. The middle class, whether independent shopkeepers or professionals with fixed incomes, highly individualistic and largely unorganized, hence unable to protect its interests in the same manner as the workers, was to a large extent bewildered and frightened by the circumstances of the time. It saw its social status as well as its possessions menaced by forces which it did not understand; but the behavior of the workers, their strikes, their demands for compensations, backed by a powerful organization, were easy to perceive" (pp. 157, 158).

[26] "Orientamenti programmatici del P.L.I.," *Risorgimento Liberale,* April 1944, p. 1. (INS)

[27] "Antifascismo-Liberalismo," *Il Secolo Liberale,* November-December 1944, p. 1. (LC)

an instrument with which to defend their position." And, the paper added, during the next two decades of the fascist era, "the material interests [of industrialists and landowners] were in fact more and more favored and protected." [28]

But the Liberal Party viewed the support given to fascism by industrialists and landowners as an error, a miscalculation that could be rectified without altering some of the essential features of the bourgeois liberal state. What was needed was a repudiation of the totalitarian conception of the state and the enactment of legislation which would free the working class from impoverishment and exploitation. Totalitarianism, not capitalism, was the enemy; a belief in freedom, not collectivism, could restore the values of democratic society and strike at the very core of fascist ideology. Aldobrando Medici-Tornaquinci, one of Florence's most prominent Liberal Party members, expressed his party's point of view in saying that the triumph of fascism was the result mainly of a temporary loss of the will to be free, of a waning of faith in liberalism after World War I, when absolutist regimes gained power not only in Italy, but also in Russia, Germany, and Spain. Viewed from the perspective of the present, said Tornaquinci, "we can safely assert that the moral debasement of our political life that fatally led to the tragic fascist experience was able to manifest itself only because in the consciousness of men at that time there was lacking a belief in the most noble liberal traditions." [29] Filippo Jacini went even further than most of his liberal colleagues in his defense of liberalism and spoke of fascism as a "sickness," with its "period of incubation" and "pathological manifestations." Liberalism and capitalism were not at fault, he said, but rather a "deficiency of character" in many Italians, "the failure of the civic conscience of the citizen," were the crucial factors.[30]

[28] "Movimento liberale e classe privilegiata," *Risorgimento Liberale,* June-July 1944, p. 1. (INS)

[29] Aldobrando Medici Tornaquinci, "Perchè ci chiamiamo 'liberali,' " *L'Opinione,* August 16, 1944, pp. 1. (ISRT)

[30] Filippo Jacini, "Carattere," *Risorgimento Liberale,* July 1, 1944, p. 1. This article is cited textually in Jacini, *Carattere,* p. 28.

Two eminent Italian historians who have developed the liberal interpretation of fascism are Federico Chabod in *L'Italia contemporanea,* and Luigi Salvatorelli in *Storia d'Italia nel periodo fascista,* cited frequently in this study. Their works are examples of essentially political and "genetic" interpretations of fascism. Chabod and particularly Salvatorelli trace in detail the day-by-day political decisions, disputes, parliamentary maneuverings, and conflicts of interest which, from 1919 to 1922, gradually brought the fascist movement into a position of prominence and finally hegemony in Italy. Salvatorelli shows how the fascists, under the skillful tactical leadership of Mussolini, exploited every sign of weakness, every moment of indecision and vacillation among the leaders of the non-fascist parties. He also

Two other aspects of the problem of Italian fascism that were rarely considered by the political press were referred to by Concetto Marchesi and Paolo Greco in the Liberation Committee organs *Fratelli d'Italia* (Padua) and *La Riscossa Italiana* (Turin). Marchesi, a communist professor of Latin literature at the University of Padua, saw fascism as merely one of the most "abject phases" of Italy's "servile history." Prior to the Risorgimento, Italy had lacked a national identity for two thousand years. This fact explained why the Risorgimento had been the work of a few heroes, while the majority of Italians continued to support the various foreign powers or their lackeys who ruled them. In view of Italy's servile history, Marchesi said, it was not surprising that in 1922 it was relatively easy for "a constitutional monarchy supported by almost the entire ruling class to hand over public power to a horde of adventurers and criminals, with the insane hope of suppressing the revolutionary energies of the proletariat." [31] Thus, whereas Eugenio Curiel, Pietro Secchia, and other Communist Party theoreticians championed the Risorgimento and limited their negative appraisal of Italian historical development to the period 1870 to 1918, Marchesi condemned the pattern of servility imposed on the Italian people by almost two millennia of foreign oppression.

The liberal Paolo Greco, on the other hand, without exculpating the Italian people, also placed blame on the shoulders of various foreign powers and their emissaries who not only failed to condemn fascism but actively encouraged its growth by according to Mussolini's regime diplomatic recognition, legal political status, and abundant amounts of praise. Influences of an international character had been brought to bear that strengthened Mussolini's power, among which, Greco said, was "a formidable amount of assistance from abroad. This is not the place to repeat the story, which in any case is well known to everyone, of the endless expressions of satisfaction and sympathy, of the innumerable examples of weakness and error in which other peoples and governments indulged themselves to the benefit of fascism." Far from being a peculiarly Italian

---

stresses the role that fascist violence played in creating an atmosphere of uncertainty and fear, and argues convincingly that the failure of Prime Ministers Nitti and Facta to repress this violence effectively broke the will to resist of many of Mussolini's opponents. As far as the actual construction of a totalitarian state is concerned, Chabod and Salvatorelli insist that this was accomplished with entirely illegal and unconstitutional methods. The basic point of view underlying the work of both historians is that fascism won power primarily through violence and clever maneuvering and not by reason of the inherent deficiencies of the liberal state or the plots of capitalists. As expressed by Chabod, "the legal and technical forms which the Fascist regime adopted in its organization . . . represented a complete break with the parliamentary regime in Italy from 1861 to 1922" (p. 63).

[31] Concetto Marchesi, "Ai giovani," *Fratelli d'Italia,* May 15, 1944, p. 1. (INS)

phenomenon, Greco concluded, fascism had found sympathizers in the highest as well as middle and lower echelons of all Western societies, a fact that rendered the task of overthrowing the dictatorship from within almost impossible.[32]

The anti-fascist journalists whose interpretations of fascism are discussed in the preceding pages employed radically different approaches to the phenomenon with which they were dealing. Yet in the final analysis there seems to be a fair degree of consensus among them regarding the reasons why fascism gained power in Italy. They tended to agree that the totalitarian character of the fascist regime grew out of deficiencies in the structure of Italian political and social life that were severely exacerbated by the crisis of World War I. Fascism was not inevitable, but the political disunity and social inequities characteristic of Italian life unquestionably were fertile soil for the rise of a fanatical movement bent on gaining total power.

There was general agreement among them concerning the susceptibility of the lower and middle strata of the Italian bourgeoisie to a mixture of chauvinistic and anti-socialist demagoguery, a susceptibility conditioned by the economic insecurity and political immaturity of this class. It was also precisely this combination of insecurity and political immaturity that encouraged a large segment of Italy's most powerful economic groups to lend financial support to the fascist movement. The question whether the magnates of heavy industry and agriculture were merely pawns in the hands of their fascist masters or whether they consciously used the fascist anti-labor squads as instruments with which to protect their own interests remained unresolved by the underground journalists. They agreed, however, that an intimate, indissoluble relationship existed between big business and fascism in Italy.

In the realm of psychological attitudes as they affect political behavior, one discovers a prevalent tendency among the writers of the underground press to attribute much importance to the feelings of powerlessness and disillusionment that afflicted millions of Italians after World War I.

---

[32] Paolo Greco, "Filofascismo estero e antifascismo italiano," *La Riscossa Italiana,* November 1943, pp. 2, 3. (CG)

With regard to Greco's contention that Mussolini's regime was enthusiastically supported by many liberals and conservatives in Western societies, American readers will find it useful to consult an article by John P. Diggins, "Flirtation with Fascism: American Pragmatic Liberals and Mussolini's Italy," *American Historical Review,* LXXI, No. 2, January 1966, pp. 487–506. Diggins presents much evidence to substantiate the assertion he makes in the opening sentence of his article, which states that "It is a strange irony of history that Mussolini's Fascist dictatorship drew more admiration from democratic America than from any other Western nation."

These feelings breed skepticism and weariness, to be sure, but they can also give rise to sudden compensatory explosions of nationalistic solidarity, as in fact happened during the early 1920's, when the fascist movement cleverly exploited the need felt by Italians of all classes for a new and cohesive sociopolitical order.

The underground journalists failed to probe several basic elements of the fascist phenomenon. For example, they did not concern themselves directly with the impact of Mussolini's "charismatic" personality on large sectors of the Italian population. Yet this factor was undoubtedly crucial, since a political leader who makes a successful effort to acquire and maintain power must necessarily embody aspirations and possess certain traits with which the people to whom he appeals can identify.[33] Also strangely absent from almost all of the analyses in the underground press is any evaluation of the component of violence in the anatomy of fascism. Yet, as we have seen, it was precisely the violence of the fascist action squads, their capacity for decisive action and defiance of the customary amenities of parliamentary procedure, that first set the stage for the fascist seizure of state power.

There can be no doubt, however, that the writers of the underground press during the years 1943 to 1945 were often remarkably perceptive and profound in their interpretations of fascism and that a careful study of their views on this question would be beneficial for scholars today who are concerned either specifically with the origin and nature of Italian fascism or with any of the other forms of twentieth-century totalitarianism.[34]

[33] Among the many studies of fascism in which the personality and impact of Mussolini are stressed are Herman Finer, *Mussolini's Italy*; S. William Halperin, *Mussolini and Italian Fascism*; Ivone Kirkpatrick, *Mussolini, a Study in Power*; and Renzo De Felice, *Mussolini il fascista*.

[34] One of the more recent studies of Italian fascism as part of a general European phenomenon is Ernst Nolte, *Three Faces of Fascism: Action Française, Italian Fascism, National Socialism,* translated by Leila Vennewitz (New York, 1966).

CHAPTER EIGHT

TOWARD A DEMOCRATIC SOCIETY

I
The Achievements of the Italian Resistance Movement

During the period between the fall of Mussolini's regime in July 1943 and the end of the war in Europe in May 1945, the Italian Resistance Movement achieved some important military, political, and social objectives.

The exact nature and extent of the military contribution made by the Italian Resistance to the Allied cause has long been a matter of controversy and will probably continue to be so for many years to come. Italians who were engaged in fighting the nazi-fascist forces as partisans and saboteurs have naturally tended to exaggerate the importance of their contribution. That the Allies would have eventually defeated the German and fascist enemy in Italy with or without the help of the partisans is beyond question. But by the same token the partisan movement undoubtedly benefited the Allied armies, saving lives and shortening the war.[1]

With respect to the political significance of the partisan movement, there can be no doubt that the authority and prestige of Mussolini's neo-fascist Republic of Salò were severely undermined by the development of an organized armed resistance in Italy. It must be emphasized here that, following the establishment of the fascist republic in late September of 1943, young men ranging in age from eighteen to twenty-one were faced with the choice either of obeying the call to arms issued by Mussolini's puppet government or of joining the partisans. Consequently, it was vitally important that anti-fascist propagandists succeed in convincing as many young men as possible to defy the fascist republic and prove their opposition to it by taking up arms on the side of the Allies. That they in fact met substantial success in this effort is borne out by an article published in *L'Unità* on May 10, 1944, at which time the Republic of Salò was deeply concerned with the problem of "the rebels," as the

[1] For an estimate of the Italian partisans' military contribution to the Allied cause, see the report of the British Special Force on p. 232.

partisans were called by their enemies. This issue of the communist newspaper published a message sent in early May to General Hans von Keitel by General Rodolfo Graziani, who had been entrusted by Mussolini with the task of mobilizing the fascist republican army. After indicating the number of men he had available for military duties, Graziani alluded to the problem of the rebels in relation to the more essential question of the neo-fascist government's political authority: "An extremely important problem," Graziani said, "is that of intensifying to the utmost of our powers the struggle against the rebels, a struggle that constitutes the necessary, indeed the indispensable precondition for the reestablishment of the authority and prestige of the [fascist] state over the people as a whole, and consequently for our success in raising an army." [2] Italians who joined the Resistance demonstrated their repudiation of the fascist state and in doing so helped to transform the latent democratic sentiments of the Italian people into an active force.

The partisan movement also played an indispensable role in reviving the tradition of local self-government in Italy. The liberation of towns, cities, and zones in central and northern Italy, often accomplished by partisan units operating independently or in conjunction with Allied troops, compelled the people living in these liberated areas to sustain and to organize themselves as best they could with the limited means at their disposal. Local administrative bodies had to be chosen; fair prices had to be set for essential foods; new schools and medical facilities had to be improvised; homeless and indigent persons had to be cared for. Many of the partisans engaged in this work realized that they were participating in crucial experiments in self-government, that one of the essential purposes of the Resistance was to rebuild the Italian people's confidence in its ability to govern itself on a democratic basis. The regional Committees of National Liberation were established for the most part by an intellectual and political élite with a long record of anti-fascist activity. These Committees provided an example to follow, but it was up to the local populations of each liberated zone to shoulder the burden of self-rule. As a result, with the decisive assistance of the partisans, democratically elected *giunte comunali* were formed in many parts of Italy from the spring of 1944 to the end of the war.

On frequent occasions the writers of the underground press referred to the newly created "partisan republics" as one of the most significant achievements of the Italian Resistance Movement. On August 24, 1944, *L'Unità* spoke of the partisan units operating in the mountains between Genoa and Piacenza as "animated by an intense commitment" to the restoration

[2] *L'Unità*, May 10, 1944, p. 2. (CG)

of democratic procedures and institutions in the areas under their jurisdiction, and on October 8 the communist newspaper praised the joint
partisan-civilian committee entrusted with political authority in Domodossola following the city's liberation in early September 1944. Domodossola was in fact an outstanding if short-lived experiment in democracy,
one which aroused the enthusiasm and support of thousands of people
in the city itself and in the smaller towns and villages surrounding it.[3]

In August 1944, Luigi Longo, the chief organizer of communist partisan
brigades, wrote an article published in the magazine *La Nostra Lotta*
concerning the accomplishments of another justifiably famous partisan
republic, that of Montefiorino, a city in the region of Emilia about
twenty miles south of Modena. Longo made mention of some of the
specific tasks performed by the *giunta popolare* responsible for governing
the newly liberated city:

> In Montefiorino the *giunta popolare* immediately solved various important
> problems. It fixed the price of grain, after having consulted with different
> segments of the population. It established the criteria that must regulate the
> furnishing of grain and other products to the partisan units. It urged the large
> landowners to make an extra contribution of grain to families whose homes
> had been burned by the Nazis during the course of a mop-up operation in
> March. . . . It saw to it that public order was maintained, and in collaboration
> with the partisans kept close surveillance on persons known to be fascist or
> pro-fascist. By reason of these activities, a new life is in ferment in the entire
> area surrounding Montefiorino: the publication of a Liberation Committee
> newspaper is being planned and lectures, meetings, discussions promote the
> political education and mobilization of the masses.[4]

The Action Party organ *Azione Contadina* also spoke with pride of
the "rebirth of democratic life" in Montefiorino, as did the newspapers
Gioventù d'Azione and *L'Italia Libera*. An article in *Gioventù d'Azione*
explained the procedures that were generally followed in setting up the
new communal governments. In most cases, two or three members of
partisan units, selected on the basis of their political maturity and understanding of local social and economic problems, held a preliminary conference with a person, usually the parish priest, who enjoyed the esteem
of the townspeople. Following this conference, various representatives of

---

[3] "Libera vita nel Val d'Ossola," *L'Unità*, October 8, 1944, p. 2. (CG) For
a complete history of the partisan republic of Domodossola, a city situated in the
northernmost tip of Italy near the Swiss border, see Anita Azzari, *L'Ossola nella
Resistenza italiana*.

[4] Longo's article is cited textually in Luigi Longo, *Sulla via dell'insurrezione
nazionale*, p. 264. On Montefiorino, see Ermanno Gorrieri, *La Repubblica di
Montefiorini: per una Storia della Resistenza in Emilia*.

the area's basic trades and occupations were invited to a public meeting, the purposes of which were to work out ways of solving the most pressing problems in the community and to elect a provisional *giunta*. Anyone of voting age (twenty-one) was eligible for election, but an effort was made to nominate at least one farmer, one worker or artisan, and one businessman in order to make sure that the interests of each major segment of the population were represented on the *giunta*.[5] Thus the new partisan republics embodied the democratic commitment of the Resistance Movement by encouraging all citizens to participate actively in the processes of government and decision-making. As defined by the newspaper *La Fabbrica,* "The fundamental task of the *giunte* was that of placing the instruments of government and administration at the disposal of the urban and rural populations," instruments which, after twenty years of dictatorship, again allowed the people "to express freely their aspirations and needs." [6]

The underground newspapers of all the major parties and groups in the anti-fascist coalition were in substantial agreement that the Resistance marked the first time in Italian history that the working classes had stood at the forefront of a *national* political movement. They agreed that the Italian working class had shown exceptional political maturity from the very beginning of the Resistance Movement and through strikes and constant organized protest had provided an example of disciplined anti-fascist action. Had there not been the strikes of March 1943 in Turin and Milan and the general strike of March 1944 extending from northern Italy into Tuscany, the Resistance Movement would not have been able to rally massive popular support; without the cooperation and solidarity of the urban proletariat the partisans would not have been able to establish the authority of the Regional Committees in the liberated areas of Italy. But the major clandestine organs indicated that the unprecedented achievement of the Resistance lay not only in the participation of the industrial workers but also in the decisive contribution made by Italian farmers. The political consciousness of both segments of the Italian working class had made it possible for the Italian people to participate in the task of national liberation.

Anticipating the judgment expressed in 1948 by the historian Gaetano Salvemini, who called the active role of Italian agricultural workers in the Resistance "the most important event in Italian history of the twentieth century," *La Nostra Lotta* declared that "never as in this period has it been demonstrated so clearly that the peasants' participation in any

[5] *Gioventù d'Azione,* July 30, 1944. (CG)
[6] "Le giunte popolari," *La Fabbrica,* September 15, 1944, p. 2. (IG)

modern movement of popular and national liberation is of decisive importance."[7] In July 1944, *L'Unità* issued a special report describing how "the farmers have helped the partisans by supplying them with food and shelter, how they have demonstrated and acted against fascist requisitions of food and men, how they have united their activities with the agitation and strikes of the workers."[8] The Action Party organ *Voci d'Officina* stated that, in defying nazi-fascist threats of repression and deportation, the industrial workers of Turin, Genoa, Milan, Padua, and other northern Italian cities had "placed themselves at the very center of the struggle for national liberation."[9] *Azione Contadina* hailed the farmers' role in supporting the partisans despite grave risks of reprisal as marking "the outset of a period in which the peasantry would become a dominant force in national political life."[10] *La Riscossa Italiana* acknowledged that, although the ideological contribution of Italy's anti-fascist intellectuals had been a necessary precondition for Resistance, "the first crucial step toward a revival of national dignity had been taken by the lower classes."[11] Even the Liberal Party newspaper *Risorgimento Liberale* paid tribute to the initiative shown by Italian workers and farmers: "Let us say with joy, since we are without envy and class prejudices, that today the place of honor in the Resistance belongs to the workers of central and northern Italy."[12]

The articles quoted above demonstrate that the ideologists of the Resistance were aware of the vital connection linking their efforts with those of the urban and rural proletariat. It was precisely this sense of interdependence that allows one to speak of the Resistance as a national movement that transcended the traditional barriers of mistrust and hostility dividing the intellectual élite from the masses of people in Italy. For the first time in Italian history, people from many different classes and walks of life were engaged in a united struggle for commonly accepted goals.

Another noteworthy achievement of the Resistance was that it brought thousands of Italian women into the arena of political and social action. Fascism had done nothing to alter the traditional Italian conception of

[7] "I contadini nella lotta di liberazione nazionale," *La Nostra Lotta,* July 1944, p. 8. (INS)
[8] "I contadini collaborano con i Partigiani in una operazione di guerra," *L'Unità,* July 2, 1944, p. 1. (ISRT)
[9] "Per una politica dei lavoratori," *Voci d'Officina,* April 1944, p. 1. (INS)
[10] "Lavoratori della terra in veste partigiana," *Azione Contadina,* July 13, 1944, p. 1. (INS)
[11] "Gli scioperi torinesi e il loro significato," *La Riscossa Italiana,* December 1943, p. 1. (CG)
[12] "Scioperi e resistenza," *Risorgimento Liberale,* March 15, 1944, p. 1. (CG)

women as inherently inferior beings whose proper role in life was to tend to domestic affairs and submit passively to a male-dominated world. The Resistance struggle dramatically demonstrated the absurdity of this attitude, since the national liberation movement was compelled to rely heavily on the reserves of energy and intelligence possessed by women of all social classes.

The testimony of numerous participants in the Resistance reveals that women took the initiative in leading many of the crucial strikes organized by Italian workers in 1943 and 1944. The majority of runners who served as liaisons between partisan units and centers of political action in the cities were women. In many instances women were the main organizers of assistance to ex-Allied prisoners of war who were liberated after September 8, 1943. A woman, Amalia Valli, served on the first provisional *giunta* of Domodossola in October and November 1944. The success of the underground press was the consequence in large measure of the courage of groups of women who, in every important urban center, functioned as liaisons between writers and printers. In Florence it was Maria Luigia Guaita who brought the clandestine newspapers of the Action Party to people living in remote areas of Tuscany, and Anna Maria Enriques was the founder of the Florentine segment of the Christian Social Movement. In Turin it was Ada Gobetti who initiated the publishing of *La Riscossa Italiana* and who at grave personal risk made contact with anti-fascist printers and distributors. Among the most active members of the *Fronte della Gioventù* in Milan was Laura Conti, who paid for her anti-fascist activities with a long period of imprisonment in a concentration camp in Bolzano.

The emergence of Italian women into the forefront of political action during the Resistance was of course due in part to the example set by women in other nazi-occupied countries, most notably France, Yugoslavia, and the Soviet Union. The underground newspapers gave prominent attention to the role that women played in the partisan movements of these countries. Yet it can also be said that Italian women rebelled against their former position of subservience by reason of their own independent evaluation of their responsibilities and in response to the challenge which the situation in Italy itself presented to them. In September 1944 the newspaper *Noi Donne,* the official organ of a national womens' organization that was founded in November 1943 and within a year numbered over thirty thousand members, commented on the significance of the contribution being made by women to the Resistance: "We now know that in a modern democratic society women can no longer play a subordinate role, but must instead take part in the life and political affairs of the nation. Therefore from this moment on we must accustom ourselves to studying and discussing; in a word, we must learn to govern." [13] The same newspaper announced with pride in March 1945 that the Bonomi government had recently granted Italian women the right to vote, a first tangible recognition of the new status of women in Italian society.

In the issue of *Nuovi Quaderni di Giustizia e Libertà* of January-August 1945, the historian Aldo Garosci, a long-time opponent of the fascist regime and a veteran of the Spanish Civil War, made a concise and realistic evaluation of the achievements of the Resistance. He first noted that, had a national liberation movement not developed in Italy, "the equation 'fascism equals Italy' would have acquired a permanent, and not only diplomatic, validity." Second, he observed that the partisan war had given the Italian people a sense of renewed dignity and had thereby prevented "an exacerbation of that national inferiority complex that under certain circumstances can suddenly be transformed into its opposite." Third, the Resistance had proven that the Italian nation was no longer "the concern of a few intellectuals, but had become a collective reality." Finally, Garosci stated his belief that the Resistance had strengthened the republican convictions of the masses of Italians and had demonstrated "in the clearest manner possible the superfluousness of the Monarchy." [14] This latter point is more open to question than the others, for in the referendum of June 2, 1946, although twelve and a half million Italians voted for a republican form of government, ten and a half million voted for the continuation of the Monarchy. It should be noted, however, that from Rome northward a majority in every region voted for the republic, whereas in the South it was exactly the opposite. In other words, wherever the German occupation lasted longest and the Resistance was an important phenomenon, there was strong anti-monarchist sentiment. Garosci's evaluation reflected of course his own personal experiences and commitments but I believe that it also represents an honest and generally acceptable appraisal of the contribution made by the Resistance to the struggle for a democratic society in Italy.

II
The Postwar Aims and Programs of the Anti-Fascist Parties

Like their counterparts in other countries of western and eastern Europe, the leaders of the Resistance Movement in Italy sought to elab-

[13] "Vita dei gruppi," *Noi Donne,* September 1944, p. 2. (IG)
[14] Aldo Garosci, "I risultati politici della guerra partigiana," *Nuovi Quaderni di Giustizia e Libertà,* January-August 1945, pp. 5–12. (ISRT)

orate concepts and programs that could form the basis of a democratic society in the postwar era.

Since Italy had been a political democracy prior to fascism, the essential problem for the various parties and movements in the anti-fascist coalition was that of seeking a balance between restoration and renewal. What aspects of the pre-fascist state and society should be restored? What features of Italian society before fascism should be altered or even repudiated entirely in favor of new ideas and ideals? These were the questions that chiefly occupied the attention of Resistance leaders concerned with Italy's future development.

As one would expect, the left-wing parties emphasized the need for a reorganization of the entire structure of Italian political, social, and economic life, while the Christian democrats and liberals believed generally that the main purpose of the Resistance was to restore the political methods and ideals that had prevailed in Italy before the advent of fascism. The actionists, communists, and socialists thought of themselves as participants in a revolutionary movement, while the Christian democrats, liberals, and representatives of many other minor parties conceived of the Resistance as the military arm of a resurgent liberalism struggling against those forces in Italian society that had temporarily suppressed the spirit of freedom. But there is no clearcut division between the parties in this regard, for the Christian democrats and liberals were also concerned with finding solutions for the social problems and inequities that had encouraged the rise of fascism and tried to construct a type of ideology that could accommodate basic reforms for the benefit of the working classes. On the other hand, the left-wing parties were aware that a total repudiation of the ideals embodied in the pre-fascist liberal state was neither feasible nor desirable and managed to keep their revolutionary enthusiasm within realistic bounds.

The general aims on which all parties and groups in the Italian Resistance reached agreement are the subject of an earlier chapter, but I refer to them again briefly before examining the separate and often radically divergent programs of the anti-fascist parties. As enunciated by the National Action Front in August 1943 and later incorporated by the Committees of National Liberation, they are (1) the destruction of the fascist state and of fascist ideology; (2) the restoration of civil and political liberties and the reestablishment of a government representing all currents of political thought; (3) the elimination of all forms of human exploitation through the enactment of democratic economic and social reforms; (4) the abolition of racism and specifically of the fascist racial laws of 1938.

But unanimous endorsement of these principles did not preclude sharp differences of opinion concerning Italy's future social order from manifesting themselves. The most important point of disagreement dividing the anti-fascist parties hinged on the question of socialism, which in turn must be seen in the context of the whole unresolved controversy over restoration versus renewal to which I alluded above.

THE PROGRAM OF THE ACTION PARTY

The actionists agreed with the communists that there was an organic connection between the insufficiencies and inequities of pre-fascist society in Italy and the triumph of fascism. They believed that a mere return to the system that had prevailed before fascism "would mean a return to a situation congenitally infected by the germs that were to provoke the pathological condition of Italian political life that lasted for more than twenty long years." [15]

The actionists differed sharply, however, with the communists in their conception of the kind of society that should ideally exist in Italy. In the August 1943 issue of *Oggi e Domani,* the Florentine representatives of the Action Party made a clear statement of their goals in an article entitled "We Want Socialism, We Want Freedom." The article first asserted that certain attitudes and ideals had gained almost universal acceptance in the course of the anti-fascist struggle: belief in the coexistence of peoples and in the common destiny of all men; peace and brotherhood; awareness of the new creative as well as destructive potentialities of science; a revulsion against absolutism; and the aspiration for an international political organization. On the basis of these attitudes and ideals, the Action Party declared that its aims were the freedom of the human person, the establishment of a Republic of Italy founded on the principle of representative government, European and eventually world federation, and a socialized, associative, cooperative economy. Instead of the "vast monopolistic complexes" that had long dominated Italian economic life, the actionists envisioned industrial enterprises in which the workers themselves assumed the responsibilities of management and production.[16]

In *La Libertà* of October 27, 1943, Carlo Ragghianti and Carlo de Cugis of the Florentine Action Party addressed a communication "to our friends of the working class" in which they sought to define their

[15] "Conquista della libertà," *Oggi e Domani,* August 1943, p. 1. (ISRT)
[16] "Vogliamo il socialismo, vogliamo la libertà," *Oggi e Domani,* August 1943, p. 2; "Il nostro programma," p. 2. (ISRT)

conception of socialism. "The Action Party is a Socialist Party in the fullest sense of the word, not only because it continues and develops from the tradition of Western and Italian socialism the profoundly ethical themes of economic redemption and of political and social consciousness within the fourth estate, but also because it supports and wants a socialized economic system as opposed to laissez faire capitalism." The article then proceeded to explain in what specific ways the Action Party's conception of socialism represented a departure from certain Marxist dogmas. Ragghianti and De Cugis said that the actionists opposed the classical Marxist doctrine of classes, which "had been invalidated by history"; that they condemned all forms of dictatorship, including the dictatorship of the proletariat; and, finally, that they wanted the workers to be free to direct their own enterprises, unimpeded by depersonalized state agencies.[17]

Some of the same ideas expressed in the article referred to above were reiterated in a different context by Tristano Codignola, the secretary of the Florentine Action Party, in the December 5, 1943, issue of *La Libertà*. In an article entitled "We and the Communists," Codignola attempted to accomplish the difficult task of defending and at the same time qualifying his party's close ties with the communists. He pointed out first that by affiliating itself, in a single popular front, with the communists and socialists, the Action Party wished to affirm its belief in a society in which all citizens who live by virtue of their own labor, whether workers, farmers, professional men, or intellectuals, have equal rights and duties. Codignola then indicated the areas of disagreement that still divided the Action Party from the Communist Party. In the first place, the actionists rejected the Marxist concept of class struggle and insisted that "bourgeois" and "proletarian" had become grossly imprecise terms. Second, they attributed far greater importance to the role played in history by individual men and women than did the communists. Third, the Action Party conceived of itself as liberal as well as socialist and therefore believed that one of the key problems in the modern world was the maintenance of individual freedom and political diversity in the transition from a capitalist to a socialist society.[18]

The problem of reconciling individual freedom and social justice was referred to in almost every statement of program issued by the Action Party during the period of the Resistance. In its report on the Action

[17] "Agli amici operai; il nostro socialismo," *La Libertà*, October 27, 1943, p. 2. (ISRT)

[18] "Noi e i comunisti," *La Libertà*, December 5, 1943, p. 1. (ISRT) For the antecedents of these ideas, see the section on the Justice and Freedom Movement in chapter III, particularly the pages dealing with the thought of Carlo Rosselli and Silvio Trentin.

Party Congress that took place in Cosenza from August 4 to 7, 1944, *L'Italia Libera* declared that the following two points were endorsed by the great majority of attending members: "(1) The Action Party is an anti-totalitarian, autonomist, and liberal socialist movement that intends to bring about socialism in our society and state while continuing its function of protecting individual freedom; (2) the original characteristic of its socialism is its conception of the coexistence of two sectors of the economy: the collective sector of mass production industries, and the private sector of individual enterprise; democratic control of the second sector will prevent the reestablishment of positions of privilege." [19] The same problem had occupied the attention of actionist spokesmen from the very inception of the party's organized activities in the early months of 1943, as evidenced in an article by Guido Calogero published in *L'Italia Libera* in April of that year: "As opposed both to conservatism that pretends to be liberal and to social extremism that does not resolve the problem of freedom, we affirm our will to struggle for the single and indivisible ideal of justice and freedom. We make our own the vindication and further development of all the institutions of democratic freedom that have permitted the growth of the modern state, but we are convinced that we can proceed in this direction only by at the same time confronting and resolving the social problem." [20]

In the previously mentioned pamphlet entitled "The Action Party and Socialism," published in December 1943, Carlo Bandi addressed himself to the problem of freedom and justice and said that if by socialism was meant Marxism, "the Action Party was obviously not a socialist party." Social classes and distinctions must not be abolished, Bandi said, for progress depended on the tensions generated by a constant interplay of various social and political forces. "The important thing is not to abolish classes, but to order political and economic life in such a way as to prevent its crystallization; to oppose decisively the tendency of every class to establish itself as such and to become oppressive and parasitic." The Action Party *was* a socialist party in two concrete ways: in its desire "to bring the workers to a constructive and direct participation in the life of the state" and in its determination "not to allow the economy to be dominated by the uncontrolled ambitions of private capitalist initiative." [21]

[19] "Il congresso meridionale del Partito d'Azione a Cosenza," *L'Italia Libera*, September 30, 1944, pp. 1, 2. (MR)

[20] This article, entitled "Precisazioni programmatiche del Partito d'Azione," is cited textually in *Difesa del liberalsocialismo*, pp. 231, 232.

[21] Carlo Bandi, *Partito d'Azione e Socialismo*, December 1943. (LC)

In August 1943, *L'Italia Libera* listed the following points in the Action Party program for postwar Italy:

(1) A republican form of government
(2) The separation of executive and judicial power
(3) Representative democratic government based on local and regional autonomy within the framework of the national state
(4) Nationalization of industrial and financial enterprises of collective interest; free initiative guaranteed to small business
(5) Agrarian reforms in conformity with the characteristics of each region
(6) Direct participation of labor unions in the managerial process
(7) Freedom of worship and belief
(8) Italian support of a European and world federation of democratic states.[22]

The need for reforms in agriculture, industry, and education was deeply felt by the actionists. With regard to agrarian reforms, the Action Party limited itself to some general recommendations, since it felt that Italian farmers themselves should work out specific solutions for their problems. In August 1944, *Azione Contadina* made the following declaration:

> The program of the Action Party looks forward to a basic reform in agriculture designed to assure the enjoyment of the fruits of the earth to those who cultivate it and to elevate the moral dignity and sense of freedom of the farmers.
>
> But what will be the nature of the relations between agricultural workers and landowners in the future? With regard to this question the party does not nor does it wish to offer an identical answer for all the regions and agricultural areas of Italy; it calls for the expropriation of large tracts of land owned by exploitative landlords, and wishes to alter the present system of sharecropping and land-rental; but it does not want to anticipate any change that might bind the will of the organized farmers, it does not want to impose solutions from above. The farmers themselves must struggle for their rights by making their situation known and by supporting the type of reforms that they want to contribute to the agrarian revolution.[23]

The actionists also took a strongly "autonomist" position with regard to the problem of industrial democracy. Their immediate proposal was for the establishment of democratically elected workers' councils through which industrial workers could participate directly in the management of the enterprises in which they were engaged. The actionists attributed the

[22] "Il nostro programma," *L'Italia Libera*, August, 1943, p. 1. (INS)
[23] "I comitati d'agitazione contadina," *Azione Contadina,* August 25, 1944, p. 1. (CG)

failure of the workers' councils formed in the factories of Turin in the early 1920's to the fact that these councils were organized by communists who looked upon them "as instruments for the conquest of power and for the establishment of a proletarian dictatorship." *Voci d'Officina* declared that "we intend to return to the idea of Factory Councils, but this time on a truly constructive revolutionary basis and no longer tied to the inadequacies of Marxist ideology. Strengthened by the experiences of the past, we are thinking of a type of Factory Council which, by its very nature, composition, and function, can constitute a basis for the concord and collaboration of all progressive social forces and for the renewal of the social and productive structure of the country." [24]

In education the actionists called for an end to the age-old dichotomy in Italy between intellectual and manual labor and for an extension of educational opportunities to all young people. The entire educational system, *L'Italia Libera* said in February 1944, had been nearly monopolized by the middle and upper bourgeoisie, which had resulted in the intellectual impoverishment of the masses. "In the new society of labor there can be no break in continuity between manual and intellectual labor. Every youth must be given a sense of the dignity of his own type of work and receive a well-balanced education commensurate with his abilities and ambitions." [25]

The actionists spoke often and with justifiable pride of their own "moral intransigence" and single-minded devotion to both freedom and justice, but this very rigidity, coupled with the profound differences of opinion between its liberal and socialist factions, prevented the Action Party after the war's end from continuing the role of leadership it had assumed from 1943 to 1945. Nevertheless, many of its programs and principles were incorporated into the Constitution of the Italian Republic promulgated in December 1947, and certain of its leading figures were destined to make important contributions to the reconstruction of Italian political life.

THE SOCIALIST PROGRAM FOR A DEMOCRATIC WORKERS' STATE

As we have seen, the Action Party was much concerned with distinguishing its program from that of the communists. The same was true of the Socialist Party, which, despite many years of close collaboration

[24] "La fabbrica; nuovo punto di partenza," *Voci d'Officina*, February 1944, p. 1. (CG)

[25] "La riforma della scuola e del costume," *L'Italia Libera*, February 20, 1944, p. 1. (ISRT)

with the communists dating back to the mid-1930's, was still in 1943 and 1944 anxious to assert its own autonomy.

The Italian socialists did not achieve unity among themselves until mid-1944. Previously there had been two groups that called themselves socialist, the Italian Socialist Party and the Italian Socialist Party of Proletarian Unity. But even before the unification of these two groups into a single party the majority of Italian socialist leaders were agreed on the necessity of rectifying the past errors made by the Italian working-class movement as a whole and in particular by the Communist Party. Their chief aims were to achieve internal party democracy and to bring about the creation of a socialist Italy in accordance with democratic procedures. The August 1, 1943, issue of *Avanti!* made these points:

In our view, a socialist party ought to do the following:
(1) while defending every positive aspect of the Italian socialist and communist tradition, it must free itself from the burdens and restrictions which that tradition often represents . . .
(2) it must be constituted democratically, from bottom to top, a real mass party, and at the same time, be a training school in autonomy, in self-government, in self-discipline for the workers who, through the party, prepare themselves to become the dominant political class . . .
(3) it will have to struggle with all its strength to provide the only possible solution for Europe, that is, the socialist solution that guarantees peace, freedom, and prosperity to an Italy and to a Europe martyred by two wars and by fascism.
(4) to achieve this end, the party must prepare itself for the complete conquest of political power, the only way of breaking definitively the bourgeois state apparatus . . .
(5) by overcoming the narrow limitations of the socialist movement as the expression only of the industrial proletariat, the party must be able to include all forces of labor—workers and farmers, technicians and white-collar workers, professional men and intellectuals—who are exploited by capitalists and who do not exploit the labor of others.[26]

The socialists spoke frankly of their intention to gain political power and to create an Italian socialist republic. On January 12, 1944, *Avanti!* appealed to its readers to join in "the struggle to liberate our country, a prelude and condition for our struggle to destroy the bourgeois state and society, for collective, planned reconstruction, for the Socialist Workers Republic. If Italy slips back into conformism it will become an Anglo-American colony condemned to survive on the crumbs of a dissolving capitalist economy. If it aligns itself with the revolutionary countries,

[26] "Unità proletaria," *Avanti!*, August 1, 1943, pp. 1, 2. (CG)

with the Soviet Union in the lead, it will rediscover the joy of living in a creative effort to build a new civilization." [27] And in July and August 1944, the Italian socialists issued an important proclamation in which they clearly identified the Resistance with the struggle to build socialism.

But the question remained as to what methods were to be used to bring about the Italian socialist republic. The socialists carried on an uninterrupted polemic on the subject of what they regarded as the undemocratic and totalitarian methods of their political allies, the communists. In an article significantly entitled "Democratic Method," *Avanti!* declared that "it wanted the state apparatus to be controlled directly by the people," that it championed "the maximum freedom for the individual," that it was unalterably opposed to all "centralized, bureaucratically dominated systems." [28] The socialists constantly took issue with the communists over methods of acquiring and wielding power. They asserted that they were opposed principally to the concept of a dictatorship of the proletariat. Why, they asked, should other segments of society be dictated to by the workers? "We have had enough dictatorships in Italy and outside of Italy. We want the freedom to think, to criticize, and also to rebel against men in positions of public authority, in Parliament as well as in the schools, in the factories as well as in the fields." [29]

THE COMMUNIST PROGRAM FOR PROGRESSIVE DEMOCRACY

Actually, the Italian communists never intended to impose with force their own ideas on the other parties in the anti-fascist coalition or on the nation at large. They did not have this intention simply because their appraisal of the balance of forces from 1943 to 1945, the main component of which was the presence of massive numbers of Allied troops in Italy, precluded the possibility of a proletarian revolution. There was no question of basic principle involved, but it must be said that the Italian Communist Party conducted itself with exemplary flexibility and intelligence in most situations of crisis that presented themselves during the course of the war. It should also be pointed out that British repression of Greek communist revolutionaries, which began in late 1944, served to validate the cooperative policy line of the Italian communists. They survived and became a powerful political force in postwar Italy because they did not incur the wrath of the many anti-communist generals in command of the British and, to a lesser extent, the American Armies.

[27] "Messaggio di capodanno ai giovani," *Avanti!,* January 12, 1944, p. 1. (ICP)
[28] "Metodo democratico," *Avanti!,* September 4, 1944, p. 2. (INS)
[29] "Socialist e Comunisti," *Avanti!,* December 22, 1943, p. 2. (ISRT)

Palmiro Togliatti repeatedly affirmed that the Italian Communist Party did not aim to establish a communist dictatorship in Italy. On the contrary, he took pains to remind party members that "the insurrection that we want does not have the purpose of imposing political and social changes in a socialist and communist direction, but has as its aim national liberation and the destruction of fascism. All other problems will be resolved by the people, tomorrow, as soon as Italy is liberated, by means of free elections and the creation of a constituent assembly." [30]

Togliatti's message was probably directed primarily to various nuclei of militantly revolutionary communist workers and partisans who found it difficult to accept the principle of interparty cooperation. One discovers in fact that certain of the clandestine organs published by communist labor unions took a position far to the left of that adopted by the Italian Communist Party. *Il Martello,* for example, one of many similar newspapers reflecting the point of view of rank-and-file communist workers in Milan, called for the complete destruction of the capitalist system and urged that all industrialists who collaborated with the fascists be immediately executed. The Communist Party was also confronted with small but tenacious and articulate groups of "international" Communists who, in their organs *Prometeo* and *Stella Rossa,* echoed Malvolio's "curse on both your houses" in attacking the followers of the Soviet Union with as much vehemence as those of Britain and the United States. This rebellion from the left compelled Italian communist leaders to make incessant pragmatic appeals to reason and common sense which, if they did not convince dissidents within their own movement, at least helped to create a basis for Resistance unity with the other non-communist parties.

The formula for Italy's future development adopted by the Italian Communist Party was therefore not dictatorship of the proletariat but rather "progressive democracy." The communists envisioned an Italy in which, within the framework of a pluralistic society and constitutional government, the working class would assume the position of national leadership it had earned for itself during the Resistance. They spoke of basic structural reforms designed to eliminate monopolistic aggregates of economic power but at the same time to protect the right of individuals engaged in small business to work independently.

Like the Action Party, the communists called for the reestablishment of workers' councils, nationalization of basic industries, agrarian reforms that would enable Italian farmers to own the land they worked, a massive program of state aid to all worthy but impoverished young people who wished to continue their education, and the complete emancipation of

[30] "Vita di Partito," *La Nostra Lotta,* January 1, 1945, p. 3. (LC)

Italian women. The models for these reforms (with the exception of those in the field of agriculture, where collectivism was not proposed) were all provided by the Soviet Union, to which the Italian communists looked with religious veneration. Yet the Italian Communist Party's admiration for the Soviet Union did not prevent it from seeing the obvious truth that Italy was not Russia, that the national traditions, history, and characteristics of the Italian people were not analogous in most respects to those of the Russian people. The Italian communist press constantly lauded the achievements of Soviet society, published the Soviet constitution along with lengthy and rhapsodic commentaries, glorified Stalin as the world's greatest political leader, yet maintained a realistic, pragmatic attitude in regard to the political situation in Italy itself. Doubtless the teachings of Italy's most outstanding communist thinker, Antonio Gramsci, who had always stressed the importance of adapting Marxist theory to the actual conditions of Italy's national life, acted as a corrective to any rigidly sectarian or dogmatic tendencies that might have manifested themselves among communist leaders during the Resistance. In any case, Palmiro Togliatti, who had been a friend and disciple of Gramsci, was a first-rate strategist known for his moderation and ability to impose his essentially "possibilistic" approach to political problems on his more militant comrades.

Togliatti, Eugenio Curiel, Luigi Longo, Pietro Secchia, and other Italian communist ideologists were acutely aware of the need for close collaboration between Italy's communist and Catholic masses. Consequently, among the principal aims of the party for postwar Italy was to create the means through which communists and Catholics could engage in dialogue and thereby clarify areas of agreement and disagreement. Religious faith, said *La Nostra Lotta,* was a matter of private conscience and should not be allowed to impede potentially fruitful cooperation between all progressive sectors of the population. This appeal to Italian Catholics formed part of the Communist Party's program for national unity and provided the rationale for its adoption of the formula "progressive democracy":

Today we are struggling not for proletarian dictatorship but for progressive democracy, which is to be distinguished from proletarian dictatorship not so much for its democratic substance as above all for its social content. Progressive democracy does not make a radical assault on the principle of exploitative capitalistic property, as does proletarian dictatorship. . . . Today we are struggling for progressive democracy because we think that it offers, in the present conditions of Italian political development, the only ground on which it is possible to bring about the national unity of all democratic and progressive forces. . . . The struggle for progressive democracy is today the only national policy because, by uniting the whole people in a fruitful and constructive effort, it allows us to overcome the catastrophe in which fascism has plunged us.[31]

The communist program for national unity, with the working class in the lead, was destined to failure almost immediately after the war's end, but there can be no doubt that from 1943 to 1945 it corresponded to the interests not only of the communists themselves but also to those of the national liberation movement as a whole.

THE CONCEPTS AND AIMS OF LEFT-WING CATHOLIC MOVEMENTS

A phenomenon that developed concurrently with the Communist Party's efforts to stimulate dialogue with Italian Catholics was the emergence in 1943 of two small but influential Catholic political movements that sought to combine the ethical teachings of Christianity with the ideals of modern socialism: the Catholic Communist Movement, led by Franco Rodano, Fedele d'Amico, and Adriano Ossicini in Rome, Felice Balbo in Turin, and Mario Motta in Milan; and the Christian Social Movement, which was founded by Gerardo Bruni in Rome in November 1941, and two years later developed an active following, particularly in Tuscany through the initiative of Anna Maria Enriques in Florence and Don Roberto Angeli in Livorno.

The Catholic Communist Movement had two clandestine organs: *Voce Operaia* in Rome and *La Voce del Lavoratore* in Turin. Both newspapers recognized the Communist Party as the leader of the Italian working class and as the political movement best able to initiate the reconstruction of Italy after the war. They based their allegiance to the Communist Party on the principle of proletarian unity, which they saw as the only sure safeguard against a resurgence of fascism in Italy. As for the problem of reconciling Catholicism and communism, both newspapers asserted that there was no fundamental principle in evangelic Christianity that was incompatible with the ideal of communism and "the study of the inner dialectic of recent historical events demonstrated [this fact]." [32] In September 1944, *La Voce del Lavoratore* proclaimed its continued allegiance to the Catholic Church, whose authority in spiritual matters was "sacred" and vivifying. But, the newspaper said, the Catholic Communist Movement was political, not religious, in character and therefore had the right

[31] "Dittatura proletaria e democrazia progressiva," *La Nostra Lotta,* November 25, 1944, pp. 2, 3. (LC)
[32] "Saluto all'Unità," *Voce Operaia,* October 4, 1943, p. 1. (ICP)

to support any program or concept of society that it felt could assist all people to achieve human dignity.[33]

The clearest policy statement issued by the Catholic Communist Movement appeared in *La Voce del Lavoratore* in March 1945. Perhaps unique among modern exponents of political syncretism, the Catholic communists declared that their aims were as follows:

[We wish to] lead the Catholic strata of the working classes, and with them all those segments of the population which, although belonging to other social classes, embrace the cause of greater social justice, to a politically constructive position by following the only path that today makes its realization possible. We may define this position as follows: the unity of the proletariat, the struggle against nazism, and the elimination of the capitalist system, the immediate and direct cause of class struggle, of imperialistic wars, and of aggressive political systems; [we call for] the consequent establishment, by means of socialization of the means of production and the creation of new political institutions, of a new order through which the right of all citizens to develop their personalities will be guaranteed.

In response to the question as to how the Catholic Communist Movement differed from the communist movement proper, *La Voce del Lavoratore* stated:

We have repeatedly declared that we do not accept the metaphysic of integral communism, the utopian ideology with its dangers of false redemption, the whole atheistic and irreligious complex of ideas tied in brief to a tradition that is more than a hundred years old and that is dead and irretrievable. We have affirmed that we do not accept every aspect of Marxism, but only those of its useful elements that are not in contrast with Catholic doctrine.[34]

Like so many similar splinter groups that arose during the course of the Resistance, the Catholic Communist Movement went into sudden decline after the liberation of Italy. Its hope for proletarian unity, its engaging but ingenuous brand of political syncretism, were simply unable to withstand the pressures of the cold war atmosphere which, in Italy from 1947 on.
as in most other European countries, was to dominate the political scene

The principal organ of the Christian Social Movement was *L'Azione,* the first issue of which appeared in Rome in October 1943. The Christian Social Movement also arose in response to the need felt by some Italian Catholics for a more radical approach to social problems than had yet

---

[33] "Che cos'è il Movimento dei Cattoloci Communisti," *Voce del Lavoratore,* September 2, 1944, p. 1. (CG)
[34] *Voce del Lavoratore,* March 5, 1945, p. 1, 2. (CG)

been provided by the main Catholic party in Italy, the Christian Democratic Party. It wished to call to the attention of lay Catholics the disturbing fact that the most advanced segments of the Italian working class had rejected the Catholic religion of love in favor of the openly materialistic doctrines of socialism and communism. The explanation for this phenomenon, according to *L'Azione,* lay "in the inadequacy and unworthiness of all those who attempt to justify, in the name of Christ, positions of political and economic privilege." [35]

The Christian Social Movement attributed World War II to a crisis of spiritual values and therefore deemphasized the importance of institutional reforms. It was concerned above all with promoting the development of a type of Christian person whose primary sense of identification was not with a particular nation, class, or race but rather with all of humanity. Yet *L'Azione* acknowledged at the same time that this sense of universal human brotherhood could not be developed in a society based on inherited and unearned privileges. Consequently, the Christian Social Movement advocated a republican form of government and the gradual replacement of capitalism with a socialist economy. In a statement of program published on October 20, 1943, the Christian Social Movement took a decidedly anti-capitalist position:

> The Christian Social Movement recognizes that the present organization of society is dominated by the abusive power of the state and of capitalism, which are the mortal enemies of freedom and of social justice: it regards state idolatry, the ideologies of nationalism and racism, and capitalist conflict, as the real causes of the present conflagration and of the decline of civilization; it affirms that only through a profound reformation of the present structure of society—to be effected in accordance with the principles of Christian morality—will the human person be able to find the necessary guarantees for a humanization of the political and economic world.[36]

THE COMPONENTS OF CHRISTIAN DEMOCRACY

One also finds a strong evangelical component, combined with a moderate form of anti-capitalism, in most of the policy declarations issued by the Christian Democratic Party during the Resistance.

Inspired chiefly by the thought of Giuseppe Toniolo and Don Luigi Sturzo, the Christian democrats announced as one of their guiding principles the belief in a necessary distinction between the state and society. The state was merely the instrument with which men ordered their political

[35] "Noi e i Cattolici," *L'Azione,* November 10, 1943, p. 3. (LC)
[36] "Il nostro programma," *L'Azione,* October 20, 1943, p. 3. (ISRT)

and juridical institutions and as such was subordinate to the higher concept of society, which was based on the myriad forms of spontaneous communion and cooperative endeavor through which individuals participated in collective life. The idea of society reflected man's inherently religious nature and derived from the principle of natural law which, as opposed to the institutional and contingent political mechanisms evolved entirely by men, was of divine origin. Both the state and society were meant to serve the needs of the individual, whose earthly happiness and ultimate salvation represented the true purpose of human existence. Under no circumstances could the state make just claim to transcendent authority over the individual, nor could the essentially religious needs of man be either satisfied or denied by the state, for it was society, existing in relation to but apart from the state, which alone gave expression to man's spiritual nature.[37]

The ideas briefly summarized above formed the philosophical basis on which the Christian democrats rejected not only the fascist concept of the totalitarian state but also the various forms of "monistic" state idolatry of which they accused the socialists, communists, and liberals. In their opinion, all of the other major political parties conceived of the state as a preeminent, absolute, self-justifying entity to which the individual had to subordinate himself. This accusation was made repeatedly by the diverse groups of Catholic intellectuals who gravitated around the newspapers *La Punta, Il Segno,* and *L'Uomo.*

Beginning in November 1943, the Christian democrats proceeded to formulate some practical proposals for the rebuilding of Italy in the postwar period. In the first place, although it tended to favor a republican form of government, the Christian Democratic Party regarded the controversy over monarchism versus republicanism as of secondary importance. The institutional question would be settled by a referendum after the war and should not be allowed to obscure the more essential question, namely, "whether the regime that will be established after the liberation will be a genuinely democratic state, in which actual sovereignty belongs not to a single person or class but—as in America and England—is given by means of the representative system to all members of the community: a regime in which the method of freedom is constitutionally guaranteed and honestly applied, a state that recognizes the rights of labor, and tends toward the abolition of the proletariat and the elimination of all forms of plutocratic feudalism, unworthy of a free people."[38]

The United States and England were also the models for the Christian

---

[37] See in particular "Il nostro Stato," *La Punta,* February 23, 1944, p. 2. (LC)
[38] "Chiarezza," *Il Popolo,* January 23, 1944, **p. 1. (ISRT)**

democrats in the economic sphere. They favored a decentralization of economic power that would be effected by giving the state the right to investigate and control existing or potentially monopolistic groups, but at the same time they took a strong stand against the collectivization of Italian economic life. Private ownership of small and medium-sized enterprises was absolutely essential, for the right to property and the value of individual initiative were indispensable prerequisites for a democratic society. This was one of the points on which the Christian Democratic Party chose to concentrate its frequent polemical attacks against the Communist Party. In January 1944 *Il Popolo,* in clarifying its own position, referred sarcastically to various communist movements "that want to take complete possession of man and claim to represent him and discipline him in all aspects of his existence. . . . This total integralism derived from a materialistic monism, which does not consider the spirit, becomes a substitute for religion and assumes the doctrinal function of a church." The Christian Democratic Party, said *Il Popolo,* was not a totalitarian party and therefore believed that the individual should be free, in the economic as well as in the political and intellectual spheres, to develop fully his unique potentialities.[39]

A series of clandestine pamphlets published in Florence in mid-1944 continued the anti-communist polemic begun by *Il Popolo* by emphasizing the differences between Italy and the Soviet Union. But if Italy was not the Soviet Union, neither was it the United States nor England, a fact that compelled the Christian democrats to examine some of the negative aspects of Italian capitalism. Indeed, one of the characteristic features of the clandestine *Il Popolo* was the socialistic component of many of its programmatic statements. The socialism of which *Il Popolo* spoke was to be sure moderate, non-Marxist, and religious in character, yet in a Roman edition of the newspaper in December 1943, the leading editorial declared: "Property must be earned by labor and controlled in accordance with principles that, without suppressing individual enterprise or private interests where they do not impede the common good, are based on the supreme concept of social welfare that will in some instances give rise necessarily to the development of socialistic, collective, and state-controlled forms of economic organization." [40] *Il Popolo* adhered consistently throughout the clandestine period to a moderate anti-capitalist position and in both its historical analyses and projections for the future spoke of classical liberalism as an idea that had outlived its usefulness.

---

[39] "Il nostro movimento e la sua ideologia," *Il Popolo,* January 23, 1944, p. 1. (INS)

[40] "Chi siamo," *Il Popolo,* December 1943, p. 1. (ISRT)

Strongly opposed to any form or degree of left-wing dictatorship, the Christian democrats were also opposed to rightist political and economic oligarchies. Their general point of view on economic matters was similar to that of Ivanoe Bonomi's Democratic Labor Party, which also recommended a middle course between the extremes of monopoly capitalism on the right and state-controlled collectivization on the left.

THE PROGRAM OF PROGRESSIVE LIBERALISM

The Liberal Party was not prepared to accept the notion that its ideology had outlived its usefulness. The liberals believed that the Resistance should aim primarily to restore the political methods and ideals that had prevailed in Italy before the advent of fascism. On the other hand, the liberals did not maintain that it would be possible to revive the liberal traditions of the past without at the same time constructing a new "open and progressive" type of liberalism that took account of the changes that had taken place in Italy since the early 1920's. The Liberal organ *L'Opinione* stated in this connection that "there can be no true freedom where the working classes are not free from impoverishment and exploitation, which humiliate the human spirit and restrict its autonomy." [41] The Liberal Party refused the labels "conservative" and "reactionary" with which it had been branded by the other parties and insisted that if the principles of liberalism were strenuously practiced in all areas of life, Italian society would make rapid progressive strides.

Administrative decentralization and the revival of local self-government were considered by the Liberal Party "the essential components of a program of reconstruction and restoration of Italian political society. For our part, we believe that freedom can exist only in those societies in which public life is free of the restrictions imposed by a rigidly centralized system." [42] The main points in the Liberal Party program were enumerated by *Risorgimento Liberale* in April 1944:

(1) Repudiation of all forms of dictatorship and totalitarianism

(2) Planned national reconstruction

(3) The establishment of new constitutional norms that guarantee the civil and political rights of all citizens

(4) The revival of communal and regional administrative autonomy

(5) School reforms designed to make secondary and higher education available to all deserving students

[41] "La nostra posizione," *L'Opinione,* August 12, 1944, p. 1. (ISRT)
[42] "Libertà e autogoverno," *L'Idea Liberale,* March 1944, p. 2. (LC)

(6) The restoration of a genuinely competitive economy in which the state may in some cases regulate but not coordinate and control private initiative.[43]

It is noteworthy that only in rare instances did the underground newspapers of the main anti-fascist parties concern themselves directly with *il problema meridionale,* the problem of Italy's impoverished and backward southern regions. The reason lies probably in the fact that during the years 1943 to 1945 the main centers of resistance were in the central and particularly the northern regions of the country. In the South, with the notable exception of the heroic revolt of the Neapolitan people in the latter part of September 1943 and occasional episodes of partisan activity in the Abruzzi region, the rapid Allied advance and the lack of an organized base of operations precluded the development of a Resistance Movement comparable to that in the North. But whatever the reason, the fact remains that the problem of the South was all but forgotten during the period of the Resistance. One of the few articles devoted to this problem appeared in December 1944 in *Combattere,* the organ of a group of Turinese students affiliated with the *Fronte della Gioventù. Combattere* affirmed that the struggle of the Resistance would not achieve its purpose unless in the postwar period the people of southern Italy was given the opportunity to participate, once and for all, in the benefits of modern political and industrial democracy. The newspaper blamed the industrialists of Turin and Milan for their exploitation of the South and for their prejudicial attitudes toward Southerners in general. An independent, free, and united Italy, said *Combattere,* would never be achieved unless southern Italy became part of the main stream of modern democratic civilization.[44]

[43] "Orientamenti programmatici del PLI," *Risorgimento Liberale,* April 1944, p. 1. (INS)
[44] "Agli studenti catanesi," *Combattere,* December 25, 1944, pp. 1, 2. (MR) It should be noted that the failure of most underground newspapers to devote attention to the problem of the *Mezzogiorno* was also probably due to the fact that traditionally most northern Italians have been unfamiliar with and little interested in the backward social and economic conditions in southern Italy.

CHAPTER NINE

THE INTERNATIONALISM OF THE ITALIAN RESISTANCE MOVEMENT

I
Initial Contacts between Italian, French, and Yugoslav Resisters (1941–1944)

Among the specific forms of thought and action through which the international commitment of the Italian Resistance Movement[1] was expressed were the agreements reached on an official level from May to July 1944 between representatives of the Italian Resistance and their counterparts in the Yugoslav and French Resistance Movements. These agreements were the culmination of a series of preparatory initiatives undertaken by many individuals and groups from 1941 to the early months of 1944.

From September 1941 through the end of 1942, activists of the Slovene Communist Party and of the Slovene National Liberation Front succeeded in establishing contact with representatives of communist and other anti-fascist movements in Trieste. At a conference held by the Slovene Communist Party in September 1941, it was announced that "among the working class of Trieste and among the Italian population of Trieste in general there are visible symptoms of ferment and discontent; a resolve to fight fascism is developing, the anti-fascist Italians are collecting matériel and food for our Resistance army, and we can report that groups of Italians have begun to volunteer for service in the Slovene partisan units." [2] As a result of these preparatory contacts, the central committee of the Slovene Communist Party spoke on January 28, 1943, of the necessity of establishing close relations with Italian anti-fascists in the entire region of Venezia Giulia.

During this same period, small groups of Italians and Yugoslavs effectively worked together to publish various underground newspapers.

---

[1] For other references to the internationalism of Italian anti-fascism and of the Italian Resistance Movement, see especially pp. 53, 68, 71, 80, 89, 116–17, 119–20, 145, 153, 155, 163–65.

[2] Aldo Bressan and Luciano Guiricin, *Fratelli nel sangue,* p. 159.

On June 1, 1942, the first issue of the bilingual newspaper *Sloboda-Libertà,* directed to the fascist troops located in Croatia, appeared in that region. Vladimir Svalbavid, a Croatian from Fiume, and Augusto Ferri, an Italian soldier who, although still in the uniform of the fascist army, won the confidence of Yugoslav partisan leaders, were the chief organizers of the newspaper. According to reliable firsthand withnesses, *Sloboda-Libertà,* as well as other joint Italian-Slavic underground newspapers such as *Il Nostro Giornale* and *Lottare,* had considerable success in persuading some Italian soldiers to desert the fascist army in 1942 and others to join various units of the Yugoslav partisan forces after September 8, 1943.[3]

In February and March 1943, a parallel phenomenon was occurring in the French region of Savoie, where some soldiers of the Italian occupying army, including both officers and enlisted men, began collaborating actively with French partisans operating in the valleys around Mont Blanc and, in addition, undertook the dangerous task of publishing a clandestine newspaper named *La Parola del Soldato.* An article in one of the first issues of the newspaper stated:

Who are we? What do we want? We are soldiers of Italy, which we want to liberate from Mussolini. We shall not fight for the Germans, no. We are not at the service of the oppressors, but rather we serve freedom. We want immediately to use our weapons to help the people of France regain its independence. . . . The people of France is preparing its just revenge. Before then, at its side, with our weapons in hand, let us as free Italians prove our brotherhood with the French people.[4]

This and other similar appeals in *La Parola del Soldato* later persuaded many soldiers of the Italian Fourth Army stationed in France to fight along with the French *maquisards* from September 1943 to the end of the war.

Beginning in January 1944, a series of events took place that further prepared the way for the unity-of-action pacts effected by representatives of the Resistance Movements of Italy, France, and Yugoslavia from May to July of that year.

A report[5] issued in June 1945 by the fourth Alpine "Justice and Freedom" division indicated that the initial military contacts between Italian and French partisans occurred in the first week of January 1944.

---

[3] *Ibid.,* pp. 223f.

[4] This article in *La Parola del Soldato* is cited textually in a broadcast from Radio London by Umberto Calosso on March 18, 1943. (CG)

[5] Giovanni Dolino and Sergio Segre, *Report on the Origin and Development of the Partisan Movement in Piedmont,* pp. 21, 22. (CG)

Six French *maquisards* crossed over the French-Italian border to a pre-designated meeting place in the valle di Lanzo, where they were received by the commanding officer of the actionist "Renzo Giua" brigade. The meeting did not have any immediate practical outcome, but it did serve the purpose of convincing the six French partisans that they could rely in the future on the support of well-organized groups of partisans on the Italian side of the border. In March and April several other such encounters between French and Italian partisans took place in the Val Pellice, where the partisan commander Antonio Prearo sought with some success to convince the visiting Frenchmen that not all Italians had supported Italy's invasion of France in June 1940 and that he and his men were eager to repair the damage done to Franco-Italian relations by helping the *maquisards* in every way possible.[6]

It is likely, however, that Prearo's expression of solidarity, although welcome to the French partisans, was less effective in cementing good relations with the French Resistance Movement as a whole than the sacrifices of five young Italian anti-fascists captured by the Gestapo in Paris on February 16, 1944. The five Italians were executed on February 21, along with the Armenian poet Misrak Manonchian and another Armenian anti-fascist, a Spaniard, eight Poles, three Hungarians, and three Frenchmen after a three-day mock trial known as "the trial of the 23," which was prominently reported by almost all French underground newspapers.[7] This event was symbolic of the international character of the resistance against nazi-fascism and was reenacted on the soils of nearly every nazi-occupied country.

Meanwhile, during this same period Italian Resistance leaders were intensifying their efforts to establish political and military contacts with the Yugoslav Resistance Movement. On February 7 and March 27, 1944, through the efforts chiefly of the communist Giuseppe Dozza, the Committee of National Liberation for northern Italy approved two important declarations which stated the intention of the Italians to solidify relations with the Yugoslav Resistance. On February 7 the CLNAI members approved a declaration directed "to the Slovene and Croatian peoples" in which they spoke of the need for both Italians and Slavs "to achieve national unity and freedom in accordance with the democratic principle of self-determination for all peoples." The document urged the Italians of Friuli and Venezia Giulia to intensify armed struggle together with their Slavic brothers and announced the intention of the CLNAI "to

---

[6] Antonio Prearo, *Terra ribelle*, p. 70.

[7] Jean Hugonnot and Gaston Laroche, "Les volontaires étrangers dans la Résistance française," *Cahiers Internationaux de la Résistance*, November 1960, pp. 8–24.

establish relations with the Slovene and Croatian Liberation Committee for the purpose of reciprocal aid and the coordination of our struggle." On March 27 the CLNAI approved a second declaration that called for "a closer understanding with the government of Marshal Tito" in order to coordinate joint military operations as well as "to create the bases for a permanent agreement after the war designed to settle all unresolved questions in a spirit of justice and respect for the respective national unity of Italy and Yugoslavia, by appealing directly to the peoples themselves." [8]

II
Appeals for International Anti-Fascist Solidarity in the Underground Press

Various Italian underground newspapers also played a decisive role in setting the stage for the accords of May, June, and July 1944, by stressing the international character of the struggle against nazi-fascism. The first issue of the partisan newspaper *Il Partigiano Piemontese* in November 1943 spoke of "the heroic exploits of partisans in all countries devoted to the same cause, the freedom and independence of their lands." On December 7, 1943, *L'Unità* referred to the existence of an international partisan front extending from "the regions of central and northern Italy to Yugoslavia, Greece, Russia, France, to all of Europe." On February 14, 1944, *Avanti!* held up the Yugoslav Resistance as an example for all Italians devoted to peace and democracy and spoke of Marshal Tito as an outstanding military and political leader. A month later *L'Italia Libera* said that the French Resistance under the leadership of General de Gaulle had paved the way for the rebirth of democracy throughout Europe and voiced the hope that "France would understand, without chauvinism, the constructive and international spirit of the new Europe." [9]

On May 20, 1944, *L'Italia Libera* published an especially significant article dealing with "Tito's Army and International Cooperation":

The liberation army under the command of Marshal Tito . . . has acquired such strength and efficiency that it has succeeded, according to recent reports, in liberating half of the Yugoslav territory. During the past several years this army has taken on a special character, of great importance for the war and for

[8] Bressan and Guiricin, *Fratelli nel sangue,* p. 161.
[9] "Partigiano," *Il Partigiano Piemontese,* November 1943, p. 1. (LC) "Guerriglia," *L'Unità,* December 7, 1943, p. 4. (IG) "La Jugoslavia di Tito," *Avanti!,* February 14, 1944, p. 2 (ICP); "La Francia alla vigilia della liberazione," *L'Italia Libera,* March 7, 1944, p. 1 (LC).

the postwar era. It is no longer a purely national army, composed only of Yugoslavs. Last September, large numbers of Italian troops located in the northeastern provinces of Italy and in Yugoslavia itself joined forces with the Yugoslav partisan army. . . . Later some Bulgarians who had rebelled against the pro-German government of Sophia as well as elements of the Bulgarian army also joined the Yugoslav partisans. And recently a Liberation Committee in Austria sent a group of Austrian patriots to fight along with the forces of Marshal Tito . . .

In truth, the presence of diverse nationalities in the same army is a common phenomenon among the United Nations. In the case of Yugoslavia, however, we are dealing with something more and different. The fact that Italians, Bulgarians, and Austrians have voluntarily decided to fight along with the Yugoslavs under Tito is not exactly analogous to the phenomenon of Englishmen, Americans, Frenchmen, and Poles fighting together on various fronts against Germany. In our case we have national groups that up to recently have been enemies and that now are struggling side by side . . . . . The significance of this is that these rival nations have understood that there is something at stake today that is more important, more crucial than their ethnic and territorial conflicts: they have understood that there is a common cause for which it is necessary to struggle together, for the common good, and that past disputes must be subordinated to this cause.[10]

III
Official Agreements between the Italian and Yugoslav Resistance Movements

The first official agreement reached by representatives of the Italian and Yugoslav Resistance Movements took place on May 7, 1944. The Italian negotiators were Mario Lizzero and Giovanni Paduan of the "Mazzini" Garibaldi battalion; the principal Yugoslav negotiator was Stefan Jöze of the partisan command of Collio and Benescia. The three men agreed that their unity of purpose was based "on the necessity, in the present hour, of a common struggle on the part of Italians and Slovenes against the German invader and the Italian fascists, for the liberation of their countries and as a premise for the peaceful solution of all problems that regard the future of the Italian and Slovene peoples in the border and nationally mixed zones." The document made mention of the impossibility of raising territorial questions at the present time, alluded to the right of anti-fascist Italians to participate on an equal basis with other peoples in the family of free nations, and concluded with a recommendation, which was in fact carried out, that "a single Italian-

[10] "L'esercito di Tito e la cooperazione internazionale," *L'Italia Libera,* May 20, 1944, p. 1. (LC)

Slovene military command be established in those areas of occcupied Yugoslavia in which Italian partisans were contributing to the struggle against the nazi invader." [11] This was the first pact of an international character signed, on an equal basis, between representatives of the Italian Resistance and an Allied country.

As a result of the May 7 agreement, the Yugoslav National Liberation Front—the *Osvobodilna Fronta*—decided to send a personal delegate of Marshal Tito, professor Anton Vratusa-Urban of the Slovene National Liberation Committee, to Milan to meet with representatives of the CLNAI. In his report to the CLNAI on June 8, Urban traced the development of the national liberation movement in Yugoslavia, emphasized the principle of national self-determination in condemning the imperialist aggression of nazi Germany and fascist Italy, and ended by outlining the political and military measures to be taken together by the Liberation Committees of Italy and Yugoslavia.[12]

In response to Urban's report, the CLNAI on June 10 issued a declaration "to the Italian population of Venezia Giulia" that began by condemning the fascist violation of Yugoslav national integrity and praising the Yugoslav partisans who had resisted the brute force of the invader. The CLNAI then called upon the Italians of Venezia Giulia to work for the cause of Italian and Yugoslav independence by establishing political and military relations with the Slovene and Croatian partisan armies.[13] This declaration of principle made it possible for the CLNAI and the Slovene *Osvobodilna Fronta* to continue negotiations, which culminated in a joint decree promulgated on July 19, 1944. This decree stated:

The CLNAI and the Slovene National Liberation Front, as the political representatives of the national liberation movements in occupied Italy and in Slovenia, assert that the purposes for which the Slovene and all Yugoslav peoples have been fighting for over three years coincide with those for which Italian anti-fascists are fighting against the Germans and the fascist traitors. They salute the unity that is developing among the masses of the two nations. . . . The CLNAI and the OF intend to make this collaboration between the Italian and Slovene liberation movements even stronger and more effective. . . . Convinced that today the first and principal duty is common struggle for the complete liberation of the two countries, the CLNAI and the OF order the National Liberation Committee for Venezia Giulia and the inter-regional Committee of the Slovene National Liberation Front to mobilize to the greatest

[11] Mario Pacor, *Confine orientale*, p. 282.
[12] Anton Vratusa-Urban, *La situazione in Jugoslavia ed i rapporti jugoslavo-italiani*, June 8, 1944. (INS)
[13] *Alle popolazioni italiane della Venezia Giulia*, June 10, 1944. (INS)

extent possible all partisan units under their command and to intensify the struggle against nazi-fascism.[14]

Although much friction and mistrust continued to characterize the relations between Italy and Yugoslavia after July 1944, there can be no doubt that the pact of July 19 facilitated the impressive accomplishments of joint Italo-Yugoslav partisan units during the remainder of the war.

IV
Official Agreements between the Italian and French Resistance Movements

The first exploratory efforts to arrange meetings on an official level between the Italian and French Resistance Movements took place in early March 1944.[15] Costanzo Picco, an experienced mountain climber and a veteran of the Italian Fourth Army, was commissioned by the Piedmontese partisan commander Tancredi "Duccio" Galimberti to go to Marseilles and Toulon and there establish contact with the *maquisards*. Picco successfully completed his mission and returned to Italy at the end of April, when he informed Galimberti of the willingness of the French partisans to hold preliminary discussions with the Italians in the near future.

At the same time another of Galimberti's contact men reached agreement with the Maquis command in the area of Ubaye concerning the advisability of a meeting between delegates of the two Resistance Movements. As a result of these contacts, delegates of the Italian and French Resistance met formally for the first time on May 12, 1944, at Col Sautron, situated between the valleys of Maira and Ubaye. The Italian representatives were Benedetto Delmastro, Luigi Ventre, Giorgio Bocca, and Costanzo Picco, all of whom held important posts in the partisan military command in Piedmont. The French delegates were Jules Sapin, Emile Aubert, and René Chabre. Delmastro and Sapin presented factual reports on the location and strength of the partisan units operating in Piedmont and in southeastern France and in a gesture of solidarity Delmastro made an offer of six machine guns to the Frenchmen. A second meeting was

---

[14] *Decreto del CLNAI e del OF*, July 19, 1944. (INS) For further information, and numerous documentary sources, concerning diplomatic relations between the Resistance Movements of Italy and Yugoslavia, see Charles Delzell, *Mussolini's Enemies: The Italian Anti-Fascist Resistance*, pp. 381–84; 444–47; 489–91.

[15] The information regarding relations between the French and Italian Resistance Movements is drawn chiefly from Mario Giovana, *Tempo d'Europa*, pp. 23–60.

set for May 20, at the French town of Barcelonette. This meeting was attended by Galimberti, Delmastro, and Bocca, who reached Barcelonette on May 22 after a twenty-mile trek across mountainous areas heavily guarded by German patrols. The French delegates were Sapin, René and Ernest Chabre, Jean Lippmann, and several other French partisan commanders. Sapin opened the meeting by saying that these contacts would benefit the Italians, but Galimberti interrupted him pointing out that the agreements "would be advantageous not only to us, but also to the cause of Franco-Italian solidarity and would strengthen our common struggle for democratic freedom." Both sides then outlined the strength and disposition of their forces, and reached formal written agreement on the following points:

(1) Intensification of liaisons between the valleys on both sides of the French-Italian frontier

(2) An officer of the French partisan units and an officer of the Italian units will establish permanent contact in order to coordinate their common actions

(3) Exchanges of war matériel will take place

(4) All means of contact with the Allied armies that are presently available to either side will be placed at the disposal of the two movements.

A third meeting between the French and the Italian partisans took place on May 30, this time on the Italian side of the frontier at Saretto. The French delegates were Lippmann, Max Juvenal, and Maurice Plantier; the Italians were represented by Dante Livio Bianco, Luigi Ventre, and Ezio Aceto. Bianco took it upon himself to approve a joint statement of commitment to a republican form of government that Galimberti and the Liberation Committee in Turin later judged to be inopportune in view of the prior decision of Italian Resistance leaders not to raise the institutional question until after the end of the war. He also made some pledges of military aid that Galimberti found to be unrealistic. Nevertheless, despite this unfortunate misunderstanding, the political accord signed by Juvenal and Bianco at the meeting of May 30 included these points on which there was general consensus:

The two delegations declare that there is no reason for resentment and hatred between the French and Italian peoples as a result of the recent political and military past, which involves the responsibility of the respective governments, and not that of the peoples themselves, both victims of oppressive and corrupt regimes.

They affirm complete French-Italian solidarity and fraternity in the struggle against nazism and fascism, and against the forces of reaction, as a necessary preliminary phase for the establishment of democratic freedom and social justice in a free European community.[16]

V
The Question of the Valle d'Aosta

Following the agreements of May 1944, and for the remainder of the war, there were significant and ever-increasing exchanges of aid on all levels between Italian and French partisans. It must also be said, however, that political relations between the Italian and French Resistance Movements became strained after August 1944, when the new Free French government under General Charles de Gaulle was reestablished in Paris. General de Gaulle and his followers were not as sympathetic as were the rank-and-file *maquisards* to the idea that a distinction should be made between the fascist regime and the Italian people, nor were they willing on most occasions to lend a helping hand to Italian partisans who went to France to seek aid from their French comrades-in-arms. Had it not been for the tactful and constructive diplomacy of various Italian Resistance leaders, it is likely that even the pacts of May 1944 would have remained ineffective.

One of the chief obstacles impeding good relations between Italian and French resisters lay in the fact that, whereas most Italian anti-fascists conceived of the Resistance as essentially an international movement, the forces behind General de Gaulle were strongly nationalistic and regarded the salvation of France and of French honor as the primary goal of their struggle. Hence friction inevitably developed whenever these two contrasting points of view were brought into the open during the course of negotiations over specific issues and joint policy statements. On September 18, 1944, *L'Italia Libera* alluded to this problem in expressing its hope that the international character of the war against nazifascism would convince de Gaulle and his followers "to overcome the too strictly national origins of the French Resistance Movement" for the sake of larger democratic aims.[17]

L'Italia Libera was referring specifically in the above-mentioned article to one of the most potentially explosive issues dividing the French and the Italians during the latter part of 1944, namely, the territorial status

---

[16] *Les accords entre résistants français et italiens dans les Alpes Maritimes.* (ISRT)

[17] "Orientamenti della lotta politica in Francia," *L'Italia Libera,* September 18, 1944, p. 4. (MR)

of the region of the Aosta Valley in northwestern Italy. Several factors rendered this question particularly complex. In the first place, as in the region of Venezia Giulia, the fascist regime had since the mid-1920's attempted to suppress the cultural identity of the *Valdostani,* many of whom were bilingual or who spoke French as their native tongue and all of whom were fiercely proud of their own regional customs and traditions. Most of the *Valdostani* thought of themselves as citizens of the Italian state but were unwilling to surrender the administrative and cultural autonomy they had enjoyed for centuries. Fascist chauvinism had thus clashed violently with the sentiments of the people of the Aosta region, some of whom took advantage of the fall of Mussolini's regime to revive the autonomist feelings of their coregionalists, while others even went as far as to advocate a complete rupture with Italy and the subsequent annexation of the region to France.

Second, in September 1944, a group of anti-fascist intellectuals in Aosta, most notably Emilio Chanoux and Ernesto Page, issued a declaration for the Aosta Valley that envisioned the restoration of administrative and cultural autonomy for the region within a federated Italian state. But this autonomist declaration was deliberately misinterpreted by many persons who claimed that it gave sanction to the complete separation of the region from Italy. There were groups of persons in the Aosta Valley under the leadership of a Frenchman named Mésard who, in July and August 1944, had entered secretly into negotiations with French government officials in Paris in order to organize a plan for the future annexation of the region to France. This idea was looked upon with some favor by General de Gaulle, and there were insistent rumors in September and October that French troops were poised for attack against Italian partisan units operating in the Valley.

It was at this point that the Liberation Committee of Turin and several influential Italians from Aosta, including the historians Federico Chabod and Alessandro Passerin-d'Entrèves, intervened and worked out a policy statement that proved to be acceptable to the majority of interested parties. On September 2, 1944, the Liberation Committee in Turin issued a special proclamation to the people of the Aosta Valley which began by recognizing the *Valdostani's* legitimate resentment against a regime that for twenty years had "brutally trampled on centuries of tradition." The proclamation then stated that "in the future the cultural autonomy of the region will be reestablished, broadened and developed, so as to make of the Aosta Valley a natural link between the Italian and French peoples who are today united in a common struggle against the same enemy. It is up to the *Valdostani* themselves to work out the forms that this autonomy will assume." [18] In late September 1944 Federico Chabod drew up a *memoriale* that reaffirmed the autonomist position taken by the Committee in Turin and that advanced a series of persuasive economic and political arguments in favor of the Aosta Valley's remaining within an Italian federation.[19]

Several of the Italian underground newspapers also contributed to a peaceful solution of the problem. The National Liberation Committee organ in Aosta, *La Vallata,* featured an article on September 8, 1944, which stated: "The problem will and must be resolved in the new democratic Italy that alone can guarantee the just aspirations of the *Valdostani* in the economic, ethnic, and cultural spheres and, in addition, make it possible for the people of the region to choose their own political representatives." [20] In this article, *La Vallata* echoed a similar policy statement published a month earlier by the partisan newspaper *Il Partigiano Alpino* that blamed the fascist regime for having confused the legitimate autonomist sentiments of the *Valdostani* with a non-existent separatism and that called upon the Resistance Movements of France and Italy to follow the principles outlined in the pacts of May 1944.[21]

Indeed, the regional autonomy that the people of the Aosta Valley enjoy today as citizens of the Italian Republic is due in large measure to the efforts of all the groups and persons mentioned above who in September and October 1944 met the challenge posed by the territorial question with firmness and reason.

VI
International Partisan Brigades in the Italian Resistance Movement

A phenomenon that developed concurrently with the negotiations and agreements referred to in the preceding pages of this chapter was the formation in many areas of central and northern Italy of partisan units composed of men from nearly every country involved in World War II. As noted by Roberto Battaglia, these multinational partisan units "furnish one of the most significant and certain proofs of the international character of the Resistance." [22] Ex-Allied prisoners of war in Italy who were liberated

---

[18] *Proclama del CLNRP ai Valdostani,* September 2, 1944. (CG)

[19] Federico Chabod, *La Valle d'Aosta-l'Italia e la Francia.*

[20] "Precisazione," *La Vallata,* September 8, 1944, p. 1. (CG)

[21] "Accordo e solidarietà fra partigiani italiani e francesi," *Il Partigiano Alpino,* August 1944, p. 2. (CG)

[22] Roberto Battaglia, "Partisans allemands dans les rangs de la Résistance italienne," *Cahiers Internationaux de la Résistance,* November 1960, p. 67.

after September 8, 1943, men who escaped from forced labor battalions brought from Germany to Italy, deserting soldiers of the German army and of nazi-satellite countries, and members of Allied Military Missions frequently joined forces with Italian partisans as fighters, tacticians, and propagandists.

The complete history of these international partisan brigades in Italy has yet to be written, but the fragmentary evidence available indicates that in almost all cases they functioned effectively in both a military and a political sense. A report issued in May 1945 by two Italian members of the *Corpo Volontari della Libertà* reveals that negotiations between Italian partisans and the Allies in August and September 1944 "were facilitated by the fact that numerous American, English, Russian, Czech, Yugoslav, and French soldiers were at that time fighting in the partisan ranks; these foreign soldiers testified to the efficiency of the units, to the hard struggle they were waging, and to the fraternal way in which they had been received" by the Italian partisans.[23]

A statement written by General Alexander in April 1945, after alluding to the indispensable assistance given to the approximately seventy-five thousand Allied prisoners in Italy by countless Italian families, makes mention of the fact that at the end of August 1944 there were still eight hundred ex-Allied prisoners in the region of Piedmont alone, of whom about four hundred chose to remain in Italy and fight along with the partisans.[24] In an account of his experiences as a partisan commander in 1944 and 1945, Dante Livio Bianco speaks of twenty Russian soldiers who escaped from a forced labor camp in July 1944 and who subsequently joined forces with the "Paolo Braccini" brigade in Piedmont.[25] Gordon Lett, a British Special Force officer who helped coordinate partisan activities in the region of Liguria in 1944 indicates that the following number of foreign soldiers were protected by Italian families and fought together with Italian partisans in the area surrounding the towns of Rossano and Arzelato: 281 soldiers from various parts of the British Commonwealth, eighteen Armenians, thirty-two Poles, nine Yugoslavs, four Dutchmen, two Frenchmen, three Belgians, twenty-five Russians, sixteen members of special British military missions, and fifty British parachutists.[26]

At the end of July 1944, according to the testimony of Luciano Bergonzini in *Quelli che non si arresero* and of Marcella and Nazarino

[23] Giovanni Dolino and Sergio Segre, *Report on the Origin and Development of the Partisan Movement in Piedmont,* p. 22. (CG)

[24] General Alexander's statement was published in a special report in connection with the *Mostra della Resistenza* in Turin on April 16, 1946. (CG)

[25] Dante Livio Bianco, *Guerra partigiana,* p. 120.

[26] Gordon Lett, *Rossano; an Adventure of the Italian Resistance,* preface.

Galassi in *Resistenza e 36a Garibaldi,* seventy-eight foreign soldiers belonged to the 36th Garibaldi brigade in the region of Emilia, including forty Russians, seven Germans, six Czechs, four Yugoslavs, five Americans, four Poles, two Dutchmen, two Frenchmen, seven Englishmen, and one Tunisian.[27] In *Vento del Tobbio,* Franzone Allessio tells the story of a Russian soldier named Griska that is typical of hundreds of his compatriots. Griska was captured during the course of the first German advance in Russia in July 1941 and was brought to a concentration camp near Berlin. In the summer of 1942 he was made a part of a labor battalion and sent to Italy to work on military installations. On September 9, 1943, he escaped with five comrades by throwing himself from a train window in a desolate area of Liguria. He found asylum with several peasant families and finally made contact with a group of Italian soldiers who immediately accepted him as a founding member of their partisan band. Several of Griska's Russian comrades were expert saboteurs, and on May 8, 1944, they and five Italians formed a special sabotage unit that they named with the initials B.I.R.S., standing for *Banda Italo-Russa di Sabotaggio.*[28] Similar experiences befell hundreds of Yugoslav soldiers who, after being captured by the nazi-fascist armies and transferred to concentration camps in Italy, escaped with the help of Italian partisans and remained in Italy to fight the Germans. A letter of thanks written in June 1945 by forty French soldiers who fought for ten months with the 14th "Sullis" partisan brigade in Piedmont is another significant indication of the extent to which non-Italians identified themselves with the international character of the Resistance Movement in Italy.[29]

Still other tangible evidences of this internationalism can be found in the underground press. In an undated issue of the newspaper *Voce Garibaldina,* an Italian partisan whose *nom de guerre* was "Lungo" published a poem written in imperfect but moving French in which he paid tribute to the many French soldiers who had fought in the ranks of Italian partisan units.[30] The partisan newspaper *Stella Tricolore* of October 29, 1944, contained an article entitled "The Brotherhood of Peoples," which was written by a Frenchman named Metz who with ten other of his compatriots had been captured and imprisoned in Italy by the fascists and then liberated by a unit of the "Garibaldi" partisans on July 5, 1944. Instead of returning to France, Metz and his comrades elected to join forces with the Garibaldini "because we were convinced that, in Italy

---

[27] *Quelli che non si arresero,* p. 112; *Resistenza e 36a Garibaldi,* p. 281.
[28] *Vento del Tobbio,* p. 77.
[29] The letter is signed "Bazin," of the Détachments Français "Milano" and "Seville." (CG)
[30] "Peuples Frères," *Voce Garibaldina,* p. 3. (CG)

too, although far from our country, we could with complete good conscience do our duty as Frenchmen by continuing our struggle against the common enemy: nazi-fascism. . . . From that moment on, we have been convinced that the struggle that we Frenchmen are waging here in Piedmont, like that which the Italian partisans are waging in France, side by side with our compatriots, will help in putting an end to all feelings of hostility." [31]

An article in the partisan newspaper *Dai Dai Dai!* in March 1945 paid homage to a group of Russian soldiers who joined the "Caio" Garibaldi brigade in the summer of 1944. The Russians fought magnificently and soon established close friendships with the Italians. These personal contacts had the immediate effect of breaking down the anti-Soviet and anti-Russian propaganda with which the fascist regime had incessantly besieged the Italian people during the years prior to World War II. The anonymous author of the above-mentioned article said that he wished the anti-Soviet propagandists "could know these Russian soldiers and compare them with the youth of Mussolini and Hitler. How many better qualities they would find in these sons of the Russian people, of this people that up to thirty years ago was a slave of the Czarist aristocracy, and that was first in the world to see the rising sun of true freedom and true human equality." [32] Similar tributes were paid by other clandestine newspapers to the gallantry of British and American soldiers, who like the Russians, had been portrayed by the fascist press as members of irremediably corrupt and decadent societies.

VII
Relations between the Italian Resistance Movement and the Western Allies

The relations between the Italian Resistance Movement and the Western Allied governments is far too vast an area of study to be dealt with here in any but cursory fashion, and I shall therefore indicate only a few of the highlights of these developments. Moreover, the diplomacy of the Italian Resistance with regard to the Allies has already been studied in some detail by Secchia and Frassati in *La Resistenza e gli Alleati* and by Charles Delzell in *Mussolini's Enemies: The Italian Anti-Fascist Resistance,* to which books the reader is referred for much valuable information on the subject.

Relations between the Italian Resistance and the Western Allies were

---

[31] "Fraternità di popoli," *Stella Tricolore,* October 29, 1944, p. 2. (CG)
[32] "Compagni russi," *Dai Dai Dai!,* March 1945, p. 5. (CG)

established on both a diplomatic and military level beginning in December 1943 through contacts between British and American intelligence officers in Switzerland and various representatives of the CLNAI in Milan. Until March 1944, the Allies mistrusted the political intentions of most Resistance leaders and therefore refused to lend substantial help to them. The situation changed in the summer of 1944, when the Allies began to grasp the importance of the partisan movement and acted accordingly by parachuting large supplies of food, guns, and ammunition to predesignated zones of central and northern Italy. A letter sent in August 1944, by John McCaffery, an official of the British Special Operations Executive in Berne, to Alfredo Pizzoni, the head of the Liberation Committee in Milan, is symptomatic of this change in attitude on the part of the Allies: "I have assured my superiors," wrote McCaffery, "that the only organization that can obtain the unity of all anti-fascist elements in occupied Italy is the Committee of Liberation in Milan." [33] As a result of the increased political stature of the CLNAI and the excellent military performances of Italian partisan units, on August 18, 1944, a United States Senate Committee issued a report signed by General Alexander that recognized that "the Italian patriots with their courage and sacrifices are making a great contribution to the liberation of Italy and the cause of all free men." [34]

In November 1944 relations between the Allies and Italian partisans again became strained as a result of an appeal sent by General Alexander to all partisans to disband their forces and return home until after the winter of 1944–45 had ended. This appeal caused widespread resentment and pessimism among segments of the Italian partisan movement, but in January 1945 General Mark Clark, who was then Supreme Commander of American forces in Italy, restored the partisans' confidence by assuring them of continued American support and by expressing his personal esteem: "As a soldier of the 5th Army," General Clark wrote, "I have seen the way in which the Italian patriots have performed their duty." [35]

General Clark's expression of esteem had been preceded a month earlier by what was undoubtedly the most important agreement reached between representatives of the Italian Resistance and the Western Allies. Subsequent to a series of preparatory negotiations in October and November, on December 7, 1944, four delegates of the CLNAI—the liberal Alfredo Pizzoni, the actionist Ferruccio Parri, the communist Gian Carlo Pajetta, and Edgardo Sogno representing the Liberal Party—met secretly

[33] Pietro Secchia and Filippo Frassati, *La Resistenza e gli Alleati*, p. 96.
[34] *Ibid.*, p. 117.
[35] *Ibid.*, p. 154.

in Rome's Grand Hotel with British General H. Maitland Wilson, Supreme Allied Commander in the Mediterranean Theatre of Operations. The purposes of this meeting were to formalize relations between the Allies and the Italian Resistance Movement, to stipulate the amount and kind of military aid to be granted to the Resistance by the Allied forces and to define the responsibilities and obligations of the Italian Resistance Movement as a whole after the war's end.

Despite the fact that the Allies refused to accord official political recognition to the CLNAI, the document signed on December 7 by General Wilson and by the four CLNAI delegates gave clear and ample evidence of the significant role assigned by the Western Allies to their Italian comrades-in-arms. The agreement of December 7 entrusted the CLNAI with the job of coordinating the activities of "all active elements in the resistance movement whether they belong to the CLNAI anti-fascist parties or to other anti-fascist organizations"; placed the military arm of the CLNAI, the Corps of Freedom Volunteers, under the direct supervision of the Supreme Allied Command; empowered the CLNAI to safeguard the economic resources of territories formerly occupied by the nazis; allocated funds on a regional basis to assist the military and political activities of Italian Resistance fighters; and required that the CLNAI and CVL consult Allied military authorities before taking action "in all matters relating to armed resistance, anti-scorch and maintenance of order." [36]

The agreement referred to above, although not entirely satisfactory to the four Italian delegates by reason of its failure to grant full political recognition to the CLNAI and its insistence on Allied control over the various activities of the Resistance Movement, was nevertheless a decisively important event in the long struggle of Italian resisters to liberate their country from fascist tyranny.

In June 1945, shortly after the end of hostilities in Europe, a report issued by the British Special Force that had worked together with various units of Italian partisans and saboteurs further cemented mutual confidence and esteem between the Allies and the Italian Resistance Movement. The report made mention of the partisans' "great contribution in the summer of 1944 in disorganizing and demoralizing the enemy at the time when France was being liberated and the Allies were advancing beyond Rome." It then listed the military contributions of the partisan movement in collaboration with the advancing Allied armies in March and April 1945:

---

[36] The full text of the agreement is cited in Delzell, *Mussolini's Enemies*, pp. 465–67.

In all more than forty thousand German and Fascist prisoners were taken including many senior officers and important officials.

Vast quantities of enemy arms and equipment were destroyed or captured

Enemy pockets in the wake of forward troops were mopped up leaving the army to advance without hindrance.

Roads were patrolled, towns garrisoned and policed, enemy prisoners and deserters were collected and caged.

Objectives such as bridges, road, and tele-communications—of vital importance to a rapid advance—were saved from destruction.

In all more than a hundred towns were liberated in the first instance by partisans.

The partisan contribution to Allied victory in Italy was a distinguished one that far exceeded the most sanguine expectations. By force of arms they helped to break the power and morale of an enemy far superior in number to themselves. Without these partisan victories there would have been no Allied victory in Italy so swift, so overwhelming or so inexpensive.[37]

It is difficult to estimate the extent to which these accomplishments helped to restore the good name of the Italian people in the minds of Allied military and political authorities. What can be said with certainty is that the partisan movement, as well as the unheralded but indispensable diplomatic work done by various political representatives of the Resistance, gave expression to the international commitment that consistently characterized Italian anti-fascism from the mid-1920's through the end of World War II.

VIII
The Campaign of Italian Federalists for European Unity

One other specific aspect of the internationalism that motivated so many Italian anti-fascists during the years 1943 to 1945 deserves mention: the work of the Italian representatives of the European Federalist Movement.

As indicated in Chapter VI, Altiero Spinelli, Ernesto Rossi, Luigi Einaudi, and Eugenio Colorni were the principal Italian exponents of European federalism during the period of the Resistance and were chiefly responsible for the program of the underground newspaper *L'Unità Europea*. A particularly important phase of the activities carried on by

---

[37] This estimate appears in the first section of a document entitled "Report on N.1 Special Forces Activities during April 1945," dated June 2, 1945, and signed by Lieut. Col. R. T. Hewitt of the HQ N.1 Special Forces. Large portions of the report were published in Italian translation by Giorgio Vaccarino in *Il Movimento di Liberazione in Italia,* November 1949, N. 3, pp. 3–23, and January 1950, N. 4, pp. 3–23.

these men is described by Charles Delzell in *Mussolini's Enemies: The Italian Anti-Fascist Resistance*. Delzell explains that in the spring of 1944 the Italian Federalists "learned of the existence of parallel groups in foreign resistance movements. They worked hard to coordinate these currents and were greatly assisted by the Reverend Dr. Willem Visser 't Hooft, the Dutch Secretary General of the World Council of Churches. They held their own version of a Dumbarton Oaks Conference in his Geneva home from March until May of 1944. At the end of that time a group representing undergrounds of eight countries—France, Italy, Netherlands, Norway, Poland, Czechoslovakia, Yugoslavia, Germany—signed a memorable International Federalist Declaration, edited by the Italians, which emphasized the need for all the European Resistance Movements to engage at once in a common struggle for European federal union. This declaration was sent covertly into the countries still under occupation and also to England." [38]

Eight issues of *L'Unità Europea* were published in Switzerland and distributed secretly in Italy from May 1943 to February 1945. One central idea ran through all the principal articles of the newspaper, namely, that a United States of Europe represented the only hope for peace and international cooperation in the postwar era. The division of Europe into autonomous and mutually hostile nation states had been the prime cause of both World Wars. This system had to be permanently repudiated in favor of European Federation based on an interlocking network of institutional, legal, political, and economic principles that would bind the various states into a cohesive and cooperative unit.

As explained by *L'Unità Europea* in August 1943, the main task of the Federation would "consist essentially of guaranteeing international peace, assuring forms of free political life to all countries, abolishing autocratic economic aggregates of power, and preventing their resurgence, establishing a single international currency, and eliminating colonial empires, that is, the exclusive possession on the part of some powers of territories rich in natural resources." [39] The Italian federalists took pains to assure their followers that they did not aim to form another political party but rather to help the already existing parties adopt a federalist position on international affairs. They intended primarily to convince as many persons as possible that "today it is not possible to speak of progress and achievements in a given country except within the framework of an international order without which peoples become the instrument of

---

[38] Delzell, *Mussolini's Enemies,* p. 282.
[39] "Carrattere della federazione europea," *L'Unità Europea,* August 1943, p. 2.
(CG)

imperialism." [40] As far as the internal political order of Italy itself was concerned, the federalists advocated the broadest possible local and regional autonomy that could be achieved within a unified Italian state. For this reason, they devoted several important articles to the regions of the Aosta Valley and Venezia Giulia, where rival nationalisms had threatened to overwhelm all the constructive efforts made by exponents of federalism and democracy in both areas.

In November 1944, *L'Unità Europea* spoke of European solidarity as an indestructible achievement of World War II paid for "by the blood, the suffering, and the sacrifices of the soldiers of the United Nations and of the volunteers and martyrs of freedom in all European countries." The negative factors working against European and international solidarity, the newspaper said, were counterbalanced by other important events: "The collaboration of Italian partisans with the men of Marshal Tito in Venezia Giulia, the more and more frequent reports of cooperation between the reborn French Army and Italian partisan units, the unity of the CLNAI after the crisis that cost the life of the first Bonomi government, the delivery of supplies parachuted to our partisans by the Allies, and the presentation of a motion in favor of a United States of Europe at a recent conference of the British Labor Party." [41]

But these encouraging events did not blind the Italian federalists to many disturbing signs of tension and conflict which, even during the latter phases of the war, were already manifesting themselves in the policy statements and political and military decisions taken by the major world powers. Neither England nor France had given any sign of a desire to abandon their colonial possessions; England had launched an offensive against revolutionary Greek Communist guerrillas late in 1944; both Churchill and Stalin were speaking in terms of "spheres of influence" and "legitimate self-interest"; Marshal Tito had delivered several truculent speeches in which he spoke of his nation's historic right to claim possession of Trieste and parts of Venezia Giulia; and even in Italy itself there were many persons who were already seeking to preserve their powers and privileges instead of working for the cause of a united and democratic Europe.

Cognizant of these divisive events, the federalists published a special manifesto in the early months of 1945 in which they expressed their concern over the future of world peace. Unfortunately, the history of the postwar era has fully corroborated the reasons underlying the federalists'

---

[40] "Movimento o partito?," *L'Unità Europea,* August 1943, p. 3. (CG)
[41] "La solidarietà europea," *L'Unità Europea,* November-December 1944, p. 1. (LC)

concern in 1945 and compels us to end this study with the words of warning they spoke even as World War II was being brought to a successful conclusion. The defeat of Germany, the federalists said, will not lead automatically to the kind of civilization to which men of peace and good will aspire. Reactionary elements in all the nations of Europe, as well as in America and the Soviet Union, will seek to profit by the disorder of the postwar period to regain their power and to suppress the international sentiments of the masses. If these reactionary forces succeed in their efforts, the federalists warned, "there will be a resurgence of national jealousies and each state will seek to satisfy its needs by reliance on the force of arms. Their principal task will again become that of transforming their peoples into armies. The problem that must be resolved, and without whose resolution all progress in other spheres is merely illusory, is the definitive abolition of the division of Europe into sovereign national states." [42]

The editors of *L'Unità Europea,* like the thousands of men and women associated on various levels with other underground newspapers that circulated in Italy during the period of the Resistance, gave expression to the ideas and aspirations of people throughout the world who conceived of World War II as an international struggle against the forces of aggression and race hatred. They helped restore the good name of their country by reestablishing a sense of interdependence with the great family of free peoples that defended human dignity in combat with nazism and fascism. Many of their hopes and ideals have not been realized. Yet their commitment to democracy and internationalism provides us today with an example to follow, with a precedent for militant action in behalf of peace, freedom, and justice for all men.

[42] "I compiti del dopoguerra," *Quaderni del Movimento Federalista Europeo,* p. 13. (LC)

APPENDIX

Some Key Aspects of the Laws and Principles Governing the Exercise of Freedom of the Press in Italy after Fascism

Since this study is concerned with the ideas, programs, and struggles of the Italian anti-fascist press from 1919 to 1945, the reader may find it useful to examine the translations given below of some key documents relevant to the issue of freedom of the press in postwar Italy.

As in many other areas of Italian life in the post-fascist era, the history and vicissitudes of freedom of the press since 1945 are complex, at times unclear and ambiguous. One would wish to report that freedom of speech and press have been militantly defended in postwar Italy by all of the country's political, intellectual, and religious leaders. That this has not been the case becomes all too evident to anyone who examines the historical record, especially during the mid-1950's, when, as noted by Norman Kogan, steadfastly conservative political administrations combined with reactionary groups in the Vatican hierarchy created a situation in which "setbacks were suffered by the forces of democratic liberalism." [1] Professor Kogan observes correctly that despite the generally consistent climate of freedom that has prevailed in postwar Italy one cannot but be disturbed by the fact that at the beginning of 1965, commissions established by the Italian legislature had not yet completed the revision of the principal legal codes inherited from fascism. Nor is it very encouraging to witness the enormous power still wielded by the Catholic Church in areas that ought to be rigorously protected from the interference of religious authorities, as evidenced in the Catholic hierarchy's successful campaign to ban the performance of Rolf Hochhuth's *The Deputy* in Rome early in 1965.

Yet, essentially, the vital freedoms of speech, of assembly, of the press do exist in Italy and are safeguarded by constitutional and legal provisions that have been fairly consistently upheld since the fall of fascism. Although serious social and economic inequities remain to be rectified in Italy, the country today is a political democracy whose citizens enjoy intellectual and cultural freedom. Newpapers reflecting the full spectrum of political opinions are published without harassment and are readily

---

[1] Norman Kogan, *A Political History of Postwar Italy*, p. 91.

available to the Italian public. The men and women of the Italian Resistance Movement did not struggle in vain.

(1) Royal Legislative Decree N. 561, May 31, 1946, entitled "Norms Concerning the Confiscation of Newspapers and other Publications." [2]

In 1906, the preventive confiscation of newspapers by administrative authorities was abolished. However, fascist legislation on the press again legitimized this practice. The Royal Decree N. 561 rescinded the fascist laws, except in the case of publications guilty of offenses indicated in Article 2.

Article 1. The confiscation of newspapers or of any other publication or periodical referred to in the Edict on the Press of March 26, 1848, cannot be effected, except by virtue of an irrevocable sentence of the judicial authority.

The judicial authority may, however, proceed to the confiscation of not more than three copies of the newspaper, publication or periodical that commits a violation of the penal law.

Article 2. Notwithstanding what is established in the preceding article, confiscation may be effected of newspapers, or other publications or printed material which, in accordance with the penal law, are considered obscene or offensive to public decency, or which spread information about methods designed to prevent procreation or about methods of obtaining abortion or which illustrate the use of these methods and ways of obtaining them or which contain advertisements or letters relative to the aforesaid methods . . .

(2) Article 21 of the Constitution of the Italian Republic. [3]

The Constitution of the Italian Republic, which went into effect on January 1, 1948, was the product of a compromise between the various political groups and parties that had led the Italian Resistance Movement. It was promulgated on December 27, 1947, by the provisional head of state, Enrico De Nicola, and was countersigned by two veterans of anti-fascism, the communist Umberto Terracini, President of the Constituent Assembly, and the Christian democrat Alcide De Gasperi, President of the Council of Ministers.

The Constitution is a strange mixture of Marxist, Catholic, and liberal doctrines. For example, Marxist and liberal doctrines are juxtaposed in

[2] *Raccolta ufficiale delle leggi e dei decreti del Regno d'Italia,* vol. II (1946), pp. 1626–28.

[3] The entire Constitution of the Italian Republic has been translated into English by Norman Kogan in his *The Government of Italy* pp. 188–215. I have used his translation of Article 21, which appears on p. 191.

Article 1, which states that "Italy is a democratic republic, founded on labor. Sovereignty belongs to the people, who exercise it in the forms and within the limits of the Constitution." Marxist influence is dominant in Article 3, which declares, after asserting the equality of all citizens before the law, that "It is the responsibility of the republic to remove obstacles of an economic and social order, which, limiting in fact the freedom and equality of the citizens, prevent the full development of the human person and the effective participation of all workers in the political, economic, and social organization of the country." Catholic pressure (with strong communist support) was responsible for Article 7, which restated the validity of the Lateran Pacts of 1929 governing the relations between Church and State in Italy.

Article 21, which deals with freedom of speech and of the press, is also a compromise statement of principle combining assertions of freedoms and rights with certain concessions to bureaucratic as well as confessional demands.

Article 21. Everyone has the right freely to manifest his own thought by word, writing, and by every other means of dissemination.

The press may not be subjected to authorizations or censorship.

A distraint may be exercised only by warrant of judicial authority with statement of reasons in case of crimes, for which the press law expressly authorizes it, or in case of violation of the norms that the law itself prescribes for those designated as responsible.

In such cases, when there is absolute urgency and opportune intervention of the judicial authority is not possible, a distraint on the periodical press may be executed by police agents of the courts. These must immediately, and in any case within not more than twenty-four hours, present charges before the courts. If the judical authority does not sustain the charge within the succeeding twenty-four-hour period, the distraint is understood to be revoked and without effect.

The law may provide, with norms of a general character, that the means by which the periodical press is financed be made known.

Printed publications, entertainments, and all other manifestations contrary to good morals are prohibited. The law establishes provisions adequate to prevent and to repress violations.

(3) Law N. 47, February 8, 1948, entitled "Regulations Concerning the Press." [4]

This is the principal legislative act governing the rights and duties of the press in the Italian Republic. Most of its twenty-five articles adhere to

[4] *Raccolta ufficiale delle leggi e dei decreti della Repubblica italiana,* vol. I (1948), pp. 293–300.

standards followed, with slight changes and modifications, in democratic states. Article 1 defines the meaning of "press" and of "printed material"; Article 2 indicates in what way a publication must be identified as to date and place of publication, name of publisher and so forth; Article 3 states that every publication must have an individual legally responsible for what it prints, and that this individual must be an Italian citizen; Article 4 states that the owner of a publication must possess the required documents necessary for the right to vote in political elections; Article 8 states that every publication must publish the replies and corrections of persons who claim to have been offended or slandered; Articles 11, 12, 13, 15, 16, 17, and 19 indicate the penalties imposed on persons who have violated the penal code regarding the press: Article 13, for example, stipulates imprisonment of from one to six years for persons found guilty of defamation of character by means of the press. Article 14 declares that publishers of newspapers or magazines directed to children and adolescents are liable to criminal prosecution if they persistently publish material that may "incite to corruption, crime, or suicide," or if they "systematically and repeatedly" publish stories or illustrations that may "favor the unleashing of the instincts for violence and delinquency."

The most significant articles are numbers 5 and 20. In contrast with fascist legislation on the press, which stipulated that newspapers and other publications could not be published without the prior *authorization* of the executive power, Article 5 requires only that each publication be *registered* at the record offices of the local courts, thus freeing the press from political or administrative restraints and linking it primarily with the judicial authority. Article 20 is designed to protect newspaper publishers, editors, and journalists from the kinds of harassment inflicted on them during the fascist era, when direct physical aggression was far more frequently employed then legally sanctioned repressive measures.

Article 5. No newspaper or periodical can be published unless it has been registered at the record office of the court in whose district its printing and publication are to take place . . .

The head of the court or a judge delegated by him, having verified the documents presented, orders, within fifteen days, the inclusion of the newspaper or periodical in a registry kept by the court record office.

The registry is public.

Article 20. Whoever removes, destroys, or damages printed material for which the prescriptions of the law have been observed, for the purpose of preventing its sale, distribution, or diffusion, will be punished, if the act does not constitute a more serious crime, with from six months to three years imprisonment.

The same punishment will be applied to anyone who with violence or threats prevents the printing, publication, or distribution of periodicals, for which the prescriptions of the law have been observed.

The punishment will be increased if the offense is committed by groups of persons gathered together either in a public place or at printing establishments, newsstands, agencies, or other places where business is done with the public.

(4) Joint statement of principle of the National Federation of the Italian Press and the Italian Federation of Newspaper Publishers (1957).[5]

(1) The freedom to secure information, the freedom to obtain the news, to publish it, and to submit it to the test of criticism, in conformity with the substantial truth of the facts, is an inalienable right of journalism.

(2) The practice of journalism must respect the right of the people to be informed in an objective and complete manner, independently of every unlawful interest.

(3) The exigencies of truth, the impartial interpretation of facts and the faithful communication of news must be scrupulously observed.

(4) In the life of the free institutions of the democratic state, it is incumbent upon us to cooperate in the proper formation of public opinion.

(5) Journalistic activity must be performed in harmony with the respect of the personality, both public and private, of individuals and institutions in the exercise of their legitimate functions.

(6) The publication of news and comments must not disturb the moral conscience of the people.

(7) Unhealthy instincts and morbid feelings must never be fomented.

(8) We are duty-bound to correct news reports that have been shown to be inexact, to rectify the errors committed, and to orient properly a poorly or badly informed public opinion.

(9) Journalists and publishers must strictly observe professional secrecy concerning the sources of information, and in particular with regard to information obtained in trust.

(10) Journalists and publishers are morally committed to cultivate the spirit of solidarity between colleagues, to promote cooperation between journalists and publishers, and to build trust between the press and the reading public.

Having reaffirmed this, the National Federation of the Italian Press and the Italian Federation of Newspaper Publishers intend to establish a Court of Honor composed of an equal number of members of both Federations with a President to be nominated by both Federations. The Court will be charged with the responsibility of providing for the application of the principles of professional ethics for the self-discipline of the press.*

[5] Gaetano Napolitano, *Vincende di una libertà,* pp. 39–40.
* The Court of Honor was constituted in May, 1958.

BIBLIOGRAPHY

I. Works on the Underground Press in Italy

Arfé, Gaetano. *Storia dell'Avanti!*. Vol. II. Milan-Rome, 1958.

Baccino, Renzo. *Contributo alla storia della Resistenza di Genova* Genoa, 1955.

Barbieri, Orazio. *Un anno di lotta contro il nazismo e il fascismo*. Rome, 1944.

Bianco, Dante Livio. *Guerra partigiana*. Turin, 1955.

Bizzarri, Libero. "La stampa clandestina antifascista," *Mondo Operaio*, April 23, 1955, 30, 31.

Botteri, Guido. *I cattolici triestini nella Resistenza*. Udine, 1960.

Branca, Vittore. "La stampa clandestina in Toscana," *Il Ponte*, August 1945, 444–49.

Caffarelli, Ernesto Vergara. "Stampa clandestina," *Mercurio*, December 1944, 241–45.

Caputo, Giorgio. "La Resistenza della scuola romana," *Il Movimento di Liberazione in Italia*, April-June 1962, 3–30.

Caracciolo, Alberto. *Teresio Olivelli*. Brescia, 1947.

Carli-Ballola, Renato. "Per una bibliografia generale della stampa periodica clandestina antifascista," *Il Movimento di Liberazione in Italia*, January 1953, 38–40.

————. *Storia della Resistenza*. Milan-Rome, 1957.

Castellani, Emilio. "La stampa partigiana delle G. L. piemontesi," *Nuovi Quaderni di Giustizia e Libertà*, July 1945, 193–97.

Conti, Laura. "La stampa clandestina della Resistenza in una raccolta documentaria," *Il Movimento di Liberazione in Italia*, N. 58 (1960), 3–23.

Curiel, Eugenio. *Classi e generazioni nel secondo Risorgimento*, edited by Enzo Modica. Rome, 1955.

Dal Pont, Adriano, Alfonso Leonetti, and Massimo Massara. *Giornali fuori legge*. Rome, 1964.

Dal Pra, Mario. "Venti mesi di stampa clandestina," *Mercurio*, December 1945, 227–32.

Delle Piane, Mario. *Funzione storica dei comitati di liberazione*. Florence, 1946.

Delzell, Charles F. *Mussolini's Enemies: The Italian Anti-Fascist Resistance*. Princeton, 1961.

Farini, Carlo, and Gaetano Salvemini. "Giornali clandestini," *L'antifascismo italiano*, edited by Paolo Alatri. I, 159–99. Rome, 1961.

Francovich, Carlo. *La Resistenza a Firenze*. Florence, 1961.

————. "La stampa a Firenze dall'armistizio alla liberazione," *Il Ponte*, September 1954, 1459–79.

Gaddi, Giuseppe. *Saggio sulla stampa clandestina della Resistenza veneta.* Bologna, 1955.

Ginzburg, Leone. *Scritti,* edited by Norberto Bobbio. Turin, 1964.

Gont, Mario. "L'Unione Nazionale della Democrazia Italiana nel periodo clandestino," *Mercurio,* December 1944, 198–201.

Jacini, Filippo. *Carattere.* Milan, 1947.

La Resistenza in Italia, edited by Laura Conti. Milan, 1961.

Lizzadri, Oreste. *Quel dannato marzo 1943,* Milan, 1962.

Longo, Luigi. *Sulla via dell'insurrezione nazionale.* Rome, 1954.

Lombardi, Foscolo. *Il socialismo fiorentino dall'azione clandestina agli albori della libertà.* Rome, 1944.

Massola, Umberto. *Marzo 1943 ore 10.* Rome, 1963.

Meneghetti, Egidio. *Scritti clandestini.* Padua, 1946.

Miani, Ercole. "La Resistenza nella Venezia Giulia," *Il Ponte,* April 1948, 339–45.

Muscetta, Carlo. "La sventurata 'Italia Libera,' " *Mercurio,* December 1944, 212–17.

Nenni, Pietro. *Taccuino 1942.* Milan-Rome, 1954.

Pertini, Sandro. "Il PSI e la Resistenza," *Avanti!,* February 25, 1955, 3.

Piscitelli, Enzo. *Storia della Resistenza romana.* Bari, 1965.

Piscitelli, Enzo. "La stampa clandestina," *Capitolium,* June 1964, 352–57.

Platone, Felice. "Vita e miracoli della stampa clandestina," *La Settimana,* March 8, 1945, 6.

Ragghianti, Carlo Ludovico. "La politica del Partito d'Azione in un giornale clandestino in Firenze," *Il Movimento di Liberazione in Italia,* September 1951, 3–19.

Repaci, Antonio. "Non Mollare;" *Il Movimento di Liberazione in Italia,* May 1956, 39–47.

Secchia, Pietro. *I comunisti e l'insurrezione.* Rome, 1954.

Spano, Velio. "Grande come un fazzoletto *l'Unità* minava il fascismo," *L'Unità,* January 21, 1951, 3.

Tomaselli, Salvo. *Storia della stampa clandestina.* Rome, 1951.

Una lotta nel suo corso, edited by Sandro Bonaccossi and Licia Ragghianti Collobi. Venice, 1954.

Vaccarino, Giorgio. "Il movimento operaio torinese nei primi mesi della crisi italiana," *Il Movimento di Liberazione in Italia,* July 1952, 3–47.

Valiani, Leo. *Tutte le strade conducono a Roma.* Florence, 1947.

Ventura, Carlo. *La stampa a Trieste 1943–1945.* Udine, 1958.

———. "La stampa clandestina a Trieste dal maggio 1945 all'inizio dell'amministrazione alleata," *Il Movimento di Liberazione in Italia,* N. 47 (1957), 3–12.

Ventura, Franco. "Cronache della crisi italiana; la stampa clandestina," *Nuovi Quaderni di Giustizia e Libertà,* May–June 1944, 98–101.

———. "La stampa a Trieste dal luglio 1943 al 1 maggio 1945," *Il Movimento di Liberazione in Italia,* N. 46 (1957), 3–28.

Venturi, Franco. "La stampa clandestina torinese," *Torino,* April 1955, 82–85.

II. List of Principal Works Consulted

Agnoletti, Enzo Enriques. "La politica del CTLN," *Il Ponte,* August 1945, 414–29.

Alatri, Paolo. *Le origini del fascismo.* Rome, 1963.

Albertini, Alberto. *Vita di Luigi Albertini.* Milan, 1945.

Albrecht-Carrié, René. *Italy from Napoleon to Mussolini.* New York, 1950.

Alessio, Franzone. *Vento del Tobbio.* Genoa, 1952.

Almond, Gabriel, and Sidney Verba. *The Civic Culture.* Princeton, 1963.

Alvesi, Fabrizio. *La ribellione degli Italiani.* Rome, 1956.

Amendola, Giovanni. *La democrazia italiana contro il fascismo.* Milan-Naples, 1960.

Amicucci, Ermanno. *La stampa della rivoluzione e del regime.* Milan, 1938.

Angeli, Don Roberto. *poi l'Italia è risorta.* Livorno, 1953.

Antonicelli, Franco. "Il movimento di liberazione e la storia d'Italia," *Il Movimento di Liberazione in Italia,* November 1952, 3–17.

———. *I valori della Resistenza.* Cuneo, 1949.

Aspetti della Resistenza in Piemonte. Turin, 1950.

Assante, Arturo. *Contributo ad una critica di il giornale ed il giornalismo di stato.* Naples, 1937.

Azzari, Anita. *L'Ossola nella Resistenza italiana.* Domodossola, 1954.

Basso, Lelio, and Laura Conti. "Sul carattere nazionale e internazionale della Resistenza italiana," *Il Movimento di Liberazione in Italia,* January-March 1963, 3–22.

Battaglia, Roberto, and Giuseppe Garritano. *Breve storia della Resistenza italiana.* Turin, 1955.

———. "Partisans allemands dans les rangs de la Résistance italienne," *Cahiers Internationaux de la Résistance,* November 1960, 67–75.

———. "Il problema storico della Resistenza italiana," *Società,* January 1948, 64–87.

———. "La Résistance italienne: des memoires à l'exposé historique," *Cahiers Internationaux da la Résistance,* November 1960, 92–105.

———. *Storia della Resistenza italiana.* Turin, 1964.

———. *Un uomo, un partigiano.* Rome, 1945.

Bedeschi, Lorenzo. *Giuseppe Donati.* Rome, 1959.

Bergonzini, Luciano. *Quelli che non si arresero.* Rome, 1957.

Bocca, Giorgio. *Partigiani della montagna.* Borgo San Dalmazzo, 1945.

Borsa, Mario. *La libertà di stampa.* Milan, 1925.

Bravo, Anna. *La repubblica partigiana dell'Altomonferrato.* Turin, 1964.

Bressan, Aldo, and Luciano Guiricin. *Fratelli nel sangue.* Lubiana, 1964.

Buozzi, Bruno. *Scritti dell'esilio,* edited by Alessandro Schiavi. Rome, 1958.

Calamandrei, Piero. *Uomini e città della Resistenza.* Bari, 1955.

Calogero, Guido. *Difesa del liberalsocialismo.* Rome, 1945.

Cammett, John. *Antonio Gramsci and the Origins of Italian Communism.* Stanford, 1967.

———. "Communist Theories of Fascism, 1920–1935," *Science and Society,* Spring 1967, 149–163.

Catalano, Franco. *Storia del CLNAI.* Bari, 1956.

Cattaneo, Carlo. *Stati Uniti d'Italia,* edited by Norberto Bobbio. Turin, 1943.

Cesarini, Marco. *Moderna M Modena P.* Rome, 1955.

Cessi, Roberto. *La Resistenza nel Bellunese.* Rome, 1960.

Ceva, Bianca. *Tempo dei vivi.* Milan, 1954.

Chabod, Federico. *A History of Italian Fascism.* London, 1963.

Clark, Mark. *Calculated Risk.* New York, 1950.

Codice della stampa e degli autori, edited by Giulio Benedetti. Milan, 1930.

Collotti, Enzo. *L'amministrazione tedesca dell'Italia occupata.* Milan, 1963.

Communism in Western Europe, edited by Mario Einaudi. Ithaca, 1951.

Cotta, Sergio. *Interpretazione della Resistenza.* Trieste, 1962.

Cottone, Giovanni. "Discussioni storiche sulla Resistenza," *Belfagor,* May 3, 1955, 328–38.

Croce, Benedetto. *La storia come pensiero e azione.* Bari, 1938.

———. *Pagine sparse.* Vol. II. Naples, 1943.

———. *Propositi e speranze.* Bari, 1944.

———. *Storia d'Italia dal 1871 al 1915.* Bari, 1928.

Cuomo, Giuseppe. *Libertà di stampa ed impresa giornalistica nell'ordinamento costituzionale italiano.* Naples, 1955.

Curina, Antonio. *Fuochi sui monti dell'appennino toscano.* Arezzo, 1957.

Deakin, Frederick. *The Brutal Friendship.* New York, 1962.

De Bosis, Lauro. *The Story of my Death,* translated by Ruth Draper. New York, 1933.

Dedijer, Vladimir. *Tito parle.* Paris, 1953.

De Jaco, Aldo. *La città insorge.* Rome, 1956.

Denmark during the German Occupation, edited by Borge Outze. Copenhagen, New York, London, 1946.

Donati, Giuseppe. *Scritti politici,* edited by Giuseppe Rossini. Rome, 1956.

Ercole, Francesco. *Storia del fascismo.* Milan, 1939.

———. *La rivoluzione fascista.* Palermo, 1936.

European Resistance Movements. New York, Oxford, London, Paris, 1960.

Exposition de la Presse Antifasciste Italienne. Paris, 1928.

Fascismo e antifascismo 1936–1948. Milan, 1962.

Francovich, Carlo. "Filologia e Resistenza," *Il Ponte,* August-September 1963, 1057–68.

Fromm, Erich. *Escape from Freedom.* New York, 1941.

Galante Garrone, Alessandro. *Lo stato siamo noi.* Turin, 1960.

Galassi, Marcella, and Nazarino Galassi. *Resistenza e 36a Garibaldi.* Rome, 1957.

Garosci, Aldo. *La vita di Carlo Rosselli.* Florence, 1946.

———. *Storia dei fuorusciti.* Bari, 1953.

Germino, Dante L. *The Italian Fascist Party in Power.* Minneapolis, 1959.

Ginzburg, Leone. "La tradizione del Risorgimento," *Il Ponte,* January 1961, 42–57.

Giovana, Mario. *La Resistenza in Piemonte.* Milan, 1962.

———. *Tempo d'Europa.* Turin, 1952.

Gobetti, Ada. *Diario partigiano.* Turin, 1956.

Gramsci, Antonio. *Il materialismo storico e la filosofia di Benedetto Croce.* Turin, 1953.

———. *Il Risorgimento.* Turin, 1949.

Gramsci, Antonio. *2000 pagine di Gramsci.* Milan, 1964.

Guérin, Daniel. *Fascism and Big Business.* New York, 1959.

Hoffer, Eric. *The True Believer.* New York, 1952.

Hughes, H. Stuart. *The United States and Italy.* Cambridge, 1965.

Hugonnot, Jean. "Les volontaires étrangers dans la Résistance française," *Cahiers Internationaux de la Résistance,* November 1960, 8–24.

Il fascismo, edited by Costanzo Casucci. Bologna, 1961.

Il secondo Risorgimento, edited by Aldo Garosci. Rome, 1955.

Kogan, Norman. *The Government of Italy.* New York, 1962.

———. *Italy and the Allies.* Cambridge, 1956.

———. *A Political History of Postwar Italy.* New York, 1966.

La legislazione fascista 1922–1928, edited by Annibale Alberti. Rome, 1929.

La Resistenza al fascismo, edited by M. Milan and F. Vighi. Milan, 1955.

Lampe, David. *The Danish Resistance.* New York, 1957.

L'antifascismo italiano, edited by Paolo Alatri. 2 vols. Rome, 1961.

Le riviste di Piero Gobetti, edited by Lelio Basso and Luigi Anderlini. Milan, 1961.

Les idées politiques et sociales de la Résistance, edited by Henri Michel and Boris Mirkine-Guetzévitch. Paris, 1954.

Leto, Guido. *Ovra, fascismo, antifascismo.* Rocca San Casciano, 1952.

Lett, Gordon. *Rossano: an Adventure of the Italian Resistance.* London, 1955.

Lettere di antifascisti dal carcere e dal confino, edited by Giancarlo Pajetta. Rome, 1962.

Lettere di condannati a morte della Resistenza italiana, edited by Piero Malvezzi and Giovanni Pirelli. Turin, 1952.

Lipset, Seymour Martin. *Political Man.* New York, 1959.

Longo, Luigi. *Le brigate internazionali in Ispagna,* Rome, 1956.

———. *Un popolo alla macchia.* Verona, 1947.

Luraghi, Raimondo. *Il movimento operaio torinese durante la Resistenza.* Turin, 1958.

Luzzatto, Riccardo. *Unknown War in Italy.* London, 1946.

Malvestiti, Piero. *Parte Guelfa in Europa.* Milan, 1945.

Michel, Henri, and Boris Mirkine-Guetzévich. *Les courants de pensée de la Résistance.* Paris, 1962.

Mussolini, Benito. *La dottrina del fascismo.* Milan-Rome, 1933.

―――. *Opera Omnia,* edited by Eduardo and Duilio Susmel. Vols. 19–22. Florence, 1956–58.

―――. *Scritti e Discorsi.* Vols. I and II. Milan, 1934.

Napolitano, Gaetano. *Vicende di una libertà.* Milan, 1958.

No al fascismo, edited by Ernesto Rossi. Turin, 1957.

Omodeo, Adolfo. *L'eta del Risorgimento.* Naples, 1946.

Pacor, Mario. *Confine orientale.* Milan, 1964.

Pansa, Giampaolo. *Storia e documenti del primo comitato militare del CLN regionale piemontese.* Turin, 1964.

Passerin-d'Entrèves, Ettore. "Risorgimento e Resistenza," *Civitas,* April 1955, 85–91.

Pavone, Claudio, "Le idee della Resistenza," *Passato e Presente,* January-February 1959, 850–918.

Pedrazza, Piero. *Giornalismo di Mussolini.* Milan, 1937.

Pieri, Piero. "Considerazioni intorno ad una storia della Resistenza italiana," *Il Movimento di Liberazione in Italia,* September 1954, 29–57.

―――. "Fascismo e Resistenza," *Itinerari,* December 1956, 571–602.

Ravà, Franco, Giorgio Spini. "Fonti documentarie e memorialistiche per la storia della crisi dello stato italiano," *Rivista Storica Italiana,* N. LII (1949), 404–31.

Revelli, Nuto. *La guerra dei poveri.* Turin, 1962.

Rosselli, Carlo. *Scritti politici e autobiografici.* Naples, 1944.

―――. *Socialisme Libéral,* translated by Stefan Priacel. Paris, 1930.

Rossi, Cesare. *Il Tribunale Speciale.* Milan, 1952.

Rossini, Giuseppe. *Il fascismo e la Resistenza.* Florence, 1955.

Ruinas, Stanis. *Appunti sul problema della stampa fascista.* Rome, 1932.

Saggi storici sul liberalismo italiano, edited by Panfilo Gentile. Perugia, 1953.

Saitta, Armando. *Dal fascismo alla Resistenza.* Florence, 1961.

Salvadori, Massimo. *Storia della Resistenza italiana.* Venice, 1955.

Salvatorelli, Luigi, and Giovanni Mira. *Storia d'Italia durante il periodo fascista.* Turin, 1959.

Salvemini, Gaetano. *Memorie di un fuoruscito.* Milan, 1960.

Salvi, Franco. "Valori morali della Resistenza," *Civitas,* April 1955, 9–14.

Schneider, Herbert, and Shepard Clough. *Making Fascists.* Chicago, 1929.

Secchia, Pietro. *Problemi e storia della Resistenza.* Rome, 1954.

―――, and Filippo Frassati. *La Resistenza e gli Alleati.* Milan, 1962.

―――, and Cino Moscatelli. *Il Monte Rosa è sceso a Milano.* Turin, 1958.

Seth, Ronald. *The Undaunted.* London, 1956.

Sogno, Edgardo. *Guerra senza Bandiera.* Milan-Rome, 1950.

Stampa dell'era fascista, edited by Francesco Flora. Rome, 1945.

Tasca, Angelo. *Nascita e avvento del fascismo.* Florence, 1949.

―――. *Le pacte Germano-Soviétique.* Paris, 1954.

Taviani, Paolo Emilio. "Il significato della Resistenza," *Civitas,* April 1955, 3–8.

Thomas, Hugh. *The Spanish Civil War.* London, 1961.

Togliatti, Palmiro. *Il Partito Comunista Italiano.* Milan, 1958.

Toniolo, Giuseppe. *Scritti scelti,* edited by Antonio Boggiano Pico. Milan, 1920.

Trent'anni di storia italiana, edited by Franco Antonicelli. Turin, 1961.

Trentin, Silvio. *L'aventure italienne.* Paris, 1928.

————. *Le fascisme à Geneve.* Paris, 1932.

————. *Liberare e federare,* translated by Antonio Giuriolo (unpublished, CG).

————. *Aux sources du fascisme.* Paris, 1931.

————. *Stato-Nazione-Federalismo.* Milan, 1945.

Valiani, Leo. *Dall'antifascismo alla Resistenza.* Milan, 1959.

Vitale, Maurizio. "Preliminari di metodo per lo studio della Resistenza," *Mondo Operaio,* April 23, 1955, 29–30.

Vuga, Francesco. *La zona libera di Carnia e l'occupazione cosacca.* Udine, 1961.

Webster, Richard. *The Cross and the Fasces.* Stanford, 1960.

Wiskemann, Elizabeth. "The Italian Resistance Movement," *Survey of International Affairs.* London, New York, Toronto, 1954.

Zagari, Mario. "Attualità di Colorni," *Avanti!,* May 29, 1945, 1.

Zangrandi, Ruggero, *Il lungo viaggio attraverso il fascismo.* Milan, 1962.

INDEX